OLYMPIC

A Visitor's Companion

George Wuerthner

Photographs by George Wuerthner
Illustrations by Douglas W. Moore

STACKPOLE BOOKS

Published by
STACKPOLE BOOKS
5067 Ritter Road
Mechanicsburg, PA 17055
www.stackpolebooks.com

Printed in China

Cover design by Caroline M. Stover
Cover photo by George Wuerthner

10 9 8 7 6 5 4 3 2 1

First edition

Library of Congress Cataloging-in-Publication Data

Wuerthner, George.
    Olympic : a visitor's companion / George Wuerthner ; photographs
by George Wuerthner ; illustrations by Douglas W. Moore. — 1st ed.
      p.   cm.
    Includes index.
    ISBN 0-8117-2869-2 (alk. paper)
    1. Olympic National Park (Wash.)—Guidebooks. 2. Natural
history—Washington (State)—Olympic National Park—
Guidebooks. I. Moore, Douglas W. II. Title.
F897.O5W84 1999
917.97'980443—dc21   98-32146
                                                   CIP

CONTENTS

ABOUT THE AUTHOR

George Wuerthner is a full-time free-lance photographer, writer, and ecologist. An authority on national parks and conservation issues, he has written more than twenty other books, including *Yellowstone: A Visitor's Companion*, *Yosemite: A Visitor's Companion*, *Grand Canyon: A Visitor's Companion*, *Texas's Big Bend Country*, *The Complete Guide to California Wilderness Areas: Mountains and Coastal Ranges*, *Alaska Mountain Ranges*, *The Adirondacks: Forever Wild*, and others. Wuerthner graduated from the University of Montana with degrees in wildlife biology and botany and has a master's in science communication from the University of California, Santa Cruz. Wuerthner also spent three additional years pursuing a graduate degree in geography at the University of Oregon. He has worked as a university instructor, wilderness guide, park ranger, and biologist. Wuerthner currently lives in Livingston, Montana, north of Yellowstone National Park.

PREFACE

I was barely nineteen when I first visited Olympic National Park, in June 1972. A college friend, John Wight, and I met in Berkeley. From there we hitchhiked north, taking the coastal highways along the northern California and Oregon coastline and eventually to the Olympic Peninsula.

After being unloaded off U.S. 101 at the junction with the South Quinault Lakeshore Road, we shouldered our packs and began walking down the road. There wasn't much traffic. It was already late in the day, and we were looking for a place to camp for the night. It was raining. Mist swirled in ragged patches through the black branches of trees with tops so tall they were hidden in the clouds.

Toward dusk, we heard a vehicle splashing up the road. It was an old pickup truck. A man in his thirties, a kind of back-to-the-land hippie, picked us up. He took us to his home, an old farmstead carved from the forestland he had recently bought with his wife. Giant gray cedar stumps littered the pastures. There was an old gray cedar shake barn that looked even grayer in the rain. When we jumped out of his pickup truck, he nodded toward the barn and said we could sleep in there if we wanted. We gladly accepted. After we had arranged our things among the straw, he reappeared and asked us into his house to share a hot dinner with him and his wife. After dinner, we retired to the barn and fell asleep to the steady beat of rain on the roof.

Sometime during the night, the rain stopped. The next day was brilliant. The clouds were gone, and the sunshine blazed through the trees. John and I began to walk up the road toward the park boundary. In the distance, I could see the snow-covered peaks of the Olympic Mountains. I was unprepared for their ruggedness. Glacier-clad crowns rose above the dark forests that surged about the gleaming summits like a swirling emerald river. It was as if a bit of Alaska's coastal mountains had been transported south.

With warm sunshine and the promise of a good day on the trail, we joyfully hiked up the road with a bounce in our stride. By that evening, we had hiked up the East Fork of the Quinault River Trail to the aptly named Enchanted Valley. The warmth of the sun had melted a lot of the snow on the higher ridges, and dozens of waterfalls big and small cascaded down the verdant green face of the valley walls. It wasn't just a visual feast; we were surrounded by the sound of thundering water as it boomed, crashed, and reverberated across the valley like cannon fire.

We awoke refreshed the next morning and were treated to another glorious sunny day. John and I practically ran up the valley toward the high glaciated peaks and up a long series of switchbacks to Anderson Pass. We set up base camp near the Anderson Glacier and spent several days exploring the surrounding high country. When the cloudy weather brought an end to alpine explorations, we hiked down the West Fork of the Dosewallips River and then up the East Fork to Lost Pass. We almost got lost in Lost Pass. The entire high country was still cloaked in deep snow, and no trail was visible. John had gone ahead of me, hoping to reach a wooden lean-to shelter that our topo map indicated should be just beyond the pass. It was raining hard.

I was young and foolish then and hadn't brought a raincoat, which, in the Olympic Mountains, is something akin to being in the desert without a canteen. I couldn't afford a raincoat and managed to get by without one in most situations. In this case, I decided that in order to keep my clothes dry, the best option was simply to take them off. I stopped to strip off my cotton windbreaker and T-shirt. In the meantime, John continued to hike toward the shelter, leaving me behind to follow in his tracks. Clouds swirled about us, and soon John disappeared from view. John had the map.

I hiked bare-chested, wearing only my shorts. By hiking very fast, I could almost keep warm. Then the rain changed to wet, sleety snow and began to come down harder. I was getting very cold. I was forced to put my clothes back on, and they became soaked.

I postholed through snow, trying to follow John's footprints and hoping to see something through the whiteout. I knew that in my wet condition, I had to find the lean-to soon, or I was going to be in big trouble. Just when I was beginning to doubt whether a lean-to actually existed, I made out its dark form through the swirling snow. It was with relief that I found John already in his sleeping bag. I was starting to get hypothermic. I felt as though I were drunk. My speech was slurred, and I couldn't make my mouth form words. My hands were so numb that I could barely untie my boot laces as I hurried to get into my sleeping bag. Neither of us wanted to get up to cook anything; we simply ate cold "hot" chocolate in our sleeping bags. It took a couple hours, but I eventually warmed up.

The next day we moved down Cameron Creek from Lost Pass and really did get lost. An avalanche had wiped out a portion of the trail. We worked our way around the debris but couldn't find the trail on the other side. We weren't unduly concerned. We figured we would eventually find it, and we did. But it would have been wiser to have invested just a little more time to find the path. Oh, what a horrendous time we had working our way through alder thickets, over large logs, and through the forest off-trail with packs that seemed to catch on every branch. We went about two miles in this manner before, with relief, we relocated the trail.

From Cameron Creek we hiked up to Deer Park, where we spent the night in the campground. It was raining again. The next morning, Deer Park was blanketed in fog. We set off early, hiking out the Deer Park Road. A few hours later, we managed to hitch a ride into Port Angeles, where we hit the nearest grocery store for goodies like fresh fruit and chocolate.

That first introduction to the Olympic Mountains was enough to keep me coming back again and again. Since then, I've managed to hike in all the major drainages of the park, as well as much of the coastal fringe. Although I've sampled most of the major mountain ranges of the West and Alaska, I've found that nothing duplicates the unique experience of the Olympics. No other place in the United States can you find such a grand assemblage of mountains, with a magnificent shoreline, and the forest is the most spectacular in the world. The coastal mountains of Alaska may come close, but they don't have the network of trails, nor is the weather as good as that on the Peninsula in summer.

Protecting the park was not easy, nor is the work finished today, but we can be thankful that early conservationists worked diligently and hard to pass on to us something that is special and unique in the entire world. Every time I hike among the park's magnificent forests, I silently thank those conservation pioneers for saving at least a fraction of the Olympic virgin forests. If the park didn't exist, no doubt the entire Peninsula would have been logged from coast to coast.

In the meantime, I am passing on the Olympic tradition to the next generation. My wife, Mollie Matteson, worked as a backcountry ranger in the park. During a chance meeting in the halls while I was in graduate school, she mentioned that she had worked the previous summer in the Olympic wilderness. That was enough to pique my interest in her, and I asked her to go hiking with me the following weekend.

Mollie and I now return to the park to share the experience with our children. My daughter was hiking up to four miles a day on Olympic Mountain trails when she was just two, and my son went on a couple overnight backpacks in Olympic before he was three weeks old. And perhaps they in turn will take their children to this gem of a wildlands and let them discover the same pleasures that I found in my youth.

INTRODUCTION

The Olympic Peninsula is one of the most beautiful corners of the United States, with wild beaches, magnificent forests, and spectacular mountain scenery. Measuring about 60 by 90 miles, or 5,328 square miles, it is slightly larger than the state of Connecticut. One could spend years exploring the area.

The Olympic Peninsula, a giant thumb of land at the northwestern corner of Washington, is bordered by the Pacific Ocean on the west, the Strait of Juan de Fuca to the north, and Hood Canal to the east. The Chehalis River, which drains into Grays Harbor, is generally recognized as the southern boundary of the Peninsula. Surrounded by water on three sides, the Peninsula has been geographically isolated for eons.

Olympic National Park encompasses the rugged mountainous interior of the Peninsula, plus a sliver of the coast. The Olympic Mountains rise abruptly from the surrounding lowlands, reaching a height of 7,965 feet on the summit of Mount Olympus. Although the elevation is not high by Rocky Mountain standards, the overall relief from the base of the mountains to the top of Mount Olympus is greater than the rise of Grand Teton above the valley at Jackson Hole. Some thirty-seven other peaks also rise over 7,000 feet in elevation.

Moisture from storms driving in from the Pacific falls on these high mountain ranges, which receive record amounts of rainfall annually. The summit of Mount Olympus receives around 200 inches of precipitation each year, more than any other area in the contiguous United States. Most of this precipitation falls as snow at higher elevations, feeding more than 60 glaciers. The heavy precipitation also nourishes eleven major rivers that radiate out from the mountains like spokes of a wheel.

Although the Olympics are known for their rain, with forest valleys on the southwestern slopes averaging 145 to 167 inches of moisture annually,

Mount Olympus, at 7,965 feet, is the highest peak in the Olympic Mountains and is mantled by glacial ice. The bedrock exposed on the peak is composed primarily of sandstone and silty shales originally laid down in ancient seas.

there are also some relatively dry areas. In the rain shadow of the mountains near Sequim, average precipitation drops to 17 inches. This variation of landscape and climate creates an incredible diversity of habitat for flora and fauna.

Although Olympic National Park is the centerpiece of this landscape, another 632,324 acres of federal lands on the Peninsula are managed by Olympic National Forest. The national forest blankets the foothills of the Olympic Mountains, circling the park, which lies mostly in the Peninsula's rugged, mountainous interior. Along two-thirds of their boundaries, excluding the ocean park strip, the park and forest share a common border. Nevertheless, they have vastly different management philosophies. National forest lands are administered by the National Forest Service under the U.S. Department of Agriculture. The Olympic National Forest has a forest supervisor and staff headquartered in Olympia and four ranger districts managed by district rangers located at field offices in Hoodsport, Quilcene, Forks, and Quinault. National forest lands are supposed to be managed to protect and perpetuate a wide variety of resources, including good-quality water, wildlife habitat, scenic beauty, fisheries, and timber. However, the agency failed to sufficiently protect any of these resources as a result of its focus on timber production. Only recently has it come to be appreciated that the heavy timber cutting may have even

Lichen-encrusted boulder on Blue Mountain frames Elk Mountain and the headwaters of Cameron Creek.

jeopardized future timber supply because of the near devastation of the forest ecosystem.

Fortunately, part of the Peninsula has been managed by the National Park Service, a division of the Department of Interior that was established by Congress in 1916 "to promote and regulate the use of the national parks, monuments and reservations" in accordance with their purpose, which is "to conserve the scenery and the natural and historic objects and the wildlife therein . . . by such means as will leave them unimpaired for future generations." Even the Park Service hasn't always been very good at resisting the timber industry's attempts to log every last stand of old growth in the mountains, but in general the lands under Park Service management have fared far better than those managed by the Forest Service.

Besides the rugged, mountainous center portion, Olympic National Park also spans a small coastal strip along the west coast of the Peninsula. A park superintendent is stationed at the headquarters office in Port Angeles, and there are eight ranger stations around the Peninsula to assist in the management of the park. Eight Native American tribes hold roughly 235,000 acres of land on the Peninsula, some immediately adjacent to the park. Another 364,700 acres are managed by the Washington Department of Natural Resources primarily for timber production. There are fourteen state parks on the Olympic Peninsula, totaling 4,172 acres. The National Oceanic and Atmospheric Administration (NOAA) administers the Olympic Coast National Marine Sanctuary, established in June 1994 and encompassing 3,300 square miles. Finally, there are some 915,000 acres, an area nearly equal in size to Olympic National Park, controlled by large timber companies.

Olympic National Park itself comprises 922,651 acres, including 574 acres of private land. Concentrations of privately owned tracts occur in the Lake Crescent area, along the north shore of Lake Quinault, and at Oil City, near the coast. There are also 8,790 acres of nonfederal public lands within the park. Some mineral claims still exist.

Olympic National Park is an area of exceptional natural beauty, with fifty-seven miles of spectacular coastline and numerous offshore islands, heavily forested mountain slopes, alpine parklands, and glacier-capped mountains. It contains the largest and best example of virgin temperate rain forest in the Western Hemisphere, the largest intact stand of coniferous forest in the contiguous forty-eight states, and the largest truly wild herd of Roosevelt elk. Twelve major rivers and 200 smaller streams provide a rich habitat for fish and other aquatic creatures.

Olympic National Park was established in 1938 primarily as a wildlife refuge to protect dwindling herds of Roosevelt elk. In the process, park protection also saved a representative sample of the primeval forests of Sitka spruce, western hemlock, Douglas fir, and western red cedar that once blanketed the entire Olympic Peninsula in one of the most magnificent forests found anywhere on earth. Tragically, much of this ancient forest has been logged in the past century, severely straining the ecological fabric of the region, and many species, ranging from salmon to spotted owl, have been extirpated or endangered. The impact of overharvest and nonsustained yield cutting has led to the closure of many timber mills as well.

Because of its scientific and scenic values, Olympic National Park has twice received international recognition. The park was named a biosphere reserve by UNESCO in 1967 for its scientific value as a major reserve of temperate rain forests and a large, protected and unmanipulated ecosystem.

The park was also named a world heritage site by the World Heritage Convention on October 27, 1981. Based on the notion of the Seven Wonders of the Ancient World, most nations of the modern world have agreed by treaty to give special recognition to important natural and cultural areas by recognizing them as world heritage sites. Other world heritage sites include ancient Thebes, with its pyramids, in Egypt; Serengeti National Park in Tanzania; Great Barrier Reef in Australia; and the world's first national park, Yellowstone.

Surrounded on three sides by water and crowned by alpine glaciers, the Olympics retain the distinctive character that developed from their isolation. The park contains more than 1,200 higher plants, 300 species of birds, and 70 species of mammals, some unique to the Olympic Peninsula and found nowhere else in the world. These are examples of how genetic diversification occurs when there is geographical isolation. The most striking example is the Olympic marmot. Others are the Olympic chipmunk, Olympic snow mole, Olympic torrent salamander, Cope's giant salamander, and Beardslee rainbow trout and Crescent Lake cutthroat trout. Endemic plant species include Flett's fleabane, Flett's violet, Piper's bellflower, Olympic Mountain synthyris, Olympic Mountain milkvetch, Olympic Mountain rockmat, and Thompson's wandering fleabane.

RECORD TREES IN OLYMPIC NATIONAL PARK

The record-size trees of many species have been found in Olympic National Park. These trees are recognized by the American Forestry Association as the largest living specimens of the species on their list of approximately 750 national champions. Following are the sizes and locations of Olympic's record trees.

ALASKA CEDAR

Circumference: 452 inches
Height: 120 feet
Spread: 27 feet
Total points: 579

Location: Quinault subdistrict. Approximately 40 feet north of Big Creek Trail and 1 mile east of Three Lakes, at approximately 3,000 feet elevation.

DOUGLAS FIR (co-champ)

Circumference: 533.5 inches
Height: 212 feet
Spread: 47.5 feet
Total points: 757

Location: Up Queets River Trail. You must ford the river, then go 2.4 miles to old Kloochman Rock Trail at Coal Creek; turn left at the junctions. The big fir is 0.2 mile along this trail. There is a sign where you leave the trail and one at the tree. The trail is on the north side of the river.

DOUGLAS FIR (co-champ)

Circumference: 448 inches
Height: 298 feet
Spread: 64 feet
Total points: 762

Location: South Fork Hoh River Trail, 0.25 mile inside the park boundary, 40 feet south of the trail.

GRAND FIR

Circumference: 229 inches
Height: 251 feet
Spread: 43 feet
Total points: 491

Location: Along the Duckabush River Trail, 7.5 miles from the trailhead or 1.5 miles from the park boundary, 100 yards past second stream crossing within park on southeast side of the trail.

SUBALPINE FIR

Circumference: 253 inches
Height: 129 feet
Spread: 22 feet
Total points: 388

Location: About 300 feet east-southeast of Cream Lake, which is located at the head of the Hoh River drainage. There is no maintained trail into the area. There is a sign at the tree.

WESTERN HEMLOCK (co-champ)

Circumference: 270 inches
Height: 241 feet
Spread: 67 feet
Total points: 528

Location: Along the Hoh River Trail, 100 yards west of Cougar Creek crossing on the north side of the trail.

WESTERN HEMLOCK (co-champ)

Circumference: 316 inches
Height: 202 feet
Spread: 47 feet
Total points: 530

Location: On east side of Wynoochee Trail, 1.2 miles from the road's end.

VINE MAPLE

Circumference: 35 inches
Height: 62 feet
Spread: 31 feet
Total points: 105

Location: North side of South Fork Hoh River Trail, 2.5 miles past the park boundary, across from a large cottonwood.

LODGEPOLE PINE

Circumference: 157 inches
Height: 43 feet
Spread: 44 feet
Total points: 211

Location: By Deer Ridge Trail, about 1 mile east of Deer Park Campground, on uphill side of trail.

Conversely, there are a number of species common elsewhere in western Washington but not native to the Peninsula, such as the noble fir, grizzly bear, wolverine, red fox (those found here today are from introduced animals), pika, lynx, mountain sheep, and mountain goat (introduced).

Wilderness Use

Because of its early protection as a park, development within the park area was largely precluded, and in 1988 nearly 95 percent of Olympic National Park (876,669 acres) was designated by Congress as federal wilderness. A designated wilderness precludes motorized vehicle access, logging, and most other kinds of development. About a third of the park is trailless and rarely visited, including most of the Bailey Range, a large core area centered on Mount Olympus and the headwaters of the Queets River, and much of the drainage divide between the Quinault and Elwha Rivers. In addition, much of the land immediately east of Olympic National Park is managed by the U.S. Forest Service as wilderness in five wilderness areas.

About 40 percent of the total overnight wilderness use in the park is along the coastal strip. Parkwide, most overnight use occurs on Friday and Saturday nights (40 percent), and in July and August (49 percent). There is increasing off-season use, however, especially in west-side valleys and along the coast. Winter activities such as cross-country skiing and snowshoeing are also increasing in popularity. Quotas on overnight campers have been implemented in a few areas, including Lake Constance, Flapjack Lakes, the Sand Point and Cape Alava area, Seven Lakes Basin, and Grand Valley.

A Geographic Tour

Elwha River

The Elwha River Valley near Port Angeles is the part of the Olympics first explored by Europeans. The 1889–90 Press Expedition went up the Elwha during its historic winter crossing of the Olympic Mountains, and many places in the Elwha Valley were named by or for expedition members. Geyser Valley was named by members who thought they heard geysers going off there. Goblin Canyon and Convulsion Canyon were named by expedition members as well. Hayes River is named for an expedition member, and the Press Valley is an obvious reference to the expedition itself.

The Elwha is the largest watershed in the park, covering approximately 175,000 acres. It contains some of the best examples of old-growth Douglas fir forests in the park, with many trees eight feet or more in diameter. The Elwha is largely a wilderness river, and beyond Lake Mills, access is by trail. The valley is flanked on the west by the Bailey Range and high peaks from Obstruction Point to Mount Anderson on the south. To the south lies Low Divide, at 3,662 feet the lowest trans-Olympic pass in the park, providing access into the Quinault drainage. Major tributaries of the Elwha include the Lillian, Lost, Goldie, and Hayes Rivers. Creeks include Boulder, Cat, and Long.

The Elwha was once the single largest producer of salmon on the Peninsula, until dams creating Lake Aldwell and Lake Mills were constructed, blocking upstream passage of fish. There are proposals to remove the dams and recover the salmon runs.

Lake Crescent

Eight-mile-long Lake Crescent is one of the largest lakes in Olympic National Park and certainly one of the most beautiful. The lake was created by ice-age glaciers that scoured out its basin and dammed its outlet with moraine. The lake was originally named Lake Everett after a local trapper, but the name was later changed to refer to its crescent shape. The trail up Mount Storm King provides the best overview of Lake Crescent.

Shortly after the retreat of the glaciers that carved the lake, a huge landslide cut off the lake's outlet from the ocean, creating Lake Sutherland in the process. Fish in the lake were isolated, leading to the development of two unique species: the Beardslee rainbow trout and the Crescent Lake cutthroat trout. Both fish have subsequently been hybridized out of existence by introductions of other varieties of rainbow and cutthroat trout. Nevertheless, the lake is still considered a good place to fish.

Soleduck River

This river has two spellings: Soleduck and Sol Duc, both of which are used. *Soleduck* is Indian for "sparkling waters," and it's an appropriate name. This beautiful stream flows clear down a heavily forested canyon full of trout, and in the appropriate season, there are salmon runs as well. The Soleduck drains the northwest part of the park, first heading north, then turning westward to join the Bogachiel River by the ocean to become the Quillayute River. The Soleduck drainage is mostly outside of the park. Its upper drainage includes the Seven Lakes Basin and the area draining off the High Divide. Many large creeks contribute to its flow within the park, but the North Fork of the Soleduck is the only major river tributary within the park. A road leading to Soleduck Hot Springs follows the river into the park.

Bogachiel River

The Bogachiel is a low-elevation drainage that was hotly contested during the formative years of the park. Timber companies and the Forest Service lobbied hard to keep the drainage and its fine stands of ancient old-growth forest out of the park and available for logging. Surprisingly, even the National Park Service fought to keep the drainage out of the park. But fortunately there was a core of dedicated conservationists who worked even harder to protect the Bogachiel forests.

The U-shaped glaciated valley of the Bogachiel River drains west from a knot of peaks on the watershed divide for the Hoh and Soleduck drainages. Since there are no glaciers in its headwaters, the river runs

The lowland forests of the slightly drier and narrower Bogachiel River Valley are dominated by old-growth Douglas fir rather than Sitka spruce.

The glacially carved upper Hoh River Valley and peaks of the Bailey Range. During the ice age, a huge glacier flowed down the Hoh Valley, nearly reaching the coast.

clear and supports good runs of salmon, steelhead, and trout. A good, easy trail follows the river to its headwaters, providing many access points for wilderness fishing, observation of elk and other wildlife, and enjoyment of the beautiful old-growth forests that cloak the valley.

Hoh River

The Hoh is the largest river in Olympic National Park. It drains the glaciers flowing off Mount Olympus and other peaks in the region. The river's upper valley is extremely steep and U-shaped, reflecting the former presence of valley glaciers. Even today the river runs milky because of glacier flour, ground-up rock coming off its glacial sources. *Hoh* is an abbreviated form of an Indian word that means "fast-moving water." Downstream from its upper glacial sources, the river meanders in braids across a broad valley as it heads west to the Pacific Ocean. The South Fork of the Hoh is a major tributary that has a road and trail along its lower section but is trailless wilderness in its headwaters.

Open to the full brunt of Pacific storms, the Hoh receives massive amounts of precipitation annually. This has contributed to the development of one of the finest examples of temperate rain forest in the world. Its magnificent rain forest, with trees 250 feet tall and up to 12 to 13 feet in diameter, is internationally renowned. The Park Service has a small visitor center in the Hoh, along with a nature trail that introduces visitors to the ecology of the old-growth rain forest. The Hoh is also a major elk winter range and a good place to see Roosevelt elk. A long trail parallels the Hoh to Blue Glacier on Mount Olympus. It's a popular trail for climbers seeking to climb the highest mountain in the park.

Queets River

The Queets River drainage is a cousin to the Hoh. It too has glacial sources on the nearby Mount Olympus and Mount Queets. Its largest tributaries are Matheny Creek, Sams River, and Tshleshy Creek. It also has tremendous rain forests of old-growth Sitka spruce, western hemlock, and Douglas fir. The Queets is less known and less visited than the Hoh, however. The road up to the primitive Park Service campground is rough and slow to drive. And unlike most rivers in the park, you have to ford the Queets River to access its trail, which dead-ends and doesn't connect with any other trails in the park.

Like the Bogachiel, protecting the Queets River old-growth corridor was a great political battle. Originally, the corridor was to extend all the way to the sea and encompass the entire drainage divide. But because of the relentless pressure of the timber industry, only a narrow, fourteen-mile strip was ultimately preserved. The last five miles of the river valley are within the Quinault Indian Reservation. Beyond this narrow corridor, the Queets Basin within the park is well protected, a timeless place where salmon still swim in the river, elk are heard bugling in the autumn, and magnificent forests cloak the mountains.

Quinault River

The Quinault drains the southwest corner of the Olympic Mountains. There are two major tributaries: the North Fork, with sources on Mount Seattle, and the East Fork, which drains glaciers on Mount Anderson. Like other westward-flowing rivers, the Quinault flows through a magnificent glacial valley cloaked with huge trees.

The upper section of the East Fork, known as the Enchanted Valley, is particularly spectacular, with dozens of waterfalls cascading down steep

Sword ferns and old-growth Sitka spruce in the Queets rain forest. Sitka spruce, along with western hemlock, dominates the low-elevation west-side forests in the lower reaches of the Queets, Quinault, Hoh, and other river valleys.

cliff faces 4,000 feet high. The mile-high rugged divide between the Queets and the drainage drained by the North Fork of the Quinault is accessed by the Skyline Trail, one of the most spectacular trails in the park.

Halfway between its headwaters and the ocean lies Lake Quinault. The lake is two by four miles and was carved by ice-age glaciers. Glacial moraine left by retreating ice tongues dammed the river to create the lake.

Queets River corridor. The Queets corridor is the only mountains-to-the-sea continuous forest strip. Less than a mile wide in places, clear-cuts define it on either side.

Skokomish River

The Skokomish River drains the southeast corner of the Olympic Mountains and empties into Hood Canal. The river has two major forks: the North Fork and the South Fork. The North Fork drains into Lake Cushman. The North Fork upstream from Lake Cushman is within Olympic National Park. The Sawtooth Range, as well as other peaks like Mount Stone, Mount Skokomish, and Mount Henderson, separates the North Fork from the Hamma Hamma drainage to the east. A very small amount of the South Fork lies within Olympic National Park by Sundown Pass, but most of the drainage is within the Olympic National Forest. Rainfall is heavy in this section of the park, and though not rain forest, the valley of the North Fork of the Skokomish still contains some of the finest western red cedar and Douglas fir in the park.

Hamma Hamma River

The Hamma Hamma River drains eastward to Hood Canal. The headwaters of the river lie in Olympic National Park, draining Mount Washington, Mount Pershing, and Mount Cruiser. The twin summit of The Brothers, one of the most impressive Olympic peaks seen from across Puget Sound, marks the northern bounds of the Hamma Hamma drainage. The Brothers lie just eight miles from Hood Canal, yet climb to 6,866 feet. Most of the Hamma Hamma lies within Olympic National Forest, and clear-cuts and logging roads outside the park have marred the scenic beauty of the lower slopes of these mountains. *Hamma Hamma* is Indian for "big stink," a reference to the smell of dying salmon that once was prevalent along this stream. Lena Creek is the largest tributary and is followed upstream to Lena Lake by a popular hiking trail.

Duckabush River

The headwaters of the Duckabush River drain the southeastern portion of Olympic National Park, while the lower portion of the river flows through Olympic National Forest. Steep mountains define the Duckabush drainage. The Brothers, Mount Lena, Mount Steel, and Mount Duckabush define the southern divide of the drainage, and Mount Jupiter, Mount LaCrosse, and White Mountains form the northern edge of the river basin. O'Neil Pass, at the headwaters, provides passage into the Quinault River drainage. It was first used by Lt. Joseph O'Neil in an exploration of the mountains in 1890. There are numerous meadows in the higher basins, but no glaciers, hence the river runs clear. Cascades and falls are numerous in the swift river.

Dosewallips River

The Dosewallips is yet another river that drains into Hood Canal from the eastern portion of the Olympic Mountains. There are two major forks: Main and West. Most of the drainage within the park consists of high-elevation meadow and cirque basins. Silt Creek, a major tributary of the Dosewallips, drains Mount Anderson and its glaciers. The beautiful, flower-studded Thousand Acre Meadow lies at the headwaters of the main Dosewallips. The Dosewallips drainage provides access to numerous other major rivers in the park via a series of passes, including Hayden Pass, Lost Pass, Gray Wolf Pass, Constance Pass, and Anderson Pass.

Dungeness River

The beautiful, clear waters of the Dungeness River drain the northeastern Olympic Mountains. Except for where it cuts across the foothills on its journey to the ocean by Sequim, the Dungeness drainage is almost entirely within the Olympic National Forest's Buckhorn Wilderness. The only parts of the Dungeness drainage within Olympic National Park are Royal Creek, the spectacular Royal Basin, and a tiny part of its head-waters near Constance Pass. Encircling the river headwaters are several high peaks, including Iron Mountain and Buckhorn Mountain on the east and Mount Constance, Mount Deception, the Needles, and Mount Clark on the west. Trails follow the main river valley as well as accessing Royal Basin. The Dungeness and its nearby sister, the Gray Wolf drainage, lie in the rain shadow of the high Olympics and as a consequence are the driest part of the Peninsula.

Gray Wolf River

The Gray Wolf River is a transparent stream of unsurpassed clarity flow-ing off the eastern slopes of the Olympic Mountains and is the largest tributary of the Dungeness. The upper parts of the river lie within Olym-pic National Park, while the lower portions of the river flow through Olympic National Forest. The river cascades and drops 5,000 feet from its headwaters near Gray Wolf Pass to its confluence with the Dungeness in only twenty-five miles. It's one of the swiftest rivers in the Olympic Mountains. Grand Creek and Cameron Creek are the two largest tribu-taries of the Gray Wolf River and are nearly as large as the main branch. The three converge at Three Forks Shelter. The Needles and Gray Wolf Ridge form the eastern bounds of the drainage, both well over 7,000 feet, while Obstruction Peak, Grand Ridge, and Cameron Ridge hem in the southwest, western, and northern fringes of the drainage.

Morse Creek and Hurricane Ridge

Morse Creek and its major tributary, Maiden Creek, drain the northern slope of the Olympics near Port Angeles. Hurricane Ridge forms the southwestern edge of the Morse Creek drainage and is perhaps the best-known part of the park because of the Hurricane Ridge Road and Visitor Center.

The views from Hurricane Ridge are outstanding. Looking north, one can see the Strait of Juan de Fuca and Vancouver Island; to the south lies the Elwha and Lillian River drainages, crowned by a knot of high, glacial-clad peaks surrounding Mount Olympus and its neighbors.

Whitebark pine and subalpine fir frame Gray Wolf Ridge and Mount Deception. Both trees grow only in the drier rain shadow in the eastern portion of the Olympic Mountains.

The eastern side of the Morse-Maiden Creek drainage is accessed by a road to Deer Park, a former ski area. Blue Mountain, a former lookout site, offers one of the most commanding views of Puget Sound, and the Strait of Juan de Fuca lies just above Deer Park and is accessible most of the way by road.

The Coastal Strip

The sixty-mile-long coastal strip is divided into three segments: Queets-Hoh, Hoh-Quillayute, and Quillayute to Shi Shi Beach south of Cape Flattery. The most southerly coastal section is the twelve-mile portion lying between the Queets River and the Hoh River, better known as the Kalaloch area. For most of this distance, the coast is paralleled by U.S. 101. This is an area of sand beaches flanked by bluffs. Short trails lead from parking areas to the beach, which can easily be walked for miles. U.S. 101 pulls away from the coast at Ruby Beach, which lies just south of the mouth of the Hoh. Ruby Beach is slightly different from the other beaches, with a number of sea stacks and tidepools.

The twenty-mile-long midsection of the coastal strip, sometimes called the South Beach area, lies between the Hoh and Quillayute Rivers, neither of which can be waded. There is road access to the mouth of the Hoh by Oil City and to La Push on the Quileute Indian Reservation lying at the south side of the Quillayute River, but nowhere in between. This is one of the wilderness coastal strips. La Push is the only port between Cape Flattery and Grays Harbor.

For the most part, this section of coast is a series of headlands separated by long stretches of sand beach. There are a number of small offshore islands and sea stacks; among the most spectacular are the Quillayute Needles, just a few miles south of La Push and accessible by a half-mile trail from the La Push Road.

The twenty-nine-mile-long northern strip lying between Shi Shi Beach and the mouth of the Quillayute River is known as the North Coastal Strip. A road to Ozette Lake, about three miles from the coast, lies in the middle of this coastal strip, and another road dead-ends on the ocean at Mora–Rialto Beach on the south. Eight-mile-long Ozette Lake is the largest in the park and the third largest in Washington. This section of coast is similar to the South Wilderness Coast, with numerous rocky headlands separated by long, sandy beaches, often with flanking bluffs.

Humans on the Peninsula

Native Americans occupied the Peninsula shortly after the ice-age glaciers retreated. Different tribal groups came and went, often displaced by new people. This changing human tide was accelerated by the settlement of the region by Euro-Americans in the 1880s. Early commercial activities consisted of subsistence farming, fishing, logging, and some mining. The isolation, wet weather, dense forests, and steep terrain of the Peninsula's mountains slowed development and buffered the area from the urbanization of the Puget Sound region. This lack of urbanization, combined with the protected landscape found in Olympic National Park, is increasingly attracting people to the area for recreation and retirement. The eastern edge of the park is only thirty to forty miles west of the Seattle-Tacoma area, with over 2 million people. Olympic National Park is the primary travel objective on the Peninsula, receiving over 4.6 million visits in 1995 and having one of the highest overnight use rates of all parks in the country. Although visitation occurs throughout the year, the vast majority of people arrive in the drier months of summer and early fall.

Economics and Demographics

Although the Peninsula was one of the first parts of Washington to be settled by Euro-Americans, it has remained largely unpopulated. The largest population centers on the Peninsula are the Aberdeen-Hoquiam area, with a combined population of roughly 25,000; Forks, 3,000; Port Angeles, 19,000; Sequim, 3,600; and Port Townsend, 7,700; plus smaller settlements and outposts including Hoodsport, Clallam Bay, Gardiner, and Quilcene.

Historically, fishing, tourism, government, and wood products were the primary employers. That has changed in recent years, with a marked decline in the wood products industry and an increase in tourism. In the Pacific Northwest as a whole, tourism is the fourth-largest and one of the fastest-growing basic industries. Only the food, defense, and forest products industries are larger employers. The natural beauty and diversity of the region are essential parts of its appeal. On the Olympic Peninsula, steady growth in visitation translated into over 3,200 tourism-generated jobs in Clallam and Jefferson Counties in 1993, according to the North Olympic Visitor and Convention Bureau.

Visitation to Olympic National Park has fluctuated annually in close rhythm with trends throughout the national park system. However, weekend patterns in the off season and daily patterns from June through September are geared more closely to the weather predictions for Puget Sound. Although weather can differ greatly from one area of the park to another, radio and television predictions for the greater Seattle area seem to affect whether people visit the Peninsula. In other words, if sunshine is predicted for Seattle, it doesn't matter much what is happening in Port Angeles or Forks, people pack up the car and head out to the Peninsula.

Visitation is highest in August and lowest in the winter. There is a trend toward more visitors in fall, particularly from September to mid-October. Because much of the park is at lower elevations, visitors also come throughout the year. Much of Olympic's winter visitation is to the coastal strip. Kalaloch, Mora, and Ozette all have year-round appeal, as visitors are drawn by both winter storm events and low tides.

As much as 67 percent of visitors come from no farther away than the greater Puget Sound, including the Olympic Peninsula. Average length of stay varies around the park, from as long as 3.5 days to a quarter hour. The park's 906 campsites and the nearly 2,400 campsites operated privately and by other government agencies are filled on major holidays and sunny weekends in summer. Visitor and convention bureau figures for 1995 show that average campers spend about $66 per party per day on food, recreation, campsites, transportation, and shopping. Those who stay in commercial lodging spend over $150 per day. And fully 25 percent of Olympic visitors stay overnight, compared with the 10 percent national average for overnight use in most national parks.

Visitors traveling to the north Olympic Peninsula are an essential part of the region's economy. The money they spend has been increasing steadily at an average of nearly 6 percent a year, reaching $208 million in Clallam and Jefferson Counties in 1993, according to North Olympic Visitor and Convention Bureau figures. These dollars translate into jobs and business sales. Since Olympic National Park is a major attraction for most of the Peninsula's visitors, it plays an important role in the economic health of the region.

PARK VISITATION BY THE MONTH IN 1998			
January	173,036	July	806,942
February	205,197	August	890,142
March	213,114	September	582,197
April	307,309	October	291,254
May	340,890	November	169,013
June	503,064	December	139,572
	Total visitors	4,621,730	

CLIMATE AND WEATHER

The green luxuriant vegetation cloaking the Olympic Peninsula is evidence that the climate is dominated by abundant precipitation. The climate of the Olympic Peninsula is classified as a marine type with cool summers, mild but cloudy winters dominated by moist air, and a small daily range in temperatures.

The climate of the Olympic Peninsula is controlled by three factors: the close proximity of the Pacific Ocean, which surrounds it on three sides; the high mountains that form the core of the Peninsula; and the broader climatic controls exerted by the shifting influence of high and low pressure cells in the Northern Pacific.

Of the three, perhaps the greatest influence upon the region's climate is the almost ubiquitous presence of the ocean. Water has the ability to store tremendous amounts of heat and release it slowly. The Pacific Ocean and the many arms of Puget Sound, which surround the Peninsula on three sides, form a huge heat sink, storing solar radiation from the sun as heat and slowly releasing it to the surrounding atmosphere. The moderating effect of the ocean means that winter temperatures are seldom cold and summer temperatures are equable.

By comparison, inland continental locations experience far greater extremes in both daily and annual temperatures. Consider that the Olympic Peninsula is at the same latitude as Montana. Great Falls, Montana, has a continental climate, characterized by temperature extremes and generally low precipitation. In an average year, Great Falls experiences 155 days when the temperature dips below 32 degrees Fahrenheit. The average summer high is in the mid-80s, with a record of 107 degrees F once recorded. The average January temperature is 10 degrees, with the record low of minus 49 recorded in 1936. Because of its location in the rain shadow of the Rockies and the overall cold temperatures that

Clouds cling to the forest along the Bogachiel River. The west side of the Olympic Peninsula receives in excess of 200 inches of precipitation a year, sustaining the lush rain forests of the Hoh, Queets, Quinault, and Bogachiel Valleys.

dominate so much of the year, annual precipitation is minimal. Clear skies and sunshine prevail. Great Falls receives a scant fifteen inches of moisture a year—less than the total reported in a typical winter month along the Hoh River.

Quillayute, near Forks, on the Olympic Peninsula, represents the opposite extreme. It receives rain an average of 210 days a year. Only Hilo, Hawaii, and some small coastal communities in Alaska receive more rain annually. This generous dose of moisture averages 103 inches of precipitation annually—more in really wet years! Yet Quillayute is not the wettest recording station on the Peninsula. Quinault, slightly south and east and closer to the mountains, receives 132 inches annually. Still, none of these communities can match the 184 inches that deluged Wynoochee Oxbow, on the southern edge of the mountains northeast of Aberdeen. That's an average of more than half an inch of moisture a day! Although there are no record stations to verify it, it is estimated that more than 200 inches fall annually in the higher parts of the Olympic Mountains.

All the moisture and heavy cloud cover moderate the temperature. Depending on the season, it's either warm or cool. Clouds not only trap heat in, but reflect the sun's heat back into space as well. Western Washington has the lowest heat budget of any place in the continental United States.

Quillayute has never experienced temperatures below zero or above 100 degrees F. On very rare occasions, a blast of frigid arctic air will invade the Northwest, dropping temperatures far below normal. A record 5 degrees has been recorded in Quillayute. Similarly, in summer, hot air from the interior of North America manages to cross the Cascades, bringing high summer temperatures. This accounts for the record high of 99 degrees F once recorded at Quillayute.

Despite the generalization that precipitation is abundant, there is great variation in annual rain and snow fall as a consequence of the high barrier created by the Olympic Mountains. Sequim, in the rain shadow of the Olympic Mountains on the northeast side of the Peninsula, receives an average of about seventeen inches of precipitation a year—the lowest annual precipitation of any location in western Washington. The rain shadow effect of the high mountain barrier is also felt elsewhere on the Peninsula. Port Angeles receives only a scant twenty-five inches recorded annually. This is considerably less than the fifty-seven inches that falls on Miami or even the forty-three inches that New York City receives.

When most people think of the "rainy" Olympic Peninsula, of course, they are thinking of the western valleys of the Olympic Mountains, where the full brunt of Pacific storms is experienced. Air masses attempting to move inland run into the barrier of the mountains, cool, and drop even more moisture on the slopes. Forty airline miles to the west of Sequim, the rain forest valleys in the park are drenched with an average 140 to 167 inches of precipitation per year. At the higher elevations of the Olympics, between 350 and 500 inches of snow falls in a typical winter.

Fortunately for those interested in visiting Olympic National Park, there is great seasonality to the precipitation, with 76 percent falling during the six months between October 1 and March 31. In summer, when most people choose to visit the park, the weather is typically warm and relatively dry.

Global Climatic Influences

The Pacific Northwest lies astride the mid-latitude cyclonic storm belt. Major climatic influences affecting the entire Pacific Northwest are controlled by two major air mass systems: the North Pacific High and the Aleutian Low. The center for the North Pacific High lies about 1,000 miles off the coast of San Francisco and is responsible for California's wonderful dry, sunny climate. The Aleutian Low lies off the Gulf of Alaska and Bering Sea. It generates wet, cool weather and frequent stormy conditions, as anyone who has visited Alaska's Aleutian Islands can testify. Where these two pressure systems meet, there is a prevailing westerly wind.

In winter, the Aleutian Low intensifies and moves southward, bringing wet storm fronts to the Pacific Northwest. In summer, the North Pacific High advances northward, generating clear, dry weather.

The reason for these differences in weather is partly due to how these different pressure systems operate. The North Pacific High spins clockwise, with the air mass traveling across the relatively cool waters of the North Pacific in the Gulf of Alaska. As a result, the air is cooled and is unable to hold much moisture. The Aleutian Low spins counterclockwise, traveling long distances over the warmer waters of the mid-Pacific. By the time the Aleutian Low frontal systems reach the west coast, they have absorbed a tremendous amount of moisture and heat. As a result, coastal lands bathed by these prevailing winds are warmed in winter and cooled in summer. In effect, the Pacific Northwest has a natural air conditioning and heating system generated by the Pacific Ocean and prevailing winds.

On rare occasions, the prevailing westerlies are deflected north or south by invading arctic air from the east of the Cascades. When such cold fronts blast into the region, they bring record-setting cold temperatures but clear, sunny skies. In summer, invasion of hot, dry air from the interior of the continent can also occur, leading to temperatures above 90 degrees in Seattle, as well as on the Olympic Peninsula. These east winds also bring a low humidity of 20 to 30 percent.

In crossing and descending the Cascade Mountains, these air masses warm, and hence are able to absorb even more moisture. Acting like a sponge, they suck up whatever moisture there is in the landscape, further drying out the forests. By the time these east winds have crossed the Olympic Mountains to reach the western side of the Olympic Peninsula, they are even drier, since they have crossed a second major mountain barrier. The extended duration of these conditions often leads to ideal burning conditions and is responsible for the occasional large wildfires that periodically burn even rain forest.

The other major influence on the Pacific Northwest are winter cyclonic storms. Most of these storms are generated in Asia over China and Japan. They move northeast across the Pacific, taking anywhere from seven to ten days to make a landfall on our shores. These storms are spawned by the collision of moist, subtropical air masses with polar cold fronts. The moist air rises, pressure falls, and high winds with heavy rains are generated.

The jet stream, high-altitude winds that circle the globe, drag these storms to the Pacific coast. The centers of these winter storm fronts usually pass to the north of Washington, crashing into the coasts of British Columbia and Alaska. Nevertheless, the southern fringes of these tempests pass over the Pacific Northwest, bringing drizzle and cloudy weather. At times, however, the center of these cyclonic storms will lash the northern California, Oregon, and Washington coasts, bringing record-breaking torrential rains and howling winds. As the low passes over the coastal region, it actually sucks up the water, creating the storm surges that can raise sea levels several feet above normal, causing flooding of low-lying areas.

The greatest rainfall and flooding typically occur when the "pineapple express" brings warm air and rain to the west coast. The name "pineapple express" refers to the origins near Hawaii of these moist, warm, southwest-flowing air masses that periodically invade the Pacific Northwest. Because warm air can hold a higher amount of moisture than cooler air, the "pineapple express" often produces days of heavy rain. Not only does the abundant rainfall melt mountain snowpacks, but the warm tropical air accelerates snowmelt. If the soils are already saturated, the end result is often extensive flooding.

Winter storms are the major ecological agent responsible for shaping coastal beaches and headlands. The battering waves shear away mussels, barnacles, and other life clinging to rocks and tidepools. At the same time, the heavy rainfall floods rivers, rearranging stream channels and riparian areas. The high winds topple and snap trees, creating small openings and snags in the forest. Winter storms are among the most important major ecological influences upon the Olympic Peninsula's life on both land and coastal strand.

El Niño Influences

One wouldn't suspect it immediately, but the weather in western Washington is often affected by what happens halfway across the globe in the South Pacific. The frequency of winter storms varies with the position of the high-elevation winds known as the jet stream. In some years, the jet stream is deflected northward by subtropical air masses called El Niño. El Niño is named for "Christ child," a name given to the phenomenon by Peruvian fishermen who noticed that the sea water off the coast of South America sometimes warmed significantly around Christmas.

Today the name refers to what scientists call the "El Niño–Southern Oscillation" or ENSO. The "Southern Oscillation" part of the name comes from observations made in the early 1900s by a British scientist, Gilbert Walker. Walker discovered that when atmospheric pressure was low around Australia, it was high to the east at Tahiti. When the pressure was high in Australia, it was low in Tahiti. This back and forth change in air pressure first observed by Walker is now known as the Southern Oscillation.

Normally, there is a huge pool of warm ocean water in the western Pacific. Normally, east-to-west trade winds push water heated by the tropical sun westward, piling it up around Indonesia and other places west of the International Date Line. However, for yet unknown reasons, the strength of the trade winds weakens occasionally and this huge pool of warm water migrates eastward across the Pacific to South America. When it reaches the South American coast, it splits into two branches. One branch heads south but the other moves north toward North America.

The warm ocean water then affects the atmosphere. Tropical thunderstorms spawned by hot, humid air over the oceans pump warm air and humidity more than 50,000 feet into the air. This then disrupts the normal flow pattern of the high-altitude jet stream winds, allowing warm tropical air masses to move closer to the west coast of North America. The result is typically more moisture in southern California, while drier winters dominate in the Pacific Northwest.

Prolonged El Niño influences bring about many ecological changes. Warmer water flows off the West Coast, allowing southern fish species to move northward, while fish requiring cold waters are pushed further north. El Niño years may also affect salmon recruitment, since less winter precipitation results in reduced winter stream flows that can jeopardize the overwinter survival of eggs in spawning beds and also affect the timing and eventual success of juvenile salmon migration to the sea. Finally, the reduced winter precipitation results in lower mountain snowpack. Forests dry out earlier in the year and are more likely to burn during the following fire season. As will be discussed in later chapters, most large fires are not a consequence of fuel accumulation, but are due to periodic drought conditions often precipitated by El Niño winters.

For most residents, the rainy winters are tolerable because the summer months are absolutely gorgeous, with many sunny days and mild temperatures. As the sun moves northward with spring, the jet stream shifts north with it. By July the weather is stable and clear. Drought, often lasting several weeks or even months, occurs most summers. Though brief, these summer droughts strongly influence which plants can survive in the Pacific Northwest and are one reason why conifers dominate the region.

Because of the nearness of the marine environment, heating of land is minimized, reducing the potential for rapidly rising air that creates thunderheads and lightning. As a result, thunderstorms are relatively rare here, unlike the southern Rockies, where afternoon thunderstorms are almost daily occurrences. Even during the height of the summer, thunderstorms develop over the Olympic Mountains only about once a month.

A common summer phenomenon in the region is fog. When summer warmed air masses come in contact with the cold coastal waters, they are chilled and the moisture in the air condenses out, forming the clouds we call fog. At night, this fog moves inland to settle in the coastal lowlands, filling valleys to 3,000 feet or so. Stringers of fog fill the valleys, while the higher ridges and peaks remain fog-free. With the warming of the air the following day, the fog dissipates.

Even in midsummer, the sky over many lowland sites, particularly on the western slopes, is clear only about one-fourth of the time. Partly cloudy conditions prevail for another fourth of the time, while the other half of the days, clouds or even rain occurs. This changes, however, if you climb higher in the mountains above the fog belt. Higher basins and ridges above 3,000 feet often experience clear weather for weeks at a time.

Mountains as Weather Machines

The presence of high mountains in the center of the Olympic Peninsula also influences regional weather patterns. Air temperatures usually drop an average of 3.5 degrees for every 1,000-foot gain in elevation. Thus, if you climb or drive higher up into the mountains, the air temperature cools. Hurricane Ridge may be as much as 15 degrees cooler than Port Angeles. The actual temperature change is contingent upon many variables, including the amount of moisture in the air, the temperature of rising air masses, and other factors. Nevertheless, as a rule, the higher you climb, the cooler the temperature.

Though less than 8,000 feet in elevation, the Olympic Mountains nevertheless create a significant obstacle for the unrestricted movement of air masses. Clouds coming off the Pacific Ocean pile up against the mountains. In climbing over them, these air masses cool. Since cool air can't hold as much moisture as warmer air, great amounts of precipitation are wrung from the clouds by the mountains. The higher up the mountain, the more moisture typically falls. Greater amounts of moisture and cooler temperatures affect the plants that can survive at any given elevation. Not surprisingly, elevation has a significant influence upon what will grow and where.

Mountains also channel air movement. In summer, cool temperatures aloft sink rapidly down valleys, bringing nighttime cooling. In the day, warm air heated in the valleys rises, heating the upper slopes and creating gentle upslope daytime breezes. Since cool air sinks, the bottoms of alpine basins are often significantly colder than adjacent slopes and terraces— an important consideration in picking a tent site if you don't have a warm sleeping bag. The cool air flow also influences plant growth. Many alpine basins remain treeless, while adjacent slopes are treed, simply because the cold air that settles in basin bottoms creates conditions too frigid for the successful establishment of tree seedlings.

Another influence of mountains upon local weather is downslope air flow. As an air parcel begins its journey over the Pacific Ocean and moves inland as warm, moist air, it is forced to rise up and over the Olympic Mountains. As it does, it cools. This process is known as adiabatic cooling. As the air parcel cools during its upward journey, moisture is wrung out of the parcel, and precipitation usually falls over the western slopes of the mountains. This one reason why rain and snow fall are so much higher in western Washington than east of the Cascades.

As the cooled air parcel continues its journey across the mountains, it reaches the eastern slopes near Hood Canal and the Strait of Juan de Fuca. These air parcels flow down the eastern slopes of the mountains, warming as they descend. This is known as adiabatic warming. Air warms about 5.5 degrees F per 1,000 feet of descent. By the time the parcel has reached sea level, it has warmed up significantly. Not only is the air warm, but it is also very dry, having lost most of its moisture in ascending and crossing the mountains. The warm, dry air often leads to the rapid disappearance of snow. As a result, many local forecasters refer to downslope winds off the Rockies as "Chinook" winds, which means "snow eater." On the Olympic Peninsula, such warm, drying winds bring clear weather and reduced rainfall to places, such as Sequim, located on the northeast slope or in the rain shadow of the mountains.

The Olympics Through the Seasons

Winter

Winters on the Olympic Peninsula are wet and drab. Cloudy weather lasts for weeks at a time, with nearly constant drizzle or more intense rain, particularly on the western slope of the mountains. Only about three days a month are sunny and clear.

During the winter season, afternoon temperatures are in the 40s and nighttime readings are usually in the upper 30s. In lower elevations and near the water, snow seldom reaches a depth in excess of six to ten inches or remains on the ground more than a few days. Snowfall increases dramatically with elevation, however. During the months of December, January, and February, about seven feet of very wet snow falls on the high country each month. In midwinter, the snowline is between 1,500 and 3,000 feet. Below the snowline, the majority of precipitation falls as rain; above it, snow dominates.

Spring

Springs are typically wet, mild, and often windy. Higher elevations remain cool, with snow flurries still possible. Temperatures usually range from 35 to 60 degrees F. This is a transition time for the Peninsula. Rainy days are followed by sunny days. Breaks in the clouds and duration of rainy days begin to shift toward the summer dry period.

Summer

This is the season when most people visit the park, and for good reason—it has the best weather of the year. Indeed, in many ways, the summers are exquisite. Rainfall is almost nonexistent, although right along the coast, it's not uncommon to have one or two inches of rain a month. July is the driest month, although June and August are not much different. A few thunderstorms usually occur each summer, especially in the higher elevations. More lightning storms occur on the drier eastern side of the mountains than on the western slopes. Though very little rain normally falls during the summer months, it has also been known to rain for several days during this period.

Temperatures are mild. Afternoon temperatures in the warmest summer months average from 65 to 70 degrees F, occasionally reaching 80. Because of the cooling influence of the surrounding ocean, daytime temperatures remain moderate. A temperature of 85 is considered unusually warm. Nighttime temperatures can drop as low as 45 degrees F. At higher elevations, temperatures average between 55 and 65 degrees, dropping into the low 40s and high 30s at night. Nighttime freezing temperatures are comparatively rare.

Frequently, during the latter half of the summer and early fall, fog banks and low clouds form over the ocean and move inland at night. Tops of the clouds are generally below 3,000 feet; thus, higher elevations are sometimes clear while the lower valleys are filled with fog. Fog sometimes disappears before midday. On most summer afternoons, a moderate to cool breeze can be expected near the water.

Fall

Early fall is a continuation of summer, and many people consider September to be the ideal month to visit the Olympics, since the most stable and sunny weather of the year often occurs during this month, and summer crowds have thinned. Nevertheless, as the year moves into October, there is a gradual transition back to the winter rainy season. Indeed, the greatest change in precipitation occurs between September and October. By October, more than two-thirds of the days are overcast. Early snowstorms are possible in the mountains. Temperatures usually range from 35 to 65 degrees F.

PRECIPITATION AVERAGES
(measured in inches per month)

	Spring	Summer	Fall	Winter	Average inches per year
Port Angeles	1.32	.67	2.45	3.76	24.6
Staircase (Lake Cushman)	6.60	1.70	9.40	15.71	100.25
Kalaloch (Ocean Beaches)	8.94	3.13	11.17	17.12	103.0
Hoh (Rain Forest)	12.48	3.14	13.15	15.75	133.58

WEATHER BY THE MONTH

Port Townsend, Washington—rain shadow of Olympic Mountains

Month	Average precipitation (inches)	Average high temperature	Average low temperature	Record high	Record low
January	3.72	42	34	60	11
February	4.03	45	36	60	22
March	2.08	47	38	55	26
April	0.81	53	41	65	36
May	1.1	57	46	70	38
June	0.55	61	49	80	43
July	0.59	62	51	80	46
August	0.83	62	51	80	45
September	0.78	61	49	79	42
October	2.34	54	45	65	38
November	3.77	49	41	66	34
December	1.5	45	38	61	24

Quillayute, Washington—western Oympic Peninsula

Month	Average precipitation (inches)	Average high temperature	Average low temperature	Record high	Record low
January	13.9	46	34	65	7
February	12.2	49	35	72	11
March	11.3	52	35	71	19
April	7.5	55	37	83	24
May	5.6	60	42	92	29
June	3.2	64	47	96	33
July	2.6	68	49	97	38
August	2.3	69	50	99	36
September	5.1	67	46	97	28
October	10.4	59	41	83	24
November	14.1	51	37	69	5
December	15.1	45	34	64	7

Quillayute, Washington

Variable: Annual precipitation (inches)

Highest year:	131.64	1975
Third quartile:	111.81	
Median:	101.77	
First quartile:	91.27	
Lowest year:	60.24	1985
Mean:	101.41	

ANNUAL MEAN RANKINGS 1961–1996
(Years of greatest precipitation)
(Ranked list with 29 years available)

Total inches	Year	Ranking	Total inches	Year	Ranking
131.64	1975	1	99.73	1986	16
129.42	1968	2	99.03	1988	17
127.76	1974	3	99.02	1979	18
121.00	1983	4	99.01	1991	19
119.61	1967	5	98.84	1977	20
119.58	1971	6	95.67	1969	21
117.05	1990	7	91.27	1970	22
111.81	1984	8	90.34	1992	23
109.15	1972	9	86.05	1976	24
109.15	1982	10	84.97	1989	25
105.06	1981	11	80.94	1987	26
104.54	1995	12	71.54	1978	27
103.81	1994	13	69.85	1993	28
102.11	1980	14	60.24	1993	29
101.77	1973	15			

Oceanography

The major global influences on weather, such as the circulation of air masses, also affect the movement of water in the ocean. As these air masses move across the globe, they push and drag water with them, creating currents. For instance, the prevailing westerlies that move across the Pacific Ocean at about 40 degrees latitude produce the North Pacific Drift. This current reaches the West Coast of North America just off the Pacific Northwest, where it splits, one branch swinging up along the British Columbia and Alaska coasts, the other moving southward along the Oregon and California coasts.

The prevailing winds continually push the surface waters offshore, lowering sea level immediately adjacent to shore. Removal of surface water allows deeper waters to rise toward the surface. The end result is the upwelling of colder, nutrient-rich waters close to shore. This nutrient upwelling provides fertile feeding grounds for marine mammals, seabirds, and fish. The rich variety of sea life found along the Olympic shore in summer is one consequence of this upwelling. Indeed, inshore waters are far more productive than the open ocean.

In winter, a near-shore current, known as the Davidson Current, flows northward along the Oregon and Washington coasts, pushing the southward-flowing California Current farther offshore. This reversal in near-shore currents has other consequences for the coastal environment. The Davidson Current carries the sizable freshwater plume of the Columbia River north along the Washington coast, lowering the salinity of the near-shore environment. This reversal of inshore currents also affects the development of beaches and spits. In summer, sand and other sediments are carried southward; in winter, the reverse occurs. Since this load of sediment is often deposited wherever there is a break in the shoreline, such as at the mouth of a river, currents can alternately open and close ocean access of smaller rivers and streams with the seasonal changes in inshore currents.

Tides

Anyone spending time along the shore, particularly hikers on the wild Olympic coast, must pay attention to the comings and goings of tides. The gravitational pull of the sun and moon creates tides. The surface of the ocean is pulled toward the moon, creating a bulge on both sides of the earth. At the new and full moon, the sun lines up with the moon. This magnifies the gravitational pull, causing high tides to be 10 percent higher and low tides 10 percent lower. These tides are known as "spring tides," since they switch so dramatically from one extreme to the other. When the moon is at right angles to the sun during the first and third quarters, the gravitational pull is reduced. This produces "neap tides," where the magnitude between high and low tides is reduced.

High tides and low tides occur twice a day. Each tide change is approximately six hours and twelve minutes apart, resulting in a gradual shift in tides that are fifty minutes later each day. The magnitude of each tide is not usually equal. Because of the northern location of the Olympic Peninsula and the centrifugal force of the earth's orbit, one high tide is usually greater than the other, and one low tide is lower than the other.

GEOLOGY

The Pacific Northwest is one of the most geologically active parts of the world. Earthquakes, volcanoes, mountain building, and glaciers have all shaped the appearance of the region. As many would agree, these geological processes have created one of the most scenic landscapes in North America, if not the world.

The driving force behind the Pacific Northwest's spectacular scenery is *plate tectonics*, a unifying theory that explains the creation of the world's oceans and continents. Plate tectonics provides a basis for conceptualizing the geological underpinnings of the Pacific Northwest, and Olympic National Park in particular. According to plate theory, the earth's mantle, or outer surface, consists of giant slabs or fragments that are forty to sixty miles thick and as large as entire continents. They "float," like ice pans in a river, on the molten magma that makes up the inner core of the earth. The North American continent makes up one plate, and the Pacific Ocean basin is yet another plate.

The movement of plates is driven by heat from radioactive decay deep in the earth, which rises toward the surface. Once the molten rock reaches the bottom of the plates, it is deflected parallel to the earth surface and, like a slow flow of molasses, drags the plates with it. Eventually the molten rock cools and sinks, and the process begins again.

The movements of these plates are random. Some plates move past each other; others ride up and over heavier, denser plates, which sink. Plates may break apart, and some collide. Each kind of motion results in different landscape features. These different movements create mountain ranges, crumple ocean basins, and cause earthquakes along active plate margins. The world's mountains all occur along former or active zones of plate movement. For example, the collision of the Indian subcontinent and Asian plates thrust up the Himalayan Mountains. The Andes of

South America lie along another active plate margin. California's San Andreas Fault represents two plate margins' lateral movement past each other.

The Pacific Northwest (northern California, Oregon, Washington, and British Columbia) is the site of the Cascadia subduction zone. Here the American Plate abuts the Juan de Fuca Plate, a small part of the larger Pacific Ocean Plate. The American Plate is slowly overriding the Juan de Fuca Plate, forcing it under the westward-moving North American continent.

Rocks riding upon the subducting plate are transformed by the pressure and heat into entirely new forms known as *metamorphic rock*. For example, limestone, a sedimentary rock, can be metamorphosed into marble, and sandstone into quartzite. If the pressure is sufficient, the rocks are flattened like dough under a rolling pin, with sedimentary layers being twisted and swirled to create schists and gneiss.

If the rock continues to be dragged deeper, increasing heat and pressure cause these rocks to melt completely, becoming magma. This molten magma then rises toward the surface of the earth, cooling as it rises. In some places, molten rock reaches the surface of the earth and erupts as a *volcano*. The Cascade volcanoes, including Mounts Rainier, St. Helens, Baker, and Hood, were all created by rising molten rock derived from the melted oceanic plate material.

In other places, the molten rock never reaches the earth's surface, but slowly cools in place. Such rocks are known as *plutonic*. Large crystals form under slow cooling, and microscopic crystals are created by rapid cooling when magma erupts on the surface. Plutonic rocks, when exposed at the surface, are grouped under the generic name granite. There are, however, a wide variety of granitic rocks. The great granitic bodies of California's Sierra Nevada and British Columbia's Coast Mountains were both formed deep in the earth and slowly exposed by erosion. Both volcanic and plutonic rocks are known as *igneous rock*, meaning "born of fire," recognizing their common origins.

The western coast of North America represents the leading edge of a continental plate, and the Atlantic seaboard the trailing edge. About 200 million years ago, North America was bound to Europe, Africa, and Asia in a single giant land mass. Then North and South America broke away from the Euro-Asian-African land mass, with the Atlantic Ocean opening up in its trail. A rift in the middle of the ocean floor oozed lava that

EARTHQUAKES

The Pacific Northwest—northern California, Oregon, Washington, and British Columbia—is the site of the *Cascadia subduction zone*. Here an oceanic tectonic plate, the Juan de Fuca plate, is being pulled and subducted beneath the North American continental plate. As a result of the interaction between the two plates, the continent overlying the subduction zone is the site of numerous geological changes. One manifestation of this subduction is earthquakes.

Yet there are relatively few earthquakes recorded along the *Cascadia megathrust*. In 1949, there was a quake centered on Olympia that measured 7.1 on the Richter Scale. In 1965, one in the Seattle-Tacoma area measured 6.5. Nevertheless, compared with southern California, the region experiences few large earthquakes. Still, the Pacific Northwest could be a sleeping giant that may someday suffer from a huge earthquake of devastating proportions.

Geologists speculate that the current earthquake inactivity along the coasts of Oregon and Washington is the result of a "locked" fault. Instead of having numerous small earthquakes that gradually relieve the stress resulting from plate movements, the faults defining the coastal mountains, including the Olympic Peninsula, are likely to "snap" suddenly, creating a giant earthquake. Evidence gleaned from local *tsunami* (tidal wave) deposits suggests that great earthquakes rocked the Pacific Northwest perhaps as recently as 300 years ago. Many earthquake specialists believe that an earthquake of a magnitude as large as 9 on the Richter Scale may devastate the region within the next couple hundred years.

solidified into basalt, creating a new seafloor. The rift remained stationary while the two continental masses separated. The Atlantic Ocean is still growing larger, as the distance between Europe and North America widens each year.

The geography of the North American coastlines reflects their positions on the two edges of the continental plate. A leading-edge coast tends to have a shallow continental margin, steep coastal mountains, and few bays. We see all these features on the Olympic Peninsula, which has almost no bays and a limited continental shelf but does have coastal mountains, sea stacks, and tidepools. A trailing-edge coast, such as the Atlantic seaboard, tends to be flat with little relief, and has large bays and a wide continental shelf.

Although the Olympic Mountains are similar geologically to the Coast Mountains of Oregon, they are separated from them by the Chehalis River lowlands. The radial design of the Olympic Peninsula rivers demonstrates, however, that the Olympics rose as an isolated uplift, not as part of some larger mountain chain.

The three most abundant rocks in the Olympics are basalt, sandstone, and shale. *Basalt* is usually formed as underwater lava flows. Basalt is a dense, hard rock that is usually black or very dark green in color. Most of the world's ocean basins are composed primarily of basalt. Basalt

Pillow basalt in the Dosewallips River Valley. Pillow basalts are formed when molten lava is erupted in seawater, which cools the outer surface rapidly, giving the rock a doughlike appearance. Pillow basalts are common in many parts of the Crescent Formation, a ring of basalt that encircles the northern, eastern, and southern fringes of the Olympic Mountains. A good place to view them is along the Hurricane Ridge Road and along the south shore of Lake Crescent.

originates as lava and is typically full of gases, which create tiny vesicles, or bubbles, in the rock. If basalt flows out from vents underwater, as much of the Olympic basalts did, it forms bulbous masses called *pillow basalts*. The rounded pillow basalts are created when the outer surface of the hot lava cools quickly. At other times, the basalt piles up as a collection of broken rock called *breccia*. Not all of the Olympic basalts formed beneath the sea. At times, they flowed out on land, cooling more slowly than basalts erupted underwater. These slower-cooling basalts developed cracks and *columnar joints*. The polygonal columns are formed by shrinkage inward of the cooling lava flow.

Sandwiched between these basalt flows are reddish-colored *limestones*. These limestones are composed of mud and the microskeletons of one-celled creatures called foraminifera. Their bodies were deposited on ocean floors in between basalt flows. The red color is derived from iron leached from the hot basalts that covered the limestones. These limestones also contain quantities of copper and manganese. These mineral deposits were the object of intense mining effort prior to the establishment of Olympic National Park. The Tubal Cain Mine by Buckhorn Mountain, Crescent Mine by Lake Crescent, and Elkhorn Mine on the south side of Mount Constance were all developed in the limestone layers. However, none of these ever contained enough high-quality ore to warrant commercial development. One of the best places to see red limestones from the road is along the *Hurricane Ridge Road*.

Sandstone is another major rock type found in the Olympics. As its name implies, sandstone is composed primarily of small grains of sand. Sandstone is eroded from uplands and usually transported by water to some settlement basin, either a lake or an ocean. Because the sand is laid down in horizontal layers, most sandstone exhibits *bedding*, or sequential layering. Because sand grains are heavy, they are usually deposited relatively close to shore. Sandstone is abundant in the park. It is one of the major rocks that makes up the areas around *Lost Pass* and *Mount Cameron*. Sandstone is also seen in the roadcuts up to *Deer Park*. Slabs of sandstone also make up much of the *Bailey Range*, *Mount Anderson*, *Mount Seattle*, *Mount Christie*, *Mount Olympus*, and *Seven Lakes Basin*, and all along the *High Divide*. The gorges of the *Elwha River*, including Rica Canyon and Grand Canyon of the Elwha, are carved into hard, resistant sandstone, as is the area around *Low Divide*. *Soleduck Falls* is cut into sandstone bedding that stands on edge vertically.

Shale also occurs in the Olympic Mountains. Shale is composed of solidified mud. Due to their lighter weight, mud particles are often deposited in deeper waters than sands. Sometimes there is an alternation of mud and sand deposits, forming bedded deposits such as those found on *Blue Mountain* and along parts of the coast, showing the changing depth of the ancient sea basin from shallow to deep and back again. Dark bands of shale are seen alternating with lighter sandstone outcrops all along the *Deer Park Road*.

Nearly all the rocks found on the Olympic Peninsula were formed between 15 and 55 million years ago. There are, however, a few older rocks exposed on the Olympic Peninsula. Near *Point of Rocks* on the coast are sea stacks and sea cliffs made of *gabbro*, a type of igneous rock similar to basalt, basalt, and sandstones estimated to be 144 million years of age, laid down on top of a previously eroded continental surface. These likely floated onto the edge of the Peninsula along with other younger materials.

In the inner portion of the Olympics lie core sedimentary rocks of sandstone and shales that have been faulted and partially metamorphosed. Surrounding them in a horseshoe shape are basalts of the *Crescent Formation*. These basalts were formed on the ocean floor as volcanoes or *sea mounts* (underwater volcanoes), perhaps 50 million years ago. At one time, the core sedimentary rock sat on top of the basalt formations, making up an island arc that collided with the North American continent.

Along the Pacific Northwest coast, plate movement is also responsible for the uplift of coastal mountains, including the Olympics. As the Juan de Fuca Plate has been driven under the North American Plate, oceanic sediments, along with the underlying basement basalt, have been scraped off and plastered or welded onto the leading edge of the North American Plate. In effect, the North American continental plate has been growing by addition of other plate material along its western margin. Pieces of oceanic or other continental plates added onto the main continental plate body are called *terranes*. Each terrane is separated from the others by major faults.

The rocks found today in the Pacific Northwest are, geologically speaking, very young. The earth itself is 4.5 billion years old, but the rocks that are now part of the western edge of North America did not even exist 200 million years ago. Most of what is now the western margin of North America has been added onto the continent by accretion. *Island arcs*, or microcontinents, similar to today's Japanese islands or New Zealand, rode eastward on the Pacific Plate and eventually collided with the western edge of the westward-moving North American continent. It is the accretion of these isolated island arcs that is responsible for the distinctive rocks making up Washington, Oregon, and British Columbia. More than fifty different terranes have been added to the western margin of the continent in the Pacific Northwest region. For example, the North Cascades terrane was added to North America about 50 million years ago. The Olympic Mountain terrane docked onto North America about 24 million years ago. This collision turned the rocks on end, sliding them up against the edge of the North American continent like the pages of a book stood upright.

The Olympic Peninsula consists of several terranes that have been added onto older terranes that make up Puget Sound and the Cascade Range. In the case of the Olympic Peninsula, a former island arc something like today's Hawaiian Islands, riding on the Juan de Fuca Plate as if on a conveyor belt, crashed into the North American continent between 30 and 55 million years ago. These rocks were then "welded" onto the advancing plate margin. This is one reason the rocks that make up the Olympic Peninsula are both younger than and substantially different from the rocks that make up the main body of the North American Plate, or even the older terranes that make up Vancouver Island and the North Cascades, which were themselves previously welded onto the North American continent.

The basalts are known today as the Crescent Formation. This rock group is separated from the core sedimentary rocks by a series of major faults. One of the largest is the *Calawah Fault,* which can be traced from *Crystal Ridge* to the *Soleduck River* and likely continues to the ocean. On one side of the fault lie sedimentary rocks of the inner core, and on the other side, the basalts of the Crescent Formation. Starting at the northwest corner of the Peninsula near *Cape Flattery,* another major fault parallels the Strait of Juan de Fuca, cutting eastward behind *Mount Angeles* and *Blue Mountain.* The fault then turns southward, giving rise to many of the highest peaks along the eastern border of the park from *Buckhorn Mountain* to *Mount Ellinor,* including *Mount Constance* and *The Brothers.* Near *Lake Cushman,* the fault turns west and defines the southern borders of the park, ending near *Lake Quinault.*

The Crescent Formation is thickest on the southern and eastern parts of the park and thins along the northern slope of the mountains. The section of road from *Hood Canal* along the *Dosewallips River* to the Dose-

Lake Cushman, located at the southeast corner of Olympic National Park, was created by glaciers. The lake, however, has been enlarged by the construction of a dam on its outlet.

wallips Campground is one of the best continuous exposures of the Crescent Formation in the park. It is thought that this island arc was jammed up against the Cascades and Vancouver Island and thus bent to fit the space, creating the horseshoe shape of the Crescent Formation. The force of the collision reshuffled and tipped the sedimentary and basaltic rocks on edge.

Some of the Crescent Formation was torn loose and restacked farther westward to form an inner ring of basalt on top of the core sedimentary rocks. These basalts are harder than the surrounding sedimentary formations and have eroded into spectacular jagged peaks, including the *Sawtooths* and *Needles*.

The ragged outline of the Needles, part of the Inner Basalt Ring found along the eastern border of the park, was originally laid down as lava flows in the ocean and later uplifted and tilted on end. Resistant to erosion, the basalt stands up higher as the softer surrounding rock is stripped away.

This accretion of an island arc was not accomplished gently. The rocks of this former island arc were crumpled and buckled, much like the front end of an automobile that has run into a wall. We know that this island arc first ran into the rest of North America along the eastern edge of the Olympic Mountains. Here, in the vicinity of *Buckhorn Mountain, The Brothers, Mount Pershing,* and *Mount Washington,* are rocks that were more intensely deformed than rocks in the western Olympic Mountains along the trailing edge of this island arc.

The resulting impact also reorganized the original orientation of the two major rock types making up this island arc. Originally, the islands were built up of sediments piled upon a base of basalt. The sediments, solidified as rock, include sandstones, shales, and limestones. These rested upon basalts formed by eruptions of lava deep on the floor of ocean basins. Upon collision with North America, these sedimentary rocks and basalts were then tipped on edge, so that the older basalts now lie in front of the younger sedimentary rocks like a shield that encases the sedimentary rocks on three sides. The rocks of the Olympic Mountains lying along the southern flank drained by the *Wynoochee* and *Skokomish Rivers,* on the eastern margin closest to *Hood Canal,* and on the northern edge of the mountains bordering the *Strait of Juan de Fuca* are all part of this horseshoe-shaped shield of basalts formed deep in the sea. The shield of basalts is then followed by sedimentary sandstones and shales that make up the bulk of the central and western edges of the mountains, including the highest peaks centered on *Mount Olympus* and the *Bailey Range.*

Erosion

If you look at a map of the Olympic Mountains, the rivers appear to run in all directions of the compass from a central high point near *Mount Olympus* and the surrounding peaks of the *Bailey Range.* This drainage pattern is a consequence of the dome-shaped uplift of the Olympic Mountains. Differences in both precipitation (rivers on the west had more water) and the hardness of rock strata allowed some rivers to erode deeper valleys more quickly. Rivers cutting through the softer shales could erode faster than rivers attempting to erode away the harder basalts. The more rapidly down-cutting rivers were able to "capture" the drainage basins of nearby streams. The *Elwha River,* for instance, appears to have breached several tributary drainages and captured their flow.

Glaciation

Whereas plate tectonics and the resulting features such as mountains, plains, and valleys can be thought of as the foundations, walls, and ceiling for the landscape, erosion in the form of water or ice provides the finishing touches, analogous to the furniture, paint, and interior decorations that are rearranged within the parameters dictated by the basic house structure.

Of the many erosional processes that have shaped these mountains, none have had as dramatic an effect as glaciation. Certainly, one of the chief scenic attributes of the Olympic Mountains even today is its white crown of glacial ice. The glaciers not only give the Olympics a more impressive appearance, but they also were responsible for shaping many of the park's physical features, including its rugged peaks and deep valleys. The glaciers that cap the park's mountains are tiny remnants of the massive ice blanket that cloaked these mountains during the last ice age, which ended some 10,000 years ago.

Ice ages are a relatively common event in earth's history. There have been numerous major glacial periods, some dating back to more than 2.3 billion years ago. What exactly prompts a glacial period is not clearly understood, but most scientists believe ice ages are influenced by plate tectonic movements. As continents shift and collide or separate, they change global ocean currents and climate patterns. The immediate triggering events include greater cloudiness, more precipitation, and overall cooler temperatures, though not necessarily colder winters. The most recent major glacial period, the Pleistocene Ice Age, began 1.8 million years ago. During this glacial age, there were at least twenty major ice advances and retreats. The last one, the Vashon Stade of the Fraser Glaciation, reached its height between 15,000 and 18,000 years ago.

Each new glacial period tends to obscure and destroy evidence of earlier ice advances. Nevertheless, there is evidence for at least four major glacial advances in the Olympic Mountains, called the Orting, Stuck, Salmon Springs, and Fraser Glaciations. During each of these glacial advances, the extent of alpine glaciation in the Olympics increased substantially, with glaciers not only cloaking most of the higher peaks, but also flowing down into the valleys and even out into the lowlands near present-day Forks.

In addition to this local glacial formation, giant glaciers from British Columbia, known as Cordilleran ice sheets, flowed southward toward the

Looking east from Blue Mountain across Puget Sound to the Cascades at sunrise. During the height of the ice age, a Cordilleran ice sheet swept south from the mountains of British Columbia, surrounding the Olympic Mountains on two sides. One lobe filled the Strait of Juan de Fuca, while the Puget lobe filled the lowlands to the east. During the Vashon Glaciation approximately 15,000 years ago, ice 3,800 feet thick lapped against the slopes of Blue Mountain.

Olympics. These Cordilleran glaciers had their headwaters in the Coast Mountains of British Columbia. As the ice thickened in the mountains east of what is now Vancouver, British Columbia, it overran these mountains and flowed west into the mountains of Vancouver Island. Here it combined with alpine glaciers flowing off the Insular Mountains, and together these ice rivers were deflected south. Eventually this ice sheet piled up against the northern flank of the Olympic Mountains, splitting into two prongs. One prong flowed west to the Pacific Ocean through the Strait of Juan de Fuca, while the second prong filled Puget Sound.

The most recent advance, the Vashon Stade of the Fraser Glaciation, reached its maximum extent around 14,000 years ago, more than 6,000 feet thick near the present-day U.S.-Canada border and more than 3,000 feet thick near present-day Seattle. This huge glacial ice sheet curved around the northern edge of the Olympics, surging as far south as the present town of Forks, and the Puget lobe buried the lands east of the Olympics under ice, advancing southward as far as the Black Hills south of present-day Olympia. The meltwater from the Puget lobe of this giant glacier flowed down the Chehalis River to the Pacific Ocean. Today the Chehalis River Valley is much broader than its current volume of water could create, reflecting its larger flow during the ice age. By 12,500 years ago, the Cordilleran ice sheet was already in retreat and had vanished from the Strait of Juan de Fuca and Puget Sound.

During the last ice age, horses, bison, caribou, woolly mammoths, and mastodons roamed Puget Sound. A mastodon skeleton was found near *Port Angeles*. Most of these species became extinct or were locally extirpated at the close of the last glacial event.

Besides the Cordilleran glacier, huge alpine glaciers draped the highest peaks in the Olympic Mountains and clogged the valleys with ice. The Hoh Valley had a giant glacier that reached all the way from its headwaters on Mount Olympus and the Bailey Range to the Pacific Ocean. Another glacier, in the Wynoochee River Valley, flowed twenty-five miles from its source to beyond the confines of the valley to the flats, where it spread out as a broad piedmont glacier. Other major river valleys, including the Bogachiel, Queets, Quinault, Soleduck, Elwha, Dosewallips, Duckabush, Hamma Hamma, and Skokomish, cradled valley glaciers in their upper reaches. West-side valleys, including the Bogachiel and Hoh, had larger glaciers, in part reflecting their greater ability to capture snowfall coming off the Pacific Ocean.

Once I was on Blue Mountain at dawn. Below me, to the east, the entire Puget Sound lowlands were blanketed in thick, white fog. Only the high, snowy peaks of the Cascades rose above the cloudbank. I could see the distinctive cones of such Cascade volcanoes as Mount Baker, Glacier Peak, and Mount Rainier—all cloaked in glaciers even today. Such a view does not differ much from the appearance of that same landscape when it was filled with ice of the Puget lobe. Similar fog-filled valleys seen from any of the high peaks give a feeling of what the Olympics must have looked like when the glaciers were at their maximum.

Whether alpine glaciers or Cordilleran ice sheets, all glaciers form in essentially the same way. Glaciers form when winter snowfall is greater than the amount of snow that melts during the following summer. The rate of glacial flow is quite variable. To advance downslope, there needs to be a greater accumulation of snow in winter and less melting on the glacier's terminus in summer. A series of heavy-snowfall winters, combined with cool summers, can send a glacier advancing downslope at a rapid rate. Nevertheless, compared with some glaciers in Alaska, which sometimes move up to several hundred feet in a single day, the Olympic glaciers are slow-moving.

Snow nurtures the glaciers in the *accumulation zone,* or at the origin of the ice. Most of the melting, or *ablation,* occurs near the termini, or snouts, of the glaciers. As with human finance management, glaciers work with a budget and expenditure plan. A vigorous glacier will be maintained by a heavy accumulation of snow in the winter and only average melting during the summer. The freezing point in late spring and precipitation in early fall appear to be critical in relation to this gain and loss. Excessive melt before and after the normal melt season would result in an impoverished budget for the following year.

The elevation where this occurs varies with place and time. In the Olympics today, snowline is at about 5,500 feet. Above this elevation, snow may not melt. In the Colorado Rockies, snowline is above 12,000 feet.

Some may ponder why the "low" Olympics, whose highest mountain isn't even 8,000 feet in elevation, would have glaciers at all. The mild climate of the Pacific Northwest would seem to be a less-than-ideal place for the formation of glaciers. But in truth, the formation of glacial ice is more a consequence of heavy snowfall and generally cool temperatures, not extreme cold. Indeed, in frigid places like Alaska's Brooks Range, glaciers are relatively uncommon, even though the entire range is north of the Arctic Circle. The Olympic Mountains' location immediately adjacent to the Pacific Ocean provides a ready source of moisture, and the often cloudy weather keeps daytime temperatures relatively cool, creating ideal conditions for the formation of glaciers.

More than 100 feet of snow may pile up in a single winter on the slopes of *Mount Olympus.* It is simply impossible for all this snow to melt in the short, cool summers. As a result, nine glaciers flank Mount Olympus alone. The *Blue Glacier* flows downslope to an elevation of nearly 4,000 feet, one of the the lowest elevations attained by any glacier in the United States outside of Alaska.

Besides the nine glaciers flanking Mount Olympus, there are more than sixty other major glaciers crowning the highest Olympic peaks. The largest glaciers flank Mount Olympus, covering approximately ten square

The 7,321-foot Mount Anderson, like most of the higher peaks that make up the central core of the Olympic Mountains, consists of erosion-resistant sandstones and other sedimentary rocks. The mountain also has the largest glaciers in the eastern Olympics. The knife-edged ridge in the foreground, known as an arête, was created by glaciers carving away at the rock on both sides of the mountain.

miles. Beyond the Olympic complex are the glaciers of *Mount Carrie,* the *Bailey Range, Mount Christie,* and *Mount Anderson.* Though the peaks along the eastern border are quite high, most lack glaciers due to the rain-shadow effect of the intervening higher peaks.

Glaciers are usually at least 100 feet in thickness, but can be up to several miles deep. The ice sheet covering the Greenland Ice Cap, for instance, is over 10,000 feet in thickness. Once a minimum of 100 feet of snow and ice accumulates, the glacier begins to move downhill due to gravity.

Though the bottom layer of a glacier is pure ice, it acts something like the plastic molten magma deep in the earth. The bottom part of a glacier flows something like cold toothpaste. Glaciers actually travel on a thin film of water. When forced over an obstruction, such as a boulder or bedrock, the intense pressure from above causes the ice to melt momentarily. Once it has passed over the obstruction, it refreezes immediately.

One of the hazards of glacier travel are *crevasses,* deep cracks that form on a glacier's surface. As a glacier moves downhill, it flows over uneven terrain, around corners, and down steep slopes. These cause changes in the rate of flow, reflected by fissures in the ice's surface. One can think of these crevasses as rapids on a river. Where a glacier flows over a steep embankment, not surprisingly, there are usually many crevasses. Where the flow is less steep, there are fewer crevasses.

Another structural feature is the *bergschrund,* a prominent crevasselike opening at the head of the glacier, where the ice has been pulled away from the mountain wall. Often the bergschrund is the most difficult obstacle for climbers attempting to scale a peak.

Again like a river, a glacier also carries a sediment load. Imbedded in the glacier are pieces of gravel, rock, and even giant boulders. These rocks and boulders turn the glacier into a giant rasp. As the glacier flows downhill, it scraps, sculpts, and grinds away at the underlying rock, smoothing bedrock, plucking rock from side hills, and carrying it all downhill.

This load of rock and gravel accumulates along the front and sides of the glacier as *moraine.* Moraines can be identified by their mixture of unsorted gravels and boulders. In contrast, gravels and boulders sorted by streams tend to be ordered by size, with finer sands and small rocks separated from larger boulders. Moraines are pushed or dragged by the advancing ice. When the glacier melts, these morainal deposits are dropped, forming small hills and ridges of unsorted rock. Sometimes the moraine

Crescent Lake was gorged out by ice-age glaciers.

will dam a stream, creating a lake. *Lake Quinault*, in the southwest part of the park, is a moraine-dammed lake. Other glacier-carved lakes include *Lake Ozette* and *Lake Crescent*.

Other glacial lakes have since disappeared. For instance, a former moraine-dammed lake existed in the *East Fork of the Quinault Valley*. The lake has since filled in, and the flat valley bottom in the *Enchanted Valley* is a reflection of the existence of this former lakebed.

There are many other physical reminders of these rivers of ice in the Olympic Mountains. Along the flanks of many of the higher Olympic peaks are basins that look as if a giant ice cream scoop was used to carve them out from the slopes. Many of these alpine bowls were filled with alpine glaciers, and some of these basins retain glaciers even today. As glaciers move downslope, they pluck bits of rock from the mountainside. As this is repeated over and over again, the glacier eventually creates steep headwalls and a broad, rounded basin. Such glaciated basins are known by the French word *cirque*. Cirque basins are often filled with small lakes called *cirque lakes* or, if very small, *tarns*. Nearly all the small lakes dotting the Olympic high country occupy former cirque basins. The

Seven Lakes Basin along the *High Divide Trail* is an excellent example of a recently deglaciated basin filled with cirque and tarn lakes.

When sufficient ice accumulates in these upper basins, the ice begins to flow downvalley. As it descends stream valleys, the ice continues its sculpting of the canyon walls. Acting like a giant bulldozer, the glacier flattens the valley floor while scraping away the canyon sides to create steep, clifflike walls. The resulting glaciated valley takes on a distinctive U-shaped profile. The view up the *Elwha River* from *Hurricane Ridge Visitor Center* is a good place to observe such a U-shaped valley.

The bowl-shaped basin in which Morganroth Lake sits was carved by a cirque glacier.

The finely ground rock created by the glaciers, called *glacial flour*, often makes the glaciated rivers look milky when the glaciers are melting. Rivers that carry a heavy load of glacier flour, such as the *Hoh*, run a pale blue.

These are all reminders of the past and present alpine glaciers of the Olympic Mountains. There is also evidence in the Olympic Mountains for the great Cordilleran glaciers of the ice age. The long, narrow *Hood Canal* to the east of the park is a *fjord*, a glacier-carved valley inundated by the sea.

Other evidence is less direct. For example, though there is no granite bedrock anywhere on the Olympic Peninsula, granite boulders can be found on the north slope of the Olympics. These granitic rocks were transported here by the Cordilleran glaciers from sources farther north in Canada's Coast Range.

Granite boulders and gravel found up the *Elwha River Valley* as far upstream as *Godkin Creek* are also a consequence of glaciation but were not directly deposited by the glaciers. Rather, the giant Cordilleran ice lobe filling the Strait of Juan de Fuca dammed the Elwha River, creating a temporary glacial lake. Icebergs calved from the glacier, laden with moraine and other glacial debris, spilled into the lake waters and floated up the Elwha Valley, where they melted, depositing granite boulders and gravel.

The Cordilleran ice sheet also dammed other river valleys, creating fjordlike lakes in the *Duckabush, Hamma Hamma, Skokomish,* and *Dungeness River Valleys*. The original *Lake Cushman* was formed by a moraine dam from the Cordilleran glacier, although the present lake was enlarged by a dam. Fine sediment from these lakes settled out to create unstable soil profiles. Many of the natural landslides in these valleys occur among these old lakebed soil types.

Access to all of the glaciers in the Olympic Mountains is by trails and cross-country routes. The most visited glaciers in the park are the *Blue Glacier* on Mount Olympus and *Anderson Glacier* on Mount Anderson. To reach the Blue Glacier, it is an eighteen-mile hike up the *Hoh Rain Forest Trail*. The Anderson Glacier can be reached by hiking the *Dosewallips River Trail* for eleven miles or, from the west side, by the *East Fork of the Quinault River* for sixteen miles. Visiting the other Olympic glaciers requires more mountaineering skill and time.

Travel on glacial ice requires the use of climbing ropes, ice axes, crampons, good judgment, and experienced leaders. Snow-bridged crevasses on glaciers present great hazards to climbers. Self-evacuation from a deep, steep-walled crevasse is nearly impossible.

Coastal Landforms

For many, the most dramatic and exciting part of Olympic National Park isn't the mountains or the rain forest, but the coastal strip. The sixty miles of wild Olympic coastline, punctuated by pointed headlands and sandy beaches, can be compared to a saw blade.

Waves are the most important geological force shaping the coast. Waves are generated by winds, pushing the surface water in looplike paths. As a wave approaches shore, the bottom of the loop begins to

Wave-smoothed boulder at Beach Three of the coastal strip. Most of the coastal segment of the park is made up of sedimentary rocks. Softer sedimentary rocks, easily eroded, give rise to beaches, whereas most of the rocky islands, sea stacks, and headlands are made of harder, more erosion-resistant sandstones and conglomerates.

experience friction with the seabed. The top of the wave begins to move faster than the bottom, steepens, and eventually falls, or breaks. The turbulent water that results is called *surf,* and it is surf that does most of the sediment transport, as well as erosion, along coastlines. The pounding surf exerts a tremendous amount of hydraulic force, exceeding three tons per square foot. Hydraulic force can directly break apart boulders and headlands and can compress the air in crevasses, exerting even greater force.

Waves also transport sand and other sediments at high velocity against the coast. These particles grind and smooth the surfaces of rocks and headlands. The tiny fragments of rock that are removed are carried by the surf to new locations, forming beaches and spits.

Waves act like a hydraulic saw, gradually cutting into sea cliffs, which eventually are undercut and collapse. Headlands along the Olympic coast are generally formed of volcanic rocks, which tend to be harder and more resistant to erosion. Occasionally the sea wears away part of a headland, leaving an isolated rock pillar known as a *sea stack.* There are hundreds of sea stacks along the Olympic coast.

Landslides

Evidence for landslides disappears relatively rapidly due to erosion. Nevertheless, some of the more interesting natural features in the park can be attributed to landslides. For example, the *Crescent Lake* basin was originally carved by ice-age glaciers. A giant landslide opposite *Mount Storm King* split the lake, creating *Lake Sutherland* in the process. *Jefferson* and *Lena Lakes,* both in the *Hamma Hamma River* drainage, were also created by landslides.

Most of the landslides occur where glacial deposits create unstable soils and slopes. Natural events such as saturated soil profiles can trigger slides, although the amount of landsliding in the Olympic Peninsula, and indeed, the entire Pacific Northwest, has increased dramatically due to logging and road construction, which have further destabilized slopes.

Hot Springs

Several hot springs can be found in Olympic National Park. These occur on or near the *Calawah fault zone,* a presently inactive zone extending from the southeastern Olympics to the northwest and probably into the Pacific Ocean.

One spring area can be reached by road; the others are located in more remote areas of the backcountry. The two best-known springs are *Olympic* and *Sol Duc Hot Springs*. According to Indian legend, two dragonlike creatures engaged in a mighty battle for dominance. Neither could surmount the other, and in defeat, both retreated to their lairs, where they wept hot tears of despair.

Olympic Hot Springs consist of twenty-one seeps located in a bank on *Boulder Creek*, a tributary of the Elwha River. Several have been trapped by human-made rock-lined depressions. The depth of these pools is about one foot, and water temperatures vary from lukewarm to a very hot 138 degrees F. A resort existed in the area until 1966, when the lease expired. Heavy winter snows caused many of the old buildings to collapse. They were removed, but seeps remain. Hikers now use the pools.

Sol Duc is a Native American word for "sparkling water." According to local legend, Sol Duc Hot Springs were located by Theodore Moritz, who obtained directions to the springs from an injured Indian whom Moritz had nursed back to health. Moritz staked a claim and built cedar log tubs, and soon people were coming great distances to drink and bathe in the allegedly healing waters.

Michael Earles, owner of the Puget Sound Mills and Timber Company, claimed he was cured of a fatal illness after visiting Sol Duc. When Moritz died in 1909, Earles bought the land from his heirs and built a $75,000 road to the springs from Lake Crescent. Three years later, on May 15, 1912, an elegant hotel opened.

The grounds were immaculately landscaped, and the resort offered golf links, tennis courts, croquet grounds, bowling alleys, a theater, and card rooms. A three-story building between the bathhouse and hotel held a sanatorium. With beds for 100 patients, a laboratory, and X-ray equipment, it was considered one of the finest in the West.

After only four years, in 1916, sparks from a defective flue ignited the shingle roof of the hotel. The building was consumed in flames in just three hours.

A more modest resort replaced the old hotel complex—although some might suggest it is still a rather inappropriate development for the middle of a national park. The resort is open from late spring through early fall and offers cabins (some cooking cabins), a dining room, gift shop, swimming pool, three mineral water pools, therapeutic massage, snackbar, and RV sites.

History

Early Humans

Some 12,000 years ago, the ice-age glaciers that had overrun the Puget Sound Basin were in retreat. The familiar spruce and fir forests of today had yet to colonize the Peninsula. Tundra and wetlands dominated the lower elevations of the Olympic Peninsula, and the higher peaks were still mantled with massive glaciers. Roaming the ice-free lands were caribou, bison, and elk. A nearly complete mastodon skeleton was unearthed near Sequim in 1977. This mastodon appears to have been butchered, suggesting the presence of humans; however, the evidence is sketchy.

The earliest good evidence for humans on the Olympic Peninsula dates from 9,000 to 6,000 years ago. These early human inhabitants were primarily big-game hunters. Numerous spear points and other human artifacts have been found on the northern and eastern sides of the Peninsula near Port Angeles, Sequim, and other parts of the northeastern portion of Olympic National Park. There is evidence that these early big-game hunters began to move up into the subalpine mountains about 8,000 years ago, likely following animals like elk on their annual summer migrations to the high country.

There are a number of sites on the Peninsula dating from roughly 3,000 to 1,600 years ago. All of these sites contain the remains of shellfish, fish, sea mammals, and even a few land mammals. One of the most important excavations of early human activity on the Peninsula was a fish camp near the mouth of the Hoko River, dated between 2,900 and 2,200 years ago. Most of the archaeological evidence indicates an orientation toward offshore fishing. Remains of salmon, halibut, and other fish, as well as sea mammals such as gray whale, harbor seal, and porpoise, were also found at the site.

Up until the relatively recent past, most hunting was done with spears. The bow and arrow were not introduced into the region until about 2,000 years ago. Then, about 1,000 years ago, the people of the Olympic Peninsula underwent a radical change in technology, giving up their chipped-stone spear points and arrowheads for newer fishing techniques. The primary food resource became fish, although on the outer coast, sea mammals such as whales and seals were equally important.

Wooden objects become more abundant, and the first evidence of wooden longhouses dates from around 800 years ago. These wooden houses, some up to sixty feet long, were constructed of split cedar with flat cedar boards as roofs, held in place by large boulders and logs. They were sturdy but could, if necessary, be dismantled and moved to another location. Usually three or four extended families lived in one house.

The rivers and sea of the Pacific Northwest coast provided a reliable and relatively abundant food source. This naturally attracted diverse groups of

The killer whale petroglyph at Wedding Rocks, south of Cape Alava, is thought to have been carved 500 years ago by native people inhabiting the coast. Salmon, shellfish, and sea mammals provided abundant food to coastal people, giving them time to develop a rich cultural tradition.

people. These native people were highly mobile, and numerous language groups indicate a diversity of origins for the people that resided on the Peninsula at the time of white settlement.

Although there were differences in language and some other aspects of culture, most people living along the Pacific coast, from Oregon north to Alaska, tended to rely upon marine resources for food—in particular, salmon. Marine mammals, shellfish, seabirds, and other fish also were important parts of the diet. There was specialization among the various groups, however. For instance, the Makah focused on whaling, hunting the giant animals in open canoes. Others, like the Skokomish and Quinault, spent more time inland and had a greater dependence upon elk and deer.

Most of the indigenous groups had communal winter houses where several families lived together, and most depended upon the canoe for transportation.

European Explorations

The earliest European explorations along the coast occurred nearly two hundred years before settlement. In 1592, Juan de Fuca, a Greek navigator sailing under a Spanish flag, claimed to have found the entrance to Puget Sound now bearing his name at 47 degrees N latitude, but his claim was doubted by subsequent explorers. In 1774, the Spanish sailor Juan Perez, piloting the coast, observed a snowy mountain in the Olympics, naming it La Sierra de la Santa Rosalia.

The following year, 1775, the Spanish were back again. An expedition under the leadership of Juan Francisco de la Bodega y Quadra (a strait in Alaska is named for him) and Bruno Heceta (Heceta Head on the Oregon coast is named for him) explored the Northwest coast as far north as Alaska. In July, Heceta and crew rowed ashore on the western shore of the Peninsula, becoming the first Europeans to set foot upon land that would later become the state of Washington. The same day, just a bit farther north, Quadra's ship was approached by Indians. Believing them friendly and wishing to trade, Quadra sent seven sailors ashore. The Indians killed all the men, making them the first Europeans to die in what would be the state of Washington. Relations between whites and Indians were not off to a glorious start.

In 1778, Capt. James Cook (for whom Cook Inlet in Alaska is named) passed the northwestern tip of the Olympic Peninsula, naming it Cape

Flattery because the opening along the coast "flattered" Cook with the hope of finding a harbor. Cook wrote in his logbook: "In this very latitude geographers have placed the pretended Strait of Juan de Fuca. But nothing of that kind presented itself to our view, nor is it probable that any such thing ever existed."

Nine years later, in 1787, Capt. Charles Barkley (for whom Barkley Sound off Vancouver Island is named) rediscovered the Strait of Juan de Fuca. Barkley continued southward along the coast and landed sailors near the same location as Quadra's ill-fated crew. And like Quadra's crew, some of Barkley's sailors were also murdered by the Indians. The site is commemorated by the name Destruction Island.

The next major exploration, in 1788, was led by Capt. John Meares (for whom Cape Meares on the Oregon coast is named). Meares was engaged in a fur-trading expedition, seeking to obtain sea otter pelts from the natives along the Pacific Northwest coast. On July 4, Meares sighted a high, snowy mountain on the Olympic Peninsula—Perez's Santa Rosalia Peak—which he promptly named Mount Olympus for its ethereal appearance as the abode of the gods.

In 1792, Capt. George Vancouver (for whom Vancouver Island is named) explored the entire Puget Sound Basin. On his maps, following Meares's lead, he called the entire mountain complex the Olympic Mountains. Vancouver also named many other geographical features in this region, including Dungeness, Discovery Bay, Hood Canal, and Mount Rainier. Another party of Spanish navigators also entered the strait at this time and, finding a sheltered harbor by Ediz Hook, named the place Puerto de Nuestra Senora de los Angeles, the present-day Port Angeles.

Up until this time, nearly all the exploration along the Pacific Northwest coast involved Spanish or English navigators. This dominance by European powers was challenged by a growing American interest in the region. In 1792, an American, Capt. Robert Gray, was engaged in the sea otter fur trade along the Pacific coast. Gray discovered and named Gray's Harbor and also located the mouth of the Columbia River, which he named after his ship. Gray's discoveries later helped solidify American claims to the Pacific Northwest.

Gray's discovery of the Columbia River, one of the major rivers of the West, set the stage for overland exploration. In 1793, Alexander Mackenzie (for whom the Mackenzie River in the Northwest Territories is named) crossed the Canadian Rockies and trekked overland to the Pacific

Ocean by Bella Coola, British Columbia. In 1805, Lewis and Clark rolled down the Columbia River in canoes to its mouth, becoming the first Americans to travel across the Rockies to the Pacific coast. In 1809, the American fur-trading magnate John Jacob Astor set up a fur-trading fort on the Columbia at present-day Astoria, Oregon. Shortly after its establishment, the fort was captured by the British.

With both countries vying for control of the region, conflicts began to escalate. Finally, in 1818, a treaty of joint occupation was signed, allowing both countries to settle and explore the region. It was the English who got the jump on settlement, however. By the early 1800s, the Hudson's Bay Company had opened up fur-trading posts in the region, operating Fort Vancouver near present-day Vancouver, Washington, and Fort Nisqually on Puget Sound near today's Tacoma.

The Oregon Trail and Settlement

The fur trade did not attract a large permanent white settlement to the region, and for three decades, the area, though contested, was still primarily inhabited by native peoples. This changed, however, with the opening of the Oregon Trail during the 1840s. Tens of thousands of settlers took the wagon trail to the Oregon Territory, which included Washington, Oregon, and parts of Idaho. Most settled in Oregon's Willamette Valley, though others moved northward into Washington's Puget Sound region. The first American settlement on Puget Sound was at Tumwater in 1845.

The British, no doubt realizing that it would soon lose Puget Sound to increasing American occupation, decided to negotiate a boundary settlement. In 1846, the boundary between the United States and Canada was set at the 49th parallel, thus firmly establishing the Olympic Peninsula as American territory. More settlers moved into the Puget Sound region, most of them settling on the southern ends of the waterway. The Olympic Peninsula remained unexplored and still under control of the Indians.

With the area south of the 49th parallel now U.S. territory, the Hudson's Bay Company closed its Oregon and Washington operations and moved to Vancouver, British Columbia. Working out of Vancouver, two Hudson's Bay men, John Everett and John Sutherland, were the first whites to explore the Olympic Mountains. On the advice of local Indians, these men trapped by two lakes near Port Angeles. The lakes, which they named for themselves—Lake Sutherland and Lake Everett (later renamed Lake Crescent)—are both now within Olympic National Park.

Both men eventually decided to remain in the United States and spent years exploring the Olympic, hunting, trapping, and trading.

As more American settlers moved northward, new communities appeared on Puget Sound, including Olympia and Seattle. In 1851, Port Townsend was established, the first settlement on the Peninsula. The new communities eventually led to the establishment of the Washington Territory in 1853, with the Columbia River as its southern boundary.

Early Olympic Expeditions

Although communities like Seattle and Tacoma were booming, few settlers had time to explore far from tidewater. The steep mountains, rushing rivers, and dense forests discouraged exploration. Beyond the ocean fringe, the Olympics remained terra incognita. The first attempt to cross the Olympic Mountains occurred in 1878. Five men, led by Melbourne Watkinson, left Hood Canal on September 2, hiking to Lake Cushman on the southwest corner of today's Olympic National Park. From Lake Cushman, they crossed into the Upper East Fork of the Quinault, which they descended to Lake Quinault. Here they met some Indians, who took them by canoe to the ocean. They then hiked the beach to Grays Harbor, arriving on September 14. Though the party did not cross the heart of the mountains, the traverse was still notable in that it provided the first recorded glimpses of the interior of these mountains.

O'Neil Expedition

During the early 1880s, several military expeditions attempted to cut trails across the mountains. None succeeded. The first real attempt to cross the mountains was led by Lt. Joseph O'Neil. In mid-July 1885, O'Neil landed his party of men at Port Angeles. The small party of six soldiers and one civilian, Norman Smith from Port Angeles, decided to explore the Elwha River drainage, since it appeared to lead into the heart of the mountains. It took the little party almost two weeks to cut a trail through the tangled forest to the first range of mountains. On July 27, Smith and O'Neil were able to ascend a peak and get their first view of the mountain interior. O'Neil noted that the mountains appeared to have no regularity about them but instead were "jumbled up in the utmost confusion." The men noted an abundance of elk in the higher terrain and happened upon a wolf, which they instinctively shot and wounded. They were surprised to find evidence of other human use, including an old cabin, showing that some whites had previously explored as far as the first high ranges—no doubt on hunting and trapping trips.

O'Neil and his men continued onward, heading south along the divide east of the Elwha along Hurricane Ridge. He eventually split the group in two exploring parties. One attempted to reach the Elwha but, after losing a mule on steep slopes, decided to return to the base camp. O'Neil continued southeastward on the high alpine terrain of Observation Point, eventually abandoning pack animals and continuing his exploration with a backpack. At his farthest point, he likely reached the Lost Pass area. Throughout these rambles, he was overwhelmed by the beauty of the region and nearly continually encountered elk herds. Eventually running out of supplies, O'Neil turned around and returned to his base camp. The summer nearly over, O'Neil left the mountains on August 26 and was assigned to a new post at Fort Leavenworth, Kansas.

The Gilman Explorations

O'Neil's explorations paved the way for another party of adventurers, a father and son team of Charles and Samuel Gilman. The Gilmans migrated from Minnesota to the Puget Sound country and almost immediately decided to explore the inner reaches of the Olympic Mountains. Their explorations began in Grays Harbors on October 17, 1889, well after the rainy season had commenced.

Leaving Grays Harbor in foul weather, they traveled north up the beach to the Quinault River, where they obtained an Indian guide and canoe to take them upriver. At Quinault Lake, they met several white trappers who were working the nearby forests for furs. Their guide took them as far as the confluence of the East and North Forks of the Quinault River. At this point, they shouldered packs and began hiking up the East Fork, encountering numerous elk along the way.

Living on elk they had killed, the men crossed the Enchanted Valley and ascended some peaks near the headwaters of the river, most likely in the vicinity of Anderson Pass. Fortunately, on the day they chose to climb a nearby peak, the day dawned clear. From the summit, which their barometer indicated was 6,800 feet above sea level, they could see the glittering summit of Mount Olympus, the high peaks of the Cascades, and Hood Canal, as well as south and east to Grays Harbor. Eventually the weather closed in again, and the Gilmans descended the East Fork of the Quinault by foot. Finding an old canoe, they continued down the main Quinault to the ocean and back along the beach to Grays Harbor, arriving on November 27.

The Gilmans were undaunted by the steady rain and decided to continue their explorations. This time they were sponsored by the Northern Pacific Railroad. Starting on December 9 from Port Angeles, the men began to explore southwest, seeking a possible railroad route across the western side of the Peninsula to Grays Harbor.

A few days after leaving Port Angeles, they met two other men, John Banta and Price Sharp, who were examining the country for potential homesteads. At the Gilmans' encouragement, Banta and Sharp joined the tiny expedition. Packing supplies on their backs, the men headed for the tiny settlement of Forks, passing en route through some of the finest timber any of them had ever seen. There were already quite a few settlers living in the Forks area, and the men resupplied with food and other gear and continued on their way.

After crossing the Bogachiel by canoe, they reached the Hoh. Here they obtained the services of an Indian, who ferried them down the river to its mouth on the ocean, where they encountered an Indian village of about fifty people. From here they headed south with an Indian guide, following the beach to the Queets River, which they ascended by canoe obtained from the Indians. Along the Queets, Banta found his potential homestead and later returned to colonize the area. Continuing their journey in steady rain and slushy snow, they eventually reached the Quinault, which they again descended to the sea. They obtained a wagon ride down the beach toward Grays Harbor, reaching that city on January 4, 1890.

The Press Expedition

Even before the Gilmans had completed their two treks, other men were dreaming about exploring the inner reaches of the Olympic Mountains. In November 1889, James Christie contacted the *Seattle Press*, asking for its sponsorship of a midwinter expedition across the Olympic Mountains. William Bailey, owner of the *Press*, agreed to provision the hastily organized expedition. By early December, Christie was in Port Angeles with four other companions, John Crumback, Christopher Hayes, John Sims, and Charles Barnes, ready to begin the first winter crossing of the Olympic Mountains—indeed, the first crossing of the mountains at all. The

The Elwha River Valley. The 1890 winter expedition of the Press party took six months to traverse up the Elwha River Valley, crossing the Quinault drainage via Low Pass, becoming the first group to successfully cross the interior of the Olympic Mountains.

names of these explorers and sponsor are now found sprinkled across the Olympic Mountains in the form of the Bailey Range, Mount Barnes, Mount Christie, Hayes River, and Barnes Creek.

Acting upon advice from local Port Angeles residents, the men decided to follow the Elwha River back into the mountains. To carry all the gear they would need for a months-long traverse, they spent several weeks constructing a boat. It was finally launched on January 12, 1899. Wading in the water, pulling the boat upstream, the men were almost constantly wet and cold. Often their clothes froze on their backs. After two weeks of enormous effort, they had progressed only four miles. They decided to abandon the boat and use mules for transporting goods. But snow continued to fall, making mule transport impossible. Nearly two months after starting out, they still hadn't left the lower Elwha Valley. Now they determined to strap on snowshoes and backpack all their gear up the trail in successive trips. Each man hauled 50 pounds on his back, taking up to 250 pounds per man from campsite to campsite by repeated portages. By

February 10, they had reached the forks of the lower Elwha, just above present-day Lake Mills. After shooting a wolf and bobcat near the site, they named nearby tributaries Wolf Creek and Cat Creek.

They moved a few miles upstream and set up a base camp, where they rested for a few weeks, subsisting on the abundant deer wintering in the valley. By March 20, after four months of travel, the party was still camped by today's Humes Ranch, barely beyond the foothills. They continued to ferry gear and food upriver, and by May 4, the expedition finally reached the headwaters of the Elwha River at Low Divide and could see the Quinault drainage beyond. It had taken them five months to get to the midpoint in their traverse. Supplies were getting critically low. By this point, the men had abandoned all extra food and gear and had just what they could carry on their backs.

Just beyond Low Divide, the now nearly starving men managed to kill three bears. Celebrating their good fortune, the men ate well and rested for a few days near the site of the kill. Then, with food in their bellies, they continued on snowshoes down the North Fork of the Quinault, killing another elk en route. Eventually they left the snow behind and were walking again on bare ground.

When they reached the confluence of the North and East Forks of the Quinault, they halted to construct a raft. While the work was under way, they met a trapper traveling upstream with two Indians. He informed them that it was only eight miles to Quinault Lake. Launching the raft, the explorers floated toward the lake. But rounding a bend, the raft crashed into a logjam, tossing nearly all men and gear into the river. Fortunately, the men were all able to extract themselves from the river, but everything was lost except for the pack that held the expedition's records.

The remainder of the journey was completed without further mishap. Eventually, with the assistance of the trapper and his canoe, the entire group was transported downriver to Quinault Lake. After resting at the trapper's cabin, the expedition members continued by canoe down the river to the Indian agency at the river's mouth. Here they hired a wagon to carry them toward Grays Harbor, where they arrived on May 21, after having spent six months in the mountains. The Press Expedition was the first party to successfully traverse the interior of the Olympic Mountains, and the first to do so in winter. The report of the expedition's travels and travails was published in the *Seattle Press* that July.

Second O'Neil Expedition

During the summer of 1890, a number of other explorations occurred in the Olympics. Lt. O'Neil was back again, with ten soldiers and four civilian scientists. The expedition started near Hoodsport. The men began the laborious task of constructing a trail past Lake Cushman and up the North Fork of the Skokomish. The effort was toilsome, since each section of trail took weeks to complete, with all supplies having to be transported by numerous passages over the trail from base camp to base camp. Near the headwaters of the North Fork of the Skokomish, O'Neil divided his party into four groups, ordering one to continue trail construction and sending the others off on separate explorations. One party explored the headwaters of the Duckabush and eventually descended the Dosewallips to Hood Canal. Another party sought out the headwaters of the South Fork of the Skokomish and eventually made its way to Grays Harbors along the southern flank of the mountains. The third group, under the command of O'Neil, descended the East Fork of the Quinault to Quinault Lake and out to Grays Harbor. Among the features named by the group were Mount Anderson and O'Neil Pass.

Eventually, all parties returned to Hoodsport and rendezvoused back at the base camp high in the mountains. At this point, the entire group descended the East Fork of the Quinault River, where they again split up. One party of men continued down the Quinault with the mules, with instructions to make their way to Grays Harbor. O'Neil took a second group north from the Quinault to explore some of the river drainages on the southwest corner of the mountains, including the Queets drainage, before heading down to the ocean and on to Grays Harbor. A third party, under the command of geologist Nelson Linsley, proceeded up the North Fork of the Quinault and over Low Divide into the headwaters of the Elwha River. From here they proceeded to the high country at the head of the Queets Basin and thence climbed what they thought was Mount Olympus but actually turned out to be South Peak. After completing their climb, the men descended the Queets River to the ocean and on to Grays Harbor.

So impressed was the lieutenant with the region's beauty and wildlife that in his final report on the summer's explorations, O'Neil wrote: "In closing I would state that while the country on the outer slope of these mountains is valuable, the interior is useless for all practicable purposes. It would, however, serve admirably for a national park. There are numer-

North Fork of the Skokomish River. In 1890, groups led by Lt. Joseph O'Neil and Judge James Wickersham followed the North Fork of the Skokomish River to its headwaters, then explored the high basins at the headwaters of the Ducka-bush, the East Fork of the Quinault, and the Dosewallips. At the conclusion of their explorations, both proposed creating a national park in the Olympics, thus becoming the first individuals to advocate complete protection for the region.

ous elk—that noble animal so fast disappearing from this country—that should be protected." Later in December of the same year, in a speech made in Portland, he repeated his call for creation of an Olympic National Park.

Wickersham Expedition

O'Neil's wasn't the only party exploring the Olympics in the summer of 1890. Judge James Wickersham, who later moved to Alaska, and for whom the Wickersham Wall on Mount McKinley is named, led a small party of four men through the southeast corner of the mountains. Unlike the military-style assault on the mountains of O'Neil's expedition, Wick-ersham's party was more like a group of boys off on a summer's fishing and camping adventure. Wickersham had previously ascended the North Fork of the Skokomish in 1889. In 1890, he was back, this time with a larger group, including three women, the wives and fiancee of the male members of the party. Traveling lightly, this group rapidly traversed up the North Fork of the Skokomish on the newly constructed trail made by O'Neil, and then passed the O'Neil party. The Wickersham group crossed beneath Anderson Peak, into the headwaters of the Duckabush, and eventually descended the Dosewallips to Hood Canal. Like O'Neil, Wickersham was so impressed with the wild beauty of the Olympics that he also proposed that the area be protected as a national park.

Protection Efforts

The area encompassed by Olympic National Park has always been a land apart. The current land-use controversies over logging, river restoration, wildlife restoration, and other issues are mirrors of social values and ideals. To fully understand the history of Olympic National Park, it must be placed within this contextual framework.

Efforts to protect the Olympics from exploitation and privatization began almost before the region was completely explored. As O'Neil and Wickersham both noted, the Olympics were spectacular. The magnificent forests of the Olympics were coveted by the timber industry but also engendered awe and appreciation among visitors and residents alike.

Giveaway Land Laws

In 1890, when O'Neil and Wickersham first promoted the idea of a national park, only three national parks existed: Yosemite, Yellowstone, and Sequoia. The national park system was still being defined and created. Though the momentum for creating a park in the Olympics grew over time, the first obstacle to overcome was removal of the Olympic forests from applicable public-lands disposal legislation. Up until this time, the main goal of the federal government had been to give away the public domain to anyone who wanted it as rapidly as possible. There were a number of laws that facilitated the transfer of public lands into private hands, including the Homestead Act and the Timber and Stone Act. Under these laws, after meeting certain criteria and paying a nominal fee, anyone could acquire public lands. These laws were enacted with the idea of enabling the average person an opportunity to acquire land and develop it. This was frequently abused, however, particularly by the timber and livestock industries. Often a timber company or a large ranch owner would have hired hands or mill workers file a claim for a piece of property. After the land was transferred to the individual, the company or ranch owner would purchase the land for a nominal fee or even demand the land as a prerequisite for continued employment.

It was by these tactics, particularly by use of the Timber and Stone Act, that millions of acres of heavily timbered public lands were transferred to private timber companies, usually through fraudulent means. Indeed, nearly all the private timberlands on the Olympic Peninsula today were acquired by such less-than-honest applications of these laws. These illegal activities were merely winked at by public officials in the West. At the turn of the century, nearly all western Congressional delegations were empowered and influenced by large timber and livestock interests that controlled the state's political machinery. Often the elected officials that made up western legislatures, governors, and the Congressional delegation were dominated by ranch or timber company owners themselves, and there was little political incentive to stop the gutting of the public domain.

Forest Reserves

Despite this political domination by western economic interests, a counterbalance was provided by eastern U.S. residents and politicians who viewed the public domain as a long-term legacy for the entire nation. By the 1890s, there was a growing movement in the eastern United States to curtail the large-scale giveaway of public lands for private commercial development.

The first opportunity to keep these public-domain lands in public ownership was provided less than a year after both O'Neil and Wickersham completed their Olympic Mountain explorations. In 1891, Congress passed a law that authorized the president to set aside any timbered public lands as forest reserves and to withdraw them from private acquisition under the Timber and Stone Act and other land-disposal legislation. These reserves were essentially managed much as today's national parks: no timber could be cut, no livestock could be grazed, and no mining was permitted.

After Congress passed the legislation over the objections of western politicians, Wickersham immediately sent a recommendation to John Wesley Powell, head of the U.S. Geological Service, who was then preparing a list of areas to recommend for protection as forest reserves.

Wickersham urged Powell to have the president proclaim the Olympic Mountains as a forest reserve. Wickersham noted that the majority of the Olympic forests were far from tidewater and beyond imaginable use to loggers, hence he recommended protecting the core of the Olympic Mountains as a forest reserve or park. In his letter, Wickersham noted, "The reservation of this area as a national park will thus serve the twofold purpose of a great pleasure ground for the Nation, and a means of securing and protecting the finest forests in America."

Due to the efforts of Wickersham and others, most of the Olympic Peninsula's forested land was set aside in 1897 as a forest reserve by President Grover Cleveland in a presidential proclamation. Cleveland included 2,188,800 acres in the Olympic Forest Reserve. At the same time, he created a number of other reserves in the West, including the High Sierra Reserve in California and the Yellowstone Forest Reserve in Wyoming, adjacent to Yellowstone National Park.

The Muir and Pinchot Debate

The declaration of forest reserves had replications far beyond the Olympic Peninsula. It actually led to a splintering of the fledgling American conservation movement into two philosophical camps—a schism that remains today. One side believed all public lands should be off-limits to commercial uses and protected for their ecological values. This is now known as the preservationist perspective. No one represented this philosophy better than John Muir, founder of the Sierra Club and the main advocate for the creation of Yosemite National Park, as well as other parks like Grand Canyon and Glacier Bay. At the other end of the spectrum was Gifford Pinchot, a young forester trained in Germany who advocated wise use of forests. Pinchot would become chief of the U.S. Forest Service. Pinchot's perspective is now known as the conservationist view.

It would be unfair to characterize Pinchot as sympathetic to industrial forest exploitation. Indeed, he was appalled by the practices of his day that left forests ravaged and ecologically bankrupt. He railed against commercial exploiters and even went so far as to recommend that all timberlands, both public and private, be managed by the government. He did, however, believe in using resources, albeit wisely. His motto was "the greatest good for the greatest number of people."

Though both men believed that government ownership and control of natural resources was in the best long-term interest of the nation, they diverged upon the issue of utilization. Muir believed that nature was perfect and that humans could not improve upon it. As a consequence, he believed that human use should be carefully weighed against the costs in things wild and free. He believed that all members of the natural world had an equal right to existence. He also believed that present generations had an ethical obligation to preserve resources for future generations to use or experience. Muir wrote of "the sacred duty of so using the country in which we live that we may not leave it ravished by greed and ruined by ignorance, but may pass it on to future generations undiminished in richness and beauty."

Pinchot believed that humans not only could improve upon nature, but were wise enough to do so without damage. Pinchot refuted Muir's concern for future generations and said, "The first principle of conservation is development, the use of the natural resources now existing on this continent for the benefit of the people who live here now." In this view, Pinchot had many supporters, particularly among western politicians.

The newly designated forest reserves, including the Olympic Forest Reserve, more nearly represented Muir's philosophy, since the reserves excluded commercial development and hence human manipulation. Though the reserves did not provide for use as Pinchot envisioned them, he supported their creation because they unequivocally kept these lands in public ownership, which was a crucial first step in Pinchot's empire building. He eventually wanted to be director of the national forest reserve system. At first, both Muir and Pinchot worked side by side to expand the reserve system. Indeed, Pinchot originally supported excluding commercial timber harvest and livestock grazing from reserve lands. But their different philosophies about management soon split them apart. Almost immediately, the forest reserves came under attack from western development interests. To westerners, used to unfettered access to the nation's natural riches, forest reserves not only represented an affront to their perceived right to natural resource extraction, but also symbolized the imposition of eastern big-government regulations.

Forest Reserve Controversy

It was not the timber interests, however, that were most angered by the establishment of the forest reserves. Most reserves were, as Wickersham noted, far from tidewater and in the higher mountains, which at the turn of the century were largely inaccessible. Most commercial timber harvest was on private lands close to the ocean. Since the majority of the early reserves did not unduly infringe upon their interests, protests from the timber industry were not nearly as loud as from other resource users.

It was the stockmen who fought against the forest reserves with the greatest intensity. The stockmen usually grazed their herds on the higher elevations of the public domain in summer. Setting aside forest reserves that explicitly forbade grazing brought forth a storm of protest. Then, as now, many western Congressional members were ranchers, and this powerful elite vowed to eliminate the forest reserves altogether. Pinchot, afraid he would lose his fledgling forest reserve system, capitulated to the political pressure from western livestock interests, reversing his earlier opposition to livestock grazing.

When Muir learned of Pinchot's change of heart, he was furious. To Muir, livestock were the single greatest threat to the mountains. When confronted by Muir, Pinchot acknowledged that he now supported livestock grazing in forest reserves. From that point on, Muir decided to work for national parks as the only secure way of protecting lands from exploitation, while Pinchot threw his influence and support behind expansion of the forest reserve system, but one more friendly to regulated commercial interests. For the next half century, the fate of the Olympic Mountains was debated back and forth between these two perspectives about land use. Ultimately, Muir's views won out for much of the Olympic Mountains when Olympic National Park was created. Nevertheless, the debate over land use continues to this day, both within the park and on the public and private lands beyond the park boundary.

Although most forest reserves included timbered lands inaccessible to timber interests, the Olympic Forest Reserve was an exception. The boundaries of the Olympic Forest Reserve included all of the mountain interior, the forested foothills, and even the western lowlands all the way to the Pacific Ocean. As a quick glance at a land-ownership map today reveals, much of this heavily timbered land did not long remain in public ownership. Timber interests almost immediately set about removing the most valuable timberlands from the forest reserve system.

Joining with the stockmen, the timber lobby eyed the rich timberlands of the Pacific Northwest and sought to reverse Cleveland's forest reservations. Senator Clark of Wyoming introduced an amendment to eliminate the entire forest reserve system. Only a threat of presidential veto killed the amendment. But less than two months later, President McKinley entered office and immediately set about reversing his predecessor's efforts. Sponsored by Sen. Richard Pettigrew of South Dakota, who was backed by the Homestead Mining Corporation, the amendment opened the forest reserves for one year to any claims by the mining, timber, and livestock industries. Pinchot also managed to slip in a provision that allowed cutting of dead or dying trees—a provision he would need to manage the forest reserves as he envisioned. Eastern newspapers and politicians opposed this capitulation to western resource interests, but McKinley approved the bill with Pettigrew's amendment. In response to criticism, McKinley threatened to revoke the forest reserves altogether.

Muir responded to the Pettigrew amendment—and to Pinchot. He wrote of Pinchot, "Much is said . . . about the greatest good for the greatest number, but the greatest number is too often found to be number one." Muir was invited to write articles defending the forest reserves for several influential national magazines. In an August 1897 *Atlantic Monthly*, Muir wrote: "Any fool can destroy trees. They cannot run away; and if they could they still would be destroyed—chased and hunted down as long as fun or dollar could be got out of their bark hides, branching horns, or magnificent bole backbones. Few that fell trees plant them; nor would planting avail much towards getting back anything like the noble primeval forests. During a man's lifetime only saplings can be grown in the place of the old trees—tens of centuries old—that have been destroyed."

Though Muir's essay appeared almost a hundred years ago, he could just as easily have been writing about the ongoing destruction of the last old-growth forests on the Olympic Peninsula that is occurring today.

As a consequence of Muir's popular articles, when the Senate voted in 1898 to abolish the forest reserves, the House, more nearly reflecting the sentiment of the people, voted 100 to 39 against the Senate bill. The forest reserves remained, but they were now open to regulated resource exploitation as envisioned by Pinchot.

The Olympic Forest Reserve became the focus of timber industry desires. Using a generous interpretation of the Pettigrew amendment, which declared that any lands within a forest reserve usable for agriculture had to be withdrawn from reserve status and made available for public acquisition, local officials began to lobby to withdraw large parts of the Olympic Forest Reserve in the name of agricultural development. To facilitate this removal of timber from the forest reserve, the lumber industry worked to elect one of their own as U.S. senator. In 1898, Washington senator Addison Foster, a timber company and railroad magnate, was voted by the Washington state legislature to be U.S. senator. (In those days, state legislatures voted for U.S. senators, making the Senate far more beholden to local and national corporate interests than those of today.) Senator Foster wasted no time lobbying to open up the "vast agricultural lands that had been tied up by the outrageous act of creating an Olympic Forest Reserve."

John Muir saw right through the timber industry's ruse and suspected that the magnificent forests of the Olympic Peninsula would continue to come under attack from the timber industry. He wrote prophetically, "There are trees in heaven that are safe from politicians and fire but there are none here." At least some government officials were also aware of Foster's motives. U.S. Geological Survey director Charles Walcott remarked, "It is apparent as in other cases from this region, that the purpose is not to make available for settlement, agricultural lands, but to obtain for the benefit of lumber companies and the men employed by them, the timber upon these lands, which is precisely what the government wishes to prevent in setting them off as reserves."

Then, as now, whenever industry sought to steal from the public coffers, it represented itself as aligned with the interests of ordinary rural folk. So petition after petition was forwarded to the U.S. Land Office asking for relief from the forest reserves in the name of the "poor, but honest settler" who was experiencing excessive hardship as a result of the reserve establishment. Local chambers of commerce complained that forest reserves would retard development of the region and affect the tax base. To anyone acquainted with current public land-use issues in the West, all of these arguments in favor of less government control and unrestricted access to the natural resources of public lands are all too familiar.

Despite objections from professional civil servants in the U.S. Geological Survey and even from Pinchot himself, Foster and his cronies succeeded in getting President McKinley to order a reduction in the size of the Olympic Forest Reserve. In 1900 and again in 1901, McKinley, by presidential proclamation, reduced the size of the Olympic Forest Reserve by a total of 721,920 acres. Though this reduced the forest reserve acreage by about a third, the withdrawal was focused upon the most productive timberlands and thus facilitated removal of three-fourths of the timber volume from the forest reserve. Ostensibly, this removal was done to make these lands available to farmers and settlers, but ten years later, more than 523,720 of these acres were owned by large timber corporations, nearly all having been fraudulently acquired under the Timber and Stone Act. Many of these same timber companies or their more recent incarnations still control much of the private acreage on the Olympic Peninsula today.

Not only was Muir angered by this loss of protected lands, but even Gifford Pinchot was outraged by the removal of these lands from the reserve system. He railed against the Interior Department, which he felt had capitulated to timber interests, saying that "nearly every acre of [the timber reserve removals] passed promptly and fraudulently into the hands of lumbermen."

Pinchot and the Forest Service

But Pinchot was as much a politician as those he despised. He sought to gain control of the forest reserves by removing them from control of the corrupt Interior Department and placing them under his management in the Department of Agriculture. Pinchot realized that to do so he had to neutralize opposition from western ranching and timber interests. First, in opposition to Muir's campaign to remove livestock from public lands, Pinchot fought to keep livestock grazing on forest reserve lands throughout the West. The ranchers saw a real advantage to maintaining reserve lands, since they could not be settled by homesteaders and thus would remain intact, which was essential to the free movement of grazing livestock. And as long as grazing was permitted on reserve lands, the ranchers could use them as if they owned them but without taxes or maintenance costs. Pinchot eventually won the support of the National Livestock Association.

To get the powerful timber industry leaders to support his plan for national forests under the administration of the Department of Agriculture, Pinchot argued that withdrawal of remaining public lands from private acquisition would inflate the value of the existing private timber holdings through a reduction of the timber supply available for cutting. To the large timber companies and railroads that held the majority of high-volume timberlands in the West, Pinchot's arguments made good business sense. By 1905, Pinchot had garnered sufficient support for the transfer of the forest reserves from the Department of the Interior to the U.S. Forest Service, a new agency he would manage as part of the Department of Agriculture.

Pinchot was able to expand his power and influence further by expansion of the newly created national forest system. Pinchot was President Theodore Roosevelt's main advisor on conservation issues, and he successfully lobbied the president to significantly expand the public lands under Forest Service management, adding millions of acres to the national forest system. Though this was clearly a bureaucracy-building effort on Pinchot's part, it was still not universally supported in the West, where all the newly created national forests were being carved from the existing public domain. In retrospect, Pinchot's efforts must be viewed in a positive light, since he single-handedly saved much of the most spectacular and valuable land in the West from being acquired by timber corporations and large ranching operations.

Nevertheless, the new power and land base Pinchot controlled put him in direct competition with John Muir, who continued to lobby for the creation of new national parks. Now Muir had to face the prospect of combating Pinchot, since all new parks, including any park that might be created in the Olympic Mountains, would have to come at the expense of existing forest reserves, a prospect that Pinchot and future Forest Service officials universally fought.

Park Proposals

The growing public support for the protection of the dwindling public domain as national forests and parks coincided with the near extinction of many wildlife species, from wading birds like herons and egrets killed for their plumes to deer and elk extirpated across America as a result of unrestricted market and subsistence hunting. Indeed, by the turn of the century, even animals now so abundant as the white-tailed deer had been wiped out in many eastern states. A growing sportsmen's movement, which included many wealthy and influential hunters such as President Theodore Roosevelt and George Bird Grinnell, led to the creation of hunter-conservation groups like the Boone and Crockett Club that worked to enact wildlife protection laws and protect habitat. Strong support from the Boone and Crockett Club, for instance, led to the establishment of Denali National Park.

Amid the growing concern for the future of wildlife in the nation, the Olympic Peninsula's native elk were being cut down by uncontrolled hunting. By 1903, it was estimated that there were fewer than 500 elk on the entire Peninsula. In response, Congressman Francis Cushman of

Skull of a Roosevelt elk. These elk were originally the motivating factor for the protection of the Olympic Mountains as a national park.

Tacoma introduced legislation into Congress to protect 393,600 acres as Elk National Park in order to save the last major herds of elk on the Peninsula. Cushman's bill would also protect elk habitat, banning logging within the proposed park. An opposing bill, introduced by Congressman William Humphrey from Seattle, would have protected more acres for the elk but specifically left the area open to logging—something the timber companies supported. As a result of the ensuing controversy, Cushman's Elk National Park bill was killed, and elk continued to be hunted on the Peninsula.

As a stopgap measure, the state legislature finally passed a law in 1905 prohibiting the killing of elk anywhere in the state. Although elk continued to be poached, the law effectively restricted the wholesale slaughter of elk, and the herds began to rebuild. In the meantime, Congressman Humphrey continued to reintroduce his "save the elk, cut the trees" park bill, but the bill was never enacted.

The Antiquities Act and Mount Olympus National Monument

A new vehicle for land protection was created in 1906 with the passage of the Antiquities Act. The act gave the president the power to declare "national monuments" by executive order without the consent of, or even consultation with, Congress. The original purpose of the act was to enable the president to withdraw from development small parcels of the public domain, such as the land around a pueblo ruin or a significant geological feature like a volcanic cone. The timing of this bill couldn't have been more fortuitous. President Theodore Roosevelt had been trying to protect the Grand Canyon in Arizona against development, including unrestricted mining, livestock grazing, and logging. Several attempts to enact passage of a national park bill for the canyon failed in light of powerful opposition from Arizona's extractive industries and its supporters in Congress.

Learning that there was no size limitation in the new Antiquities Act that would prevent him from setting aside the entire canyon, Roosevelt immediately declared the Grand Canyon a national monument, much to the distress of Arizona's Congressional delegation. (Since Roosevelt's time, many other national monuments have been proclaimed by presidential order, and most of our famous national parks were first national monuments, including Grand Teton, Arches, Death Valley, Denali, Joshua Tree, and Glacier Bay. More recently, President Clinton used the act to establish the Grand Staircase–Escalante National Monument in Utah.)

Nearing the end of his term as president, Roosevelt was approached by Congressman Humphrey, who sought to have a 750,000-acre national monument declared for the heart of the Olympic Mountains. Roosevelt, ever willing to protect significant national lands from overhunting and development, agreed to do this. He asked Pinchot, however, to write up the legislation. Pinchot, hoping to keep the area's trees available for logging, wrote a special clause exempting the proposed Mount Olympus

National Monument from any restrictions on timber harvest and removing 150,000 acres of the heavily timbered lower portions of the Queets, Bogachiel, Hoh, and Clearwater drainages along the western boundaries of Humphrey's proposed monument. Roosevelt signed the bill into law on March 3, 1909, creating a 600,000-acre Mount Olympus National Monument.

With the new monument under Forest Service administration, and the clause allowing logging in place, Pinchot was ready to apply forestry principles to the vast Olympic woodlands. Pinchot's plan backfired, however, when Richard Ballinger, an old foe from Seattle, was appointed the new secretary of the interior under the Taft Administration. Ballinger was no friend of conservation, but probably to spite Pinchot, he determined that the Antiquities Act called for strict preservation and said that therefore logging was banned from within the boundaries of the new national monument.

Almost immediately, plans to open the new monument to logging were developed by Washington timber interests. To facilitate logging, Congressman Humphrey introduced a national park bill as a cover-up to hide his real intent. His bill, while giving lip service to protecting the area's natural features, allowed logging if deemed necessary for "protection or improvement of the park." In addition, Humphrey's bill would allow mining, leasing of summer homes, and road construction.

Humphrey courted preservationists by pointing out that national monuments, which are proclaimed by presidential order, can also be undone by presidential proclamation. National parks offer more permanent protection, since they are designated by Congress, and the prospect that enough members of Congress could be persuaded to undesignate a national park is less likely than a president's changing a monument's status. In reality, however, Humphrey's bill was an attempt to undermine the protection conferred by national monument status. In his efforts to open up the national monument to logging, Humphrey was supported by most of the local politicians, governments, newspapers, and chambers of commerce.

Although Humphrey's bill did not pass, the timber industry and its supporters, along with the Forest Service, continued to lobby to remove all the valuable timberlands presently in the monument. In 1915, they succeeded. By presidential order, Woodrow Wilson removed 170,000 acres of heavily timbered lands from the southern flank and western valleys of Mount Olympus National Monument.

The National Park Service

The following year, the National Park Organic Act of 1916 created the National Park Service and mandated preservation of resources for the future while providing for visitor use and enjoyment of these resources. An influential millionaire, businessman Stephen Mather, was appointed by Secretary of the Interior Franklin Lane in 1914 to take charge of the national parks. Mather had no previous experience with the parks, nor a great understanding of their purpose. He was, however, a great park promoter and used his considerable fortune to finance park acquisitions and even the salaries of rangers hired to work within the new agency.

Mather's contributions to the Park Service and parks were not entirely positive. His ideas and the policies he set in motion affected the agency for many years beyond his long tenure as director. Without any ecological training, Mather basically evaluated potential and existing parks with an eye toward their scenic qualities and their potential for mass tourist development, not preservation. Mather, the former businessman, aligned himself with national park concessionaires, and his focus seemed to be on tourism.

Mather also joined forces with the Forest Service to work for the removal of any valuable timberlands from existing parks, including Sequoia and Yosemite. To fund park operations and land acquisitions, he advocated the cutting and selling of timber within parks and the killing of predators and the sale of their furs. Mather also promoted the introduction of exotic plants and animals into the parks. By 1921, the Ecological Society of America passed a resolution condemning the direction of park management under Mather's administration. In fairness to Mather, he also fought many other development schemes, from dams proposed within Yellowstone National Park to a proposed tram that would have crossed the Grand Canyon in Grand Canyon National Park. Many preservationists were deeply disappointed in the new Park Service. Unfortunately, they had no choice but to continue supporting the Park Service, since the Forest Service was increasingly becoming an agent of the timber industry.

Alarmed at how the parks were being run, Dr. Willard Van Name, curator of invertebrate zoology at the American Museum of Natural History, began writing and distributing pamphlets on park management issues. Van Name was angered that the Park Service was giving away the very lands it should have been protecting. He wrote, "If we are robbed of money we can go to work and earn more, but if we are robbed of the national parks we lose what neither time, money, labor, or regrets can replace."

In 1925, a committee that included both William Greeley, head of the Forest Service, and Stephen Mather of the Park Service produced a document recommending boundary adjustments that would free up timber to Forest Service management and potential logging. Parks scheduled for boundary adjustments included Yosemite, Crater Lake, Rocky Mountain, Mount Rainier, and Yellowstone. Van Name was appalled that any forestlands would be removed from park protection. In 1926, Van Name, using his own money, published and distributed a pamphlet, complete with maps and photos, called *Hands Off the National Parks*. In it, Van Name exposed Park Service plans to give away forested parklands and accused the agency of being more interested in promoting industrial tourist development than in protecting the nation's natural legacy.

Meanwhile, the Forest Service began to quietly dismantle the protection afforded Mount Olympus National Monument. The agency continued to view the timber within the monument as available for timber harvest, expecting local communities that were heavily oriented toward timber harvest to help generate the political pressure necessary to open up the area to logging. In addition, the agency permitted domestic sheep to graze on some of the high basins and decided that it was no longer authorized to protect elk or other wildlife from hunting and trapping.

The Forest Service surveyed roads up the Dosewallips and down the East Fork of the Quinault, and another up the Elwha River and down the North Fork of the Quinault, with the idea of using them to haul out timber once the political pressure for timber harvest permitted such extraction. If built, these roads would have cut the monument wilderness into fragments. The Forest Service was quietly redefining the meaning of the national monument legislation and turning the monument into an industrial resource.

Support for Olympic National Park

But nationwide support for a national park in the Olympics was beginning to grow. By 1928, the Park Service was regularly receiving letters from people who were advocating that Mount Olympus National Monument be redesignated a national park. There was even some support for a park among Olympic Peninsula business interests that thought national park status would increase tourism, and hence tourist dollars to local communities. Despite these supportive letters, the Park Service continued to balk at the idea of a park in the Olympics. At Mather's direction, it produced a form letter that basically stated that the Olympics, though beautiful, didn't quite measure up to national park standards.

Van Name, as a scientist, saw the national parks as the only place where natural processes and native species would be protected from exploitation, and he feared that the use of scenic quality as the only criterion for park establishment was severely limiting. Van Name, well ahead of his time in terms of his ecological understanding, appreciated the need for wildlands preservation based upon biological criteria.

Van Name was becoming so effective in his critiques that pressure to silence him was mounted against his employer, the American Museum of Natural History. When his contract at the museum was up for renewal, a clause specifically prohibited him from publishing anything that wasn't first reviewed by the editorial board of the museum.

With his job on the line, Van Name sought another outlet for his conservation writings. Van Name had recently met a conservation-minded New York matron, Rosalie Edge, who had important political and social ties. Edge joined with Van Name to form a new organization to provide a cover for his writing. They decided to call their new group the Emergency Conservation Committee (ECC). The ECC would publish Van Name's pamphlets, but with Rosalie's name and address on them.

Van Name and Edge didn't limit criticism to the Park Service. Their first campaign together as the ECC focused on the U.S. Biological Survey, which was involved in poisoning and shooting the last wolves and grizzlies in the West. Their pamphlet, titled *The United States Bureau of Destruction and Extermination: The Misnamed and Perverted Biological Survey*, exposed the bureau's predator extermination program, which included destroying wolves, mountain lions, and other carnivores in national parks, with the full cooperation of Park Service director Mather. Soon Van Name and Edge were joined by Irving Brant, a writer and editor with the *St. Louis Star* who had a strong concern for wildlife and nature. Together, the three constituted the full membership of the ECC. Never had such a small organization had so much power and influence as the ECC.

With the election of Franklin Roosevelt in 1932, new opportunities for expansion of the national park system were created. In particular, the new secretary of the interior, Harold Ickes, was very sympathetic to conservation measures. One of the first things Roosevelt did upon taking office was to put together a plan to transfer fifteen national monuments administered by the Forest Service to the Park Service. Ickes ordered the Park Service to take over management of Mount Olympus National Monument, which the Park Service continued to argue didn't merit national park status. In 1934, Van Name and the ECC published *The Proposed Olympic National Park,* which called for protection of the remaining old-growth forests on the Peninsula. The ECC enlisted the support of Irving Clark, a prominent Seattle lawyer, conservationist, and secretary to the Mountaineers, a Washington-based outing and conservation club, to help mount an Olympic Park campaign. Clark would be the local watchdog for the ECC for years.

Predictably, the Forest Service attacked Van Name's proposal and argued that if valuable timberlands were protected in a park, it would have grave consequences for the Olympic Peninsula timber industry. Olympic National Forest supervisor H. L. Plumb argued that park establishment would rob local communities of taxes, road funds, school funds, and jobs. Plumb's views reflected the Forest Service's utilitarian perspective about forests. "It must be remembered that forestry is the growing of trees for human use, and that trees reach maturity the same as any other crop and if not harvested will die and rot. The timber policy of the Forest Service is to maintain continuous production, or sustained yield." Irving Clark responded to the Forest Service's assertions that it practiced "sustained yield" by calling sustained yield "progressive destruction."

But joining the Forest Service in denouncing Van Name's park proposal was the Park Service itself, which reassured local communities that it had no intention of protecting trees that had any value as timber. Dave Madsen, recently appointed to manage the Mount Olympus National Monument, told local communities, "A National Park is not created for the purpose of conserving valuable stands of timber."

Van Name and the ECC seemed to have an impossible task. If they were going to be successful in protecting trees, they would have to overcome not only the considerable political and financial influence of the timber industry and the Forest Service, but the resistance of the Park Service as well. The odds seemed formidable: three people—two still working at full-time jobs—taking on the largest industry in Washington and the considerable resources and political connections of two major federal agencies. But if the ECC ever thought their task impossible, they didn't let on. They continued to work for a national park that included trees.

The Park Service had been ordered to produce a park proposal document. Owen A. Tomlinson, superintendent at Mount Rainier National Park, prepared the report. In its final recommendations, the agency carefully excluded any valuable timber from the park proposal. Tomlinson sought to assure the timber industry that no valuable timber would be in the report and sent an advance confidential copy to the timber industry's major lobbying organization. The report was soon copied and widely distributed, and Van Name eventually obtained a copy. Meanwhile, the report was reviewed by the Park Service and submitted to Interior Secretary Ickes, who approved it.

As soon as Van Name saw the recommendations, he caught the next train to Washington, D.C., where he arrived unannounced, demanding to see Ickes. Ickes had heard of Van Name and agreed to meet with him. As Ickes listened, Van Name poured out all his frustrations with the Park Service—in particular, its unwillingness to protect the magnificent forests of the Olympic Peninsula. Ickes responded by canceling his previous endorsement of the Park Service report and, instead, had Van Name draw up the boundaries for the new park proposal. Ickes accepted Van Name's recommendations and had them substituted for the previous Park Service documents. The Park Service was now caught in the embarrassing situation of promoting boundaries it had previously ridiculed as unreasonable.

Ickes then contacted Congressman Mon Wallgren, whose district included the Olympic Peninsula, and asked him to introduce an Olympic National Park bill with Van Name's defined boundaries. In what was quite an achievement for the ECC, the Ickes/Van Name park bill HR 7086 was introduced by Congressman Wallgren on the House floor on March 28, 1935.

To counter the park proposal, the timber industry, the Forest Service, and its allies began to promote sustained yield as the reasonable alternative to outright preservation. Of course, if the industry had actually been practicing sustained yield as it promised, it would have no need for the trees in the proposed Olympic National Park. A. E. Demaray, associate director of the Park Service, answered the sustained yield argument with unusual boldness, writing that "sustained yield has been promised to the Olympic Peninsula for twenty-five years and the yield of the Peninsula has not been sustained."

During Congressional hearings on the Wallgren bill, many factions showed up to testify. There were members of the timber industry, the ECC, and the Wilderness Society, as well as local park supporters from Washington State. When questioned during the hearings on the bill, even the Park Service changed its previous position and supported the expanded park with the inclusion of the big trees. Interior Secretary Ickes even showed up to testify in favor of Wallgren's bill. At the hearings, Ickes said, "I insist that it would be a stupid thing for this country to do, an unpardonable thing, to surrender this area to become a laboratory for the working out of a theory of multiple use which inevitably sooner or later, would mean the exhaustion of everything in the area that is capable of being converted into a money profit." The Congressional committee reported favorably on Wallgren's bill, but the bill never came up for a vote before Congress adjourned.

In 1937, Wallgren was reelected by a wide margin and reintroduced his Olympic Park bill. Despite its apparent past support during the previous Congressional hearings for the expanded park boundaries, the Park Service reversed itself again and redrew the park boundaries to exclude 138,000 acres in the heavily timbered west-side valleys, including the Bogachiel River. The new boundaries were inserted into Wallgren's bill, introduced in February 1937.

Reaction from the ECC was immediate and swift. They denounced the new boundaries and soon produced another graphic map and pamphlet to alert the public about the proposed changes. Having believed that the Park Service was the final authority, Wallgren had accepted the agency's boundary adjustments for his new bill, but upon discovering that it would remove many of the finest timber stands from protection, he abandoned the Park Service's new boundaries in favor of an expanded park as envisioned by the ECC. Wallgren even asked Rosalie Edge for copies of her pamphlet that argued against his bill to distribute in his district.

Hoping to avoid further erosion of the Wallgren bill by the Park Service, Edge wrote Ickes asking why the Park Service was apparently fighting against protection of the Olympic forests. Ickes called in Arno Cammerer, the Park Service director, for an explanation. Cammerer claimed that the agency was concerned about creating a hardship for local industry and communities by inclusion of valuable timber within the proposed park. Cammerer also used the old complaint that the west-side valleys like the Bogachiel lacked national park qualities. Ickes then grilled Cammerer, asking why the Park Service seemed to be fighting the groups working for an Olympic National Park instead of working against those opposed to it.

Even as the secretary of interior and Congressman Wallgren were rethinking their position on the reduced park boundaries, some of the local conservation groups like the Mountaineers and Northwest Conservation League were backing away from the ECC's boundary proposals in favor of the Park Service's weakened park proposal. With backing from these conservation organizations, Wallgren's bill with the Park Service's reduced boundaries sailed through the Congressional committee and was heading for a floor vote.

Presidential Support for Olympic National Park

The ECC appeared to be losing ground. But then events took an unexpected turn. President Roosevelt decided to visit the Olympic Peninsula and see for himself the cause of all the commotion.

Roosevelt arrived in Port Angeles on September 30, 1937. The entire town turned out to greet him. While waiting for the local ceremonies to end, a sign on the courthouse placed by local park activists caught the president's attention. It read: "Please Mr. President, we children need your help. Give us our Olympic National Park." Roosevelt was taken by the sign and declared in an extemporaneous speech, "I think you can count on my help in getting that national park, not only because we need it for us old people and you young people but for a whole lot of young people who are going to come along in the next hundred years of America."

That night Roosevelt stayed at Crescent Lake Lodge. After dinner, he met with Wallgren, several Park Service officials, and eventually the regional forester, Clarence Buck. Roosevelt declared to Buck, "You are not allowing a large enough National Park. I am thinking 50 years ahead when this state will have a large population and will need extensive areas for recreational purposes." Others were brought into the discussion, including Congressman Martin Smith of Hoquiam, who opposed any reduction in timber harvest on the Peninsula. When Smith argued that an expanded park boundary would cost jobs, the president responded, "Five billion board feet of timber is but a drop in the bucket compared to the 119 or 120 billion board feet already logged on the peninsula . . . there need be no worry over the comparatively small amount reserved, which is far more valuable for its recreational use than for lumber." No one in the ECC could have said it better. The president was clearly inclined to back the larger park proposal.

The next day, Roosevelt toured around the proposed park, heading south through Forks to Quinault, where they had lunch. After the lunch break, the group would be heading through some Forest Service lands. During the entire tour, the Forest Service continued to argue against an expanded park, claiming that it could manage timberlands well. In preparation for the presidential visit, the agency had moved a sign for the forest border back from some logged-over lands within the forest boundary to give the appearance that all Forest Service–managed lands were well cared for and beautiful.

The president and his entourage were completely taken in by this deception. After passing beyond what they thought was the border of the national forest, they entered a devastated moonscape of raw giant stumps and burned-over land. Roosevelt was so outraged by the devastation he saw that he turned to the others and declared, "I hope the son-of-a-bitch who logged that is roasting in hell." Little did the president know that the people responsible for this logging activity were leading his tour.

The Forest Service ruse may have worked, except that the president's son commented to *Seattle Post Intelligencer* reporters about the devastation on private lands they had seen just beyond the Forest Service boundary. Several seasonal Forest Service workers who had been involved in moving the sign read the comments and realized they had been involved in deceiving the president. One of them wrote a detailed letter to the president exposing the hoax.

The deception did not endear the Forest Service to the president. He later told Ickes that in his estimation, "eight out of ten foresters were hand in glove with the lumber interests." Ickes resolved to become directly involved in the Olympic Park issue and ordered the Park Service to amend its proposal for the park to include the big trees in the Bogachiel, Hoh, Elwha, Quinault, Skokomish, and upper Dungeness. Ickes also told the agency to include a coastal strip of wild beach as well.

Even as Roosevelt and Ickes swung clearly behind an enlarged park bill, the opposition continued to argue against inclusion of merchantable trees within the park. The timber industry and others succeeded in gaining the endorsement of the National Parks Association for a smaller park. The NPA argued against including valuable timber in the park and said that such lands lacked "park qualities" and would diminish the park's stature. The NPA's arguments were so against a larger park that they could have been written by the timber industry itself. The ECC continued its efforts, producing yet another pamphlet in favor of a national park and distributing 11,000 copies nationwide.

Roosevelt was clearly in favor of a large park, including several mountain-to-sea corridors. A meeting with representatives of the Forest Service and the Park Service, a Congressional delegation, and Irving Brant was held at Roosevelt's request to devise new park borders. What came out was a million-acre park proposal, with forested strips to the ocean along the Bogachiel and Hoh Rivers. Most of the land along these river corridors had long ago passed into private hands and thus would have to be purchased. The new boundaries did not last long. Purchasing the lands along the Hoh and Bogachiel was considered too politically risky, since it would be viewed as federal government land grab. To defuse resistance to the park, the river corridors were dropped, with the qualification that they could be added later when the park would be expanded.

Wallgren introduced yet another park bill, this one with expanded boundaries but minus the mountain-to-sea river corridors. Ickes went on the offensive and had a radio broadcast played all over Washington declaring that the president and the interior secretary were both in favor of a large Olympic National Park and appealing to the state's citizens' sense of pride by stating that he was sure that the people of Washington would want a park that ranked with other great parks and would be a credit to the state. Ickes' actions were unprecedented—never before had an interior secretary spent so much time and effort promoting a new national park.

The Wallgren bill was passed in the House and went to the Senate, where Washington's two senators were afraid to support the larger bill. As a compromise, ECC's Brant arranged for the senators to approve a smaller park boundary similar to Wallgren's earlier park proposal, but with a clause that enabled the president to expand the park by proclamation at a later date. This compromise was passed by both houses of Congress just before it adjourned on June 29, 1938. Olympic National Park was finally a reality.

But Roosevelt, Ickes, and the ECC still did not feel that the park was complete. The old-growth rain forests on the western side of the Olympic

Mountains were still outside the boundaries. Roosevelt moved quickly to exercise his option to add to the park by proclamation. With Brant's help, Ickes gave Roosevelt a list of proposed additions to the park that included 187,411 acres of forests in the Elwha, Quinault, Queets, Hoh, Bogachiel, and Calawah Valleys. Roosevelt added these areas by presidential proclamation on January 2, 1940.

Ickes then used his position as head of the Public Works Administration to declare that acquisition of the coastal strip would be a PWA project. Using federal funds and condemnation, Ickes acquired the coastal strip and then placed it under the National Park Service administration. Altogether, an additional 62,881 acres along the ocean strip and Queets corridor were added later. With these additions, Olympic National Park became the third largest in the national park system at the time.

Attacks on the Park

Though Olympic National Park and its forests were theoretically protected, the timber industry never accepted the idea that the trees within the newly established park were off-limits to logging. It continued to seek new ways to justify logging within the park. In its efforts, it was assisted by the local park administration.

After designation of the park and additions by presidential proclamation, Ickes considered the issue of forest preservation on the Olympic Peninsula settled. That was a mistake. Ickes left the management of the park to individuals who had previously fought to keep the old-growth forests outside the park boundaries, including Owen Tomlinson, who now was the regional park director for the Pacific Northwest; Preston Macy, superintendent of Olympic National Park; and Fred Overly, a former forester who identified more with timber industry values than the preservation ideals of the Park Service. None of these men accepted the idea that valuable timber should be protected within a park, and they looked to find any excuse to open up the park to new logging. Almost immediately after the old-growth forests on the west side of the park were added, Overly produced a report titled *Estimate of Timber Volumes in Olympic National Park*. He also completed a timber assessment of the Queets corridor and concluded that "it would not be objectionable to permit commercial utilization of spruce, and for that matter, other timber" in the Queets corridor.

The 1941 entry of the United States into World War II provided the perfect excuse the timber industry needed to justify logging off the park's west-side forests. In the name of the war effort, the timber industry argued that it was necessary to log the old-growth Sitka spruce inside the park to construct airplanes. In their effort, they had the help of old park foes who now held powerful positions in the War Department, including William Greeley, former head of the Forest Service, then main lobbyist for the West Coast Lumbermen's Association, now heading up the timber section of the War Production Board. Greeley wrote to the director of the War Production Board, asking for his help in opening up the Hoh, Queets, and Quinault watersheds to logging.

Interestingly, opposition to logging these forest valleys came from an unexpected source. Henry Graves, head of the Forest Service, sent figures to Newton Drury, new director of the Park Service appointed by Ickes, that demonstrated that the forests within Olympic National Park represented less than 1 percent of the volume of Sitka spruce available in Oregon and Washington, not to mention the huge volume of spruce found in Alaska's Tongass National Forest. There was, in effect, no need to log any trees in Olympic National Park. Indeed, Graves wrote to Drury, "From the foregoing it is clear that there is no real necessity to open the Mount Olympus National Park to cutting timber." He ended his letter by saying, "I am opposed to any such movement advanced under the guise of national defense."

Unfortunately, the Graves letter was never circulated, and apparently Drury never let Ickes or anyone else see it. Instead, the Northwest region of the Park Service produced another report, *The Availability of Vital Woods Which Can Be Contributed to War Needs by the National Park Service within the Olympic Peninsula*. Greeley worked behind the scenes to create the illusion that there was a shortage of timber and the only source was from within Olympic National Park. All the local chambers of commerce on the Peninsula, newspapers, and politicians loudly complained that the timber locked up in Olympic National Park was the only way to maintain mill production and at the same time serve the war effort.

In 1943, Park Service director Drury sent a memo to Ickes recommending that the Park Service "show its willingness to sacrifice" by logging 77,045 acres of the newly added west-side forests. Ickes sent the memo back to Drury with a terse message: "Not approved." A few weeks later, Drury tried again to get Ickes to approve logging in the park.

Again Ickes rejected the proposal. He wrote a letter to the War Production Board saying there was plenty of spruce for the war effort in British Columbia and elsewhere, and that all other sources should be exhausted before the forests of Olympic National Park were cut. During Congressional hearings held in Seattle later that month, statistics were released showing that the presumed shortage of timber from the mills was created more by a labor shortage, and the inability to get trees to the mills, than by any lack of trees to cut.

Nevertheless, this was ignored as hysteria over the war effort continued to be exploited by the timber industry and its allies on the War Production Board. Ickes continued to defend Olympic National Park against logging. It was good that he did, for less than three months after the War Production Board suggested there was a desperate need to log Olympic for Sitka spruce, it canceled its Alaska spruce program, citing a lack of need for the wood. Thanks to Ickes, we can still enjoy these forests today.

After the war, the park's forests were still not safe from the lumber-

Hiker admires the giant fluted buttresses of old-growth Sitka spruce along the Queets River Trail.

man's ax. William Greeley offered a new attack, saying that we now needed to log Olympic's forests to meet the demand for postwar veterans' housing. The *Seattle Post Intelligencer* took up the call, demanding that the Park Service open up its lands to logging to relieve the "extreme housing shortage."

Assistant park superintendent Fred Overly, always ready to help log the park, wrote an endorsement of the logging proposals, again reiterating that the park's western valley forests "had little to recommend it for park purposes" and recommending removal of these forests from the park to "provide materials for home building purposes." Overly produced yet another report in May 1946 arguing that 80 percent of the Hoh Valley forests should be logged economically and that 75 to 80 percent of the Bogachiel was also of timber quality. That the assistant park superintendent should continue to do timber suitability studies on the forests the agency was supposed to protect never seemed inappropriate to either the park superintendent or his superiors in Washington.

The local Park Service administration, including Overly, continued to argue that boundary adjustments were necessary on the west side to remove the forests that were not up to national park quality and improve management. By happy coincidence, all these boundary adjustments would release more than 56,000 acres of the biggest trees for cutting by the local timber industry. The Park Service's boundary adjustment study was forwarded to Congressmen Henry Jackson and Fred Norman, both staunch supporters of the timber industry, who immediately introduced legislation into Congress in 1947 to adjust park boundaries.

By this time, Ickes had retired, but he now penned a popular newspaper column. In that column, Ickes wrote that "the tree butchers, axes on shoulders, are again on the march against some of the few remaining stands of America's glorious virgin timber." Ickes then named Park Service director Newton Drury, someone he had appointed, as one of the people leading the charge upon Olympic's forest. Ickes' columns prompted public outrage, and soon the Park Service was inundated with letters demanding that the park be protected from logging. The ECC also started pumping out letters to the editors, Congress, and a new pamphlet, *The Raid on the Nation's Olympic Forests*. The Sierra Club and Wilderness Society also sent out alerts.

Fortunately for those fighting to protect the Olympic forests, momentum for boundary changes diminished. Congressman Norman died in office, and Henry Jackson, in the face of increasing public opposition to any logging of Olympic Park forests, claimed that he had only introduced a bill that the Park Service had prepared and recommended. Jackson eventually withdrew his bill.

By 1952, land originally designated by Roosevelt's proclamation to be acquired for the park along the Queets corridor and coastal strip had been purchased but had not yet officially been added to the park. In addition, a nine-mile strip along the Bogachiel River was not yet legally part of the park. After the election of Dwight Eisenhower in 1952, pro-park forces were worried that these lands would never be added. They applied pressure on President Truman to add these areas before he left office. On January 13, 1953, with just thirteen days left in his administration, Truman added the lands, including protection for the Queets corridor and ocean beaches

By now, most conservationists thought they had finally put to rest the issue of logging in the park. However, they had not counted on having Fred Overly appointed as park superintendent. Just a few years before, Overly had tried to get a job with Peninsula Plywood Corporation, but his salary demands were deemed excessive, and he missed being hired by one vote of the board of directors. He was then transferred to Washington, D.C., where he continued to work for the Park Service until he was appointed superintendent of Olympic National Park.

Now back at Olympic, Overly continued to dream up excuses for timber harvest. He ordered trail crews to cut large trees that were on trails and float them down rivers to waiting log trucks. He proposed a number of new roads, including one that would have gone up the Hoh and over High Divide and down the Soleduck, that would have generated millions of board feet of timber for local mills. He ordered salvage logging of trees knocked down by avalanches and the widening of roads with subsequent logging of old growth. He even advocated cutting a border around the park, similar to the swath that marked the 49th parallel and the border between Canada and the United States, so as to provide more wood for the local timber industry. Overly quieted critics by suggesting that the money generated from timber sales was to be used for acquisition of private inholdings within the park and other park-related programs.

Overly expanded his logging program by authorizing salvage logging ostensibly to protect the forest or visitors. Giant ancient Douglas firs were cut down as "potential safety hazards" from campgrounds, along roads, and elsewhere. Using his position as head of the Olympic Natural History Association, Overly began to assign logging contracts in the park to the association. Many Park Service staffers were outraged but felt that their jobs were at stake if they protested. Overly had less control over the seasonal park staff, however, and in the end, it was the seasonal park naturalists who were his undoing.

Paul Shepard, a seasonal naturalist, began a campaign to stop the logging. Using his contacts with the Garden Clubs of America, Shepard exposed the logging in the park. Records showed that between 1941 and 1958, when logging was finally halted, more than 100 million board feet of timber had been removed from Olympic National Park. In the end, the controversy led to the transfer of Overly from Olympic to Great Smoky Mountains National Park in 1958. Shepard was rewarded for his activities by being barred from any future Park Service employment by the regional director.

It's difficult to imagine a man more ill suited for his role as chief protector of Olympic National Park than Fred Overly. After being appointed superintendent, he had also begun a campaign to construct a highway along the coastal fringe of the park. Overly maintained that President Roosevelt had personally requested a road along the coast when he added the strip by presidential proclamation. Overly succeeded in obtaining Mission 66 funds allotted by Congress to begin construction of his highway in 1956. At this time, however, the logging controversy exploded, and in light of the unfavorable publicity, Overly was told by the Park Service director to abstain from building the road.

Conservationists decided to fight Overly's road and garner protection for more of the coast. In their fight, they had the assistance of many prominent conservationists, including Supreme Court Justice William O. Douglas, Olaus Murie, and Howard Zahniser of the Wilderness Society. In 1958, Douglas led two well-publicized beach walks with as many as seventy hikers to draw attention to the coast's wilderness qualities. The coastal highway proposal eventually died.

But Overly was persistent. Though he was transferred to Great Smoky Mountains, and the coastal highway was dropped from Park Service plans, he was not to be deterred so easily. Seven years later, with help from Sen. Henry Jackson, he succeeded in getting appointed regional director of the newly created Bureau of Outdoor Recreation (BOR). In 1964, Overly launched his road program again, suggesting that the last wilderness

Most of Olympic National Park, managed by the U.S. Park Service, is surrounded by Olympic National Forest, administered by the U.S. Forest Service. National forest lands are open to logging, mining, livestock grazing, and other forms of development typically prohibited within national parks. However, some 90,000 acres of the Olympic National Forest were given protection from future development by designation as federal wilderness by the 1984 Washington Wilderness Act. Pictured here is the Quinault River and the slopes of the Colonel Bob Wilderness, one of five Forest Service wildernesses adjacent to Olympic National Park.

beach in the United States be destroyed with a road up to Cape Alava. The road would be constructed in the name of recreation, but it would also facilitate logging on the western side of the Peninsula. Overly also proposed a number of other roads in Olympic National Park, including one from Deer Park to Hurricane Ridge, an extension of the East Fork of the Quinault Road, and a road from the Queets Valley up Tshletshy Creek and down to the Quinault drainage.

At the same time, Overly continued to lobby for deletions of the park to permit logging. In a letter to Interior Secretary Udall, Overly called for logging the Bogachiel and Calawah and removing 16,440 acres in the Quinault drainage, among other recommendations to facilitate logging.

Ten-mile-long Ozette Lake is the third largest natural lake in Washington. The lake was only added to Olympic National Park in 1986.

Concurring with Overly on these recommendations was his boss, Edward Crafts, former assistant chief of the Forest Service and a pro-logging advocate, now director of the BOR. Together they lobbied to have the old growth in the Olympics removed from the park.

By 1966, conservationists were fighting to establish a North Cascades National Park. Henry Jackson, no friend of conservation, hoped to make designation of the new park a quid pro quo for removal of old-growth forests from Olympic. But the plan fell through, as public sentiment again showed the desire to protect Olympic National Park intact.

Overly never gave up. Upon retirement from the BOR in 1972, he formed the Olympic Peninsula Heritage Council, which received huge contributions from all the large timber companies, including Weyerhaeuser, Rayonier, Simpson Timber Company, and Crown Zellerbach. Overly continued to work for the elimination of old growth from Olympic National Park until his death.

In 1976, the park was expanded by additions at Lake Ozette, Shi Shi Beach, Point of Arches, Heart o' the Hills Parkway, and the Queets. Park expansion continued. In 1986, the park boundary was extended from the beach to include the intertidal zone. Another 15,186 acres were added to the park that year through a combination of purchase and exchange with the U.S. Forest Service. Additions included the coastal beaches to low, low water line; the offshore islands that constitute the Quillayute Needles and Flattery Rocks National Wildlife Refuges; and the surface of Lake Ozette and the Ozette River.

In 1988, most of Olympic National Park was designated federally protected wilderness, barring future development of roads, logging, and any other scheme that might be hatched up by industry. In 1994, the entire coastal region was set aside as a national marine sanctuary.

I would be remiss if I left readers with the impression that the Park Service is not worthy of its role as protector of the nation's heritage. Since the 1960s, the Park Service has become increasingly concerned with protection of natural landscapes, wildlife, and processes.

Most of Olympic National Park is only accessible on foot. Here Mollie Matteson wades the bridgeless Queets River in the Olympic Park Wilderness. The park's wildlands were given legal protection against future development in 1988 when Congress designated 95 percent of the park as a federal wilderness area.

Lessons from the Olympic Park Battles

In many ways the history of Olympic National Park is the history of all our public lands. There hasn't been a national park created that wasn't fought by industry, many local people, and others with vested interests. But the saga of Olympic Park is also an inspiring story of democracy working at its best and shows how the efforts of just a few dedicated people were able to overcome the intense opposition of industry, politicians, and corrupt government officials.

If it hadn't been for the persistent and dedicated activities of individuals like Willard Van Name, Irving Brant, Rosalie Edge, and Irving Clark and public-spirited government officials like Interior Secretary Harold Ickes, we wouldn't have a national park or any old-growth forests today. These people were branded as radicals in their day because they were unwilling to compromise their position. They believed that saving some old-growth forests was worth fighting for—and they had to do it over and over again.

Unfortunately, history and politics don't always honor the right people. A wilderness area in Washington is named for Sen. Henry Jackson, who worked ceaselessly on behalf of the timber industry to open up new public lands to logging, whereas public servants like Harold Ickes and members of the ECC, responsible for saving what little of America's virgin forests we now have, are virtually ignored.

The most important lesson to be learned from the Olympic Park battles is that though battles end, the war on America's resources never ends. One cannot become complacent and assume that any place—whether a national park, wildlife refuge, wilderness area, or any other protected designation—is permanently saved. It is saved only until the next attack is begun, always with the same tired arguments.

THE GREEN WORLD

Step out of your car and walk into the Olympic rain forest, and it is like walking into a giant hall with emerald hanging gardens of ferns, mosses, and flowers. Roofed in as it is by the multilayered forest canopy, the interior of this forest may be dry even if it is raining. It is a world of lime green light and silence, broken only by the songs of varied thrushes and winter wrens. The trees stretch up to the sky, so tall you cannot see the tops without craning your neck. Although the magnificent trees command attention, in number they are just a small portion of the Olympic Peninsula's floral wealth.

The Peninsula is home to nearly 1,200 native species and varieties of plants. Nine species are endemic, found nowhere else in the world. The Olympic Peninsula is home to 28 percent of Washington's rare flora, the greatest concentration of rare plants in the state. A number of factors contribute to the diversity of flora and abundance of rare species. The Olympic Mountains create a variety of microclimates. West slopes of the mountains receive hundreds of inches of precipitation annually, whereas the area around Sequim, in the rain shadow of the mountains, receives less than twenty inches. While temperate rain forest dominates the western slope, cacti thrive near Sequim. Mountains affect vegetation in other ways as well. The higher mountains experience colder temperatures, and even arctic species can find suitable niches at higher elevations.

The flora is also influenced by the area's history. The disproportionate representation of rare species on the Olympic Peninsula is partly a consequence of geological and climatological changes over the last 12,000 years.

The advance of ice sheets during the last ice age profoundly influenced today's vegetation. During the last glacial advance, ice sheets filled Puget Sound and the Strait of Juan de Fuca. Alpine glaciers also moved down from the high peaks, filling valleys like the Hoh, Quinault, and Bogachiel with giant tongues of ice. Many of the higher peaks, however, particularly on the northeastern side of the Olympics, lacked glaciers or were only partially entombed in ice. For instance, Blue Mountain stood more than 2,200 feet above the ice, providing a refuge for plants. Likewise, an extensive strip of lowlands west and south of the mountains was never covered by glacial ice. This ice-free region may have been even larger than at present. So much of the earth's water was tied up as ice that sea level was actually lowered by several hundred feet, giving rise to a wider coastal fringe. Then, as now, the presence of the ocean and the influence of the mountains on local microclimates controlled what grew where. The eastern side of the Olympics, even then, was drier than the western lowlands adjacent to the Pacific Ocean.

Pollen analysis has enabled researchers to reconstruct past vegetation and even climatic conditions. Pollen is notably resistant to degradation and when buried in lake cores or bogs is preserved intact. Since each major genus has distinctive characteristics, analysis of pollen grains can reveal much about past vegetative communities.

Research into the floral history of the Olympic Peninsula reveals that many of the species we find in the area today were present during the last ice age. For example, the three most dominant trees—lodgepole pine, Sitka spruce, and western hemlock—were all present in abundance. There were, however, some ebbs and flows in the flora due to climatic change. For instance, during a glacial advance between 23,000 and 17,000 years ago, trees decreased while grasses and sedges increased. After the last glacial retreat approximately 12,000 years ago, the flora underwent evolution to its current state. In effect, the current plant assemblages are not very ancient. The Olympic forests that we see today are a relatively young phenomenon, no more than four or five generations old.

Another major factor affecting the flora has been the introduction of exotic species. The alien invasion of the Peninsula by exotic species, many of them with Asian or European origins, has increased substantially in the past century. Most exotics are invaders and thrive on disturbed habitat—the kinds of sites created by logging, farming, livestock grazing, road construction, and other human activities. In 1900, there were only 40 non-native species on the Peninsula. By the 1980s, the number of exotic plant species had increased to 333, or 25 percent of the flora found on the

Peninsula. Exotics often compete with native species for space and nutrients. The normal checks upon population growth that occur in the land
of origin are often missing, and exotics frequently take over, crowding out
native species and reducing overall biodiversity.

Temperate Rain Forest

Despite the spectacular wild beaches and scenic mountains, Olympic
National Park's greatest asset is its forests—the most magnificent collection of giant conifers anywhere in the world. The park's location has
much to do with its extraordinary forests. The mild climate with abundant rain enables growth. In addition, the Olympic Peninsula's location
about halfway between the equator and the pole means that it receives
abundant solar radiation during the growing season. And the soils derived
from the volcanic and sedimentary rocks that make up the Olympic Mountains are rich in nutrients. These factors all make the Olympic Peninsula
one of the best places in the world for growing trees and shrubs. Indeed,
the productivity rate per acre is greater than any other forest ecosystem in
the world, even outproducing the tropical rain forest.

The impressive forests of the Peninsula are known as temperate rain
forest. Temperate rain forests occur in only a few locations globally: the
coast of Chile, parts of northern Japan and the nearby coast of Asia, parts
of New Zealand and southern Australia, and formerly in northern Europe,
particularly the British Isles. Temperate rain forests are distinguished by
their relative scarcity of fire, their multilayered canopy, abundance of epiphytes (plants that live upon other plants), and large evergreen trees. The
dominant trees of the lowland forest are western hemlock, Sitka spruce,
Douglas fir, and western red cedar.

Broadleaf deciduous forest dominates the eastern United States and
most other temperate climates around the world. The dominance by conifers (cone-bearing trees) is unique to the Pacific coast. The Pacific Northwest has twenty-five species of conifers (not all of them found on the
Olympic Peninsula) but only twelve hardwoods. Two major factors are
responsible for the superlative conifer forests of the region: mild winter
temperatures and summer drought. Although rainfall is abundant on the
Olympic Peninsula, it is seasonal, with a summer dry spell. This is what
has created the great conifer forests of the Northwest. Conifers are far
superior to broadleaf trees in their ability to survive drought stress. All the

native broadleaf species, such as big-leaf maple, cottonwood, and red alder, are associated with year-round water sources, such as the fringes of wetlands, streams, or seeps.

The needles of conifers, unlike the leaves of deciduous trees, present a small surface area to the sun, reducing the heat load as well as evaporation through leaf pores. Reducing heat load is important, given the often hot, dry summers that characterize the Pacific Northwest, since chlorophyll is heat sensitive and begins to destabilize at high temperatures. Conifer needles also have thick, waxy cuticles that help them retain moisture in dry periods.

The large mass of the Pacific coast giants is another advantage in summer drought. Conifers can store as much as half of their daily water needs in their sapwood. A large Douglas fir may hold as much as four tons of water in its bole. Thus the trees' large size may be in part a response to summer water stress.

Conifers are able to photosynthesize throughout the year so long as temperatures are above freezing and moisture is available. In the mild Pacific Northwest, the soils seldom freeze, even at higher elevations, meaning that water is available to roots throughout the year. Since conifers retain their needles year-round, they can photosynthesize even in the winter months. Given the productive landscape and exceptional growing conditions, it's not surprising that the Olympic Peninsula supports trees of record proportions. The world's largest western hemlock, more than eight feet in diameter, is found in the Quinault River Valley. A Sitka spruce some fourteen feet in diameter grows near the Queets River campground in Olympic National Park. An even bigger giant, a Sitka spruce nineteen feet in diameter, is rooted by Lake Quinault on national forest lands. A fourteen-foot Douglas fir, the world's largest, also grows in the Queets Valley. A Douglas fir that is taller but slightly slimmer towers over the forest giants in the Hoh Valley. A western red cedar nineteen feet across can be found near the mouth of the Hoh River. The tree looks out of place surrounded by much smaller trees in the midst of a regrowing clear-cut.

Olympic Peninsula trees are also among the tallest. Only some of the California redwoods can outdo them for height. One Douglas fir in the Queets Valley is more than 326 feet in height. A Sitka spruce in the same valley rises to 305 feet. Other record trees found on the Peninsula include the largest Alaska cedar, subalpine fir, grand fir, vine maple, lodgepole pine, and western hemlock.

Although big trees are found throughout the Olympic Peninsula, they reach their greatest magnificence on the western slopes of the Olympic Mountains. The valleys of the Quinault, Queets, Hoh, and Bogachiel Rivers support the majority of remaining old-growth temperate rain forest left on the Peninsula. With their west-facing orientation, they receive the full brunt of Pacific storms, and rain falls abundantly. Average annual rainfall at the Hoh Visitor Center in the Hoh Valley is 142 inches. Condensation from fog adds another 30 inches. Coupled with nearly constant cloud cover, low evaporation rates, and moderate temperatures, the conditions are ripe for the growth of the world's tallest, largest trees.

Old-Growth Forests

But what makes the Pacific Northwest forests so unique are not just a few trees, but entire forests of giants. In the past, ignorant foresters called forests of large, older trees "decadent, overmature" timber, but today more enlightened ecologists and other specialists have come to recognize them as old-growth or ancient forests. The difference is more than just terminology. Ecologists have come to appreciate that forests dominated by large, old age-class trees have certain unique characteristics not found in younger forest stands. The idea that managed forests mimic natural forests is more industry propaganda than fact. Indeed, commercial forests dedicated to timber production are not an adequate substitution for natural old-growth forest stands. In fact, the continued existence of forests in the Pacific Northwest, not to mention salmon and a host of other wildlife, may be dependent upon the existence of ancient forests.

Ancient or old-growth forests have a multi-age-class stand structure, including trees of different age classes and species. This diversity in structure in turn fosters greater diversity of other plant and animal species associated with such forest. It is also an insurance policy for the forest, since most natural disturbance factors such as diseases, insects, and even fires seldom affect all age classes or species.

Old-growth forests are critical to many species. The controversial spotted owls rely upon the large branches found only in big, old trees for shelter from the elements. Old-growth forests provide them with shade from the summer sun and protection from winter rainstorms. In addition, the spotted owls' major food source, flying squirrels, requires the cavities that are abundant in the snags and dying trees common in older forest stands.

Roosevelt elk prefer the thermal protection provided by old-growth forest stands as shelter against the elements. In addition, some of their preferred foods grow only in the forest shade. Studies of elk forage have demonstrated that plants favored by elk that grow in old-growth stands are higher in leaf growth and digestible proteins and are more succulent than the same species growing in clear-cuts and other forest openings.

Other species dependent upon Olympic's old-growth forests are Vaux's swift, murrelet, silver-haired bat, long-eared myotis, long-legged myotis, Cope's giant salamander, Olympic salamander, Van Dyke's salamander, tailed frog, northern flying squirrel, coast mole, marten, and fisher.

Old-growth forests also sustain many species of lichens that are known as nitrogen fixers. These lichens take nitrogen from the atmosphere and chemically bind it so that it's available to other plants for growth. Rain falling through these lichens removes this nitrogen and transports it to the soil, or the lichens themselves fall to the ground, where they are incorporated in the forest litter and eventually contribute to soil nutrient enhancement. These lichens add about two to five pounds of nitrogen per acre annually. Such lichens are uncommon in younger forests, particularly those managed for timber production.

The large branches of these forest giants create their own environment for many specialized species of plants and animals. The branches support epiphytes such as ferns, mosses, and lichens, which provide food and habitat for many animals. One researcher found at least 130 species of epiphytes living upon the trees in the Hoh Valley. And more than 1,500 species of insects depend upon forest canopy for their homes.

Older forests are dominated by what forest ecologists term downed woody debris—dead logs lying on the ground. In a typical old-growth Douglas fir forest, a tree falls every two years, and half of the annual litter fall is woody debris. Dead trees and downed logs serve numerous ecological purposes. Snags are critical habitat for many species of wildlife, from fungi and bacteria to insects and spiders, cavity-nesting birds, mammals, and even reptiles and amphibians. The diverse array of animals that exploit these snags for home and food include flying squirrels, bats, wood ducks and goldeneyes, nuthatches, woodpeckers, and chickadees. Large snags provide more potential nesting sites than small trees. Cavity-nesting birds prefer trees larger than two feet in diameter.

When snags fall to the ground, they continue their useful life. Insects and other invertebrates, as well as decomposers like fungi, depend upon logs for their home and forage. Many vertebrate animals, from salaman-

Fallen logs in Royal Creek. Trees fill many important ecological roles, even after they have died.

ders to voles, find shelter under downed logs. Rotten downed logs hold moisture long into the summer drought, providing a moist environment critical to the survival of salamanders and other creatures and providing germination sites for trees.

The downed woody debris also provides a rich seed bed for fungi. Mycorrhizal fungi attach themselves to the roots of trees like Douglas fir. The fungi then aid the tree in the gathering of nutrients and water from the soil. Mycorrhizal fungi also release antibiotics that inhibit forest pathogens. The mycorrhizal fungi benefit from the tree by deriving carbohydrates from it. The soil beneath an old-growth Douglas fir forest may contain as much as two and a half tons of mycorrhizal fungi per acre.

The spores of many fungi species are spread by small rodents like voles and flying squirrels, which consume the fruiting bodies and then spread the spores in their feces. A complete circle of dependency occurs. The forest depends upon the fungi to enhance its growth, the voles and other rodents depend upon the larger logs for shelter and to provide the habitat for the fruiting of fungi, and the fungi can't be spread readily without the aid of rodents. Other animals that fed heavily upon the underground fruiting bodies of mycorrhizal fungi include mountain beavers, chipmunks, pocket gophers, mice, and tree squirrels. These all support a host of predators from marten to owl.

The logs themselves help to perpetuate the forest. In the severe competition of living plants that cover a forest floor, tree seedlings have a difficult time germinating and surviving long enough to establish a root system. Fallen logs provide sites for seedling establishment that are free of competition, as well as a source of moisture during the summer drought. Such logs are called "nurse" logs, since they aid the establishment of the trees themselves. Long colonnades of trees that all sprouted upon the same fallen nurse log are a common site in the Olympic forests.

Some snags fall into streams and rivers, where they serve structural and nutrient cycling purposes. Aquatic insects and other invertebrates live in or upon the logs, and logs also provide the structural habitat critical for fish such as salmon and trout. Studies have shown that 50 percent of the salmon and trout habitat in smaller streams is created by fallen logs.

In addition, logs in streams create a stair-step structure of pools and small falls that helps to dissipate flood energy to protect banks from erosion. The falling water also traps oxygen, helping to aerate streams by providing the oxygen so critical for the survival of fish and other organisms. Logs also trap sediment.

When those logs are washed out to sea, they provide habitat for many marine species as well. Coho salmon fingerlings, for instance, use snags as hiding habitat from predators. The logs washed up on beaches help to protect the shoreline from erosion, and others rammed by waves against headlands rip apart mussel and barnacle beds, creating new colonization habitat for other marine invertebrates. In all areas, logs serve as long-term nutrient sources as they slowly rot and break apart. Finally, in years past, sea currents carried the huge logs of the Pacific Northwest to the Hawaiian Islands and elsewhere, where they were prized by Polynesians for the construction of their huge outrigger canoes. Again, larger logs, not just any log, serve all of these multiple purposes best.

Unfortunately, most of the magnificent old-growth forest has been

Western hemlock seedlings on a nurse log.

cut during the past 100 years. Of the million acres of old-growth Sitka spruce–western hemlock that once clad the western portion of the Olympic Peninsula, less than 3 percent remains today, nearly all of it within the boundaries of Olympic National Park. More old-growth Douglas fir forest is protected, but even the majority of this forest type has fallen before the ax and chain saw.

Much of the remaining old-growth habitat is fragmented and isolated from other old-growth ecosystems. From a biological perspective, small, isolated pieces of the forest are of limited value. Though several hundred thousand roadless and uncut acres of old-growth forest exist on national forests surrounding Olympic National Park, only one parcel is larger than

10,000 acres in size. This might seem like a large chunk of land, but it's less than four miles by four miles, and such small parcels can't support many old-growth-dependent species. Given the exceptional growing conditions on the Olympic Peninsula, there is no doubt that trees will regrow on the Peninsula, as the timber corporations continually try to remind us, but trees are not the issue. Ecologically speaking, a tree farm isn't the same as a naturally functioning forest ecosystem. A forest is more than the sum of its individual parts. What have been destroyed—and likely will not be replaced within human lifetimes, if at all—are the complex ecological relationships found only in old-growth forest ecosystems.

The loss of old-growth forests as a result of clear-cutting has far more implications and serious consequences than whether a single species like the spotted owl goes extinct. The spotted owl is merely the canary in the coal mine sounding a warning about the extent of loss in these kinds of forests. Some authorities estimate that up to 90 percent of the old-growth forest that existed at the time of European colonization is now gone. Just because trees have grown back on many of these cut-over lands doesn't mean the forest ecosystem is intact or will be restored. Nor is the restoration of old-growth characteristics likely to occur in the future. Trees on lands used for commercial timber production typically are cut long before they gain old-growth proportions. The idea that timber production is compatible with forest ecosystems is suspect.

Three things are critical to restoring the forests of the Pacific Northwest. All remaining old-growth forests need to be given full protection. Commercial timber production must be halted on all public forests, and they must be allowed to return to natural conditions. And an organized effort toward acquisition of large parcels of private timberlands in the Pacific Northwest should be implemented, with these lands managed for restoration of natural forest processes and structure.

Fire is a major disturbance feature of the forest ecosystem, even in the rain-drenched Olympic Peninsula. Despite the abundance of annual rainfall, the periodic summer drought coupled with El Niño winters with their reduced precipitation can lead to very dry conditions in the forest. It is only under such conditions that fires are possible; under normal conditions, the Olympic forests are nearly flameproof. Other critical factors are wind and low humidity, as well as an ignition source, usually lightning. Under conditions of drought, wind, and low humidity, even a young regenerating clear-cut will burn well. Such conditions may occur only every few hundred years, but when they do, Olympic forests can readily burn.

It is interesting to note that Gifford Pinchot, founder of the U.S. Forest Service, on a tour of the Olympic forests near the turn of the century near Lake Crescent, noted the effects of fires upon the forest composition. In his book *Breaking New Ground,* Pinchot wrote, "But the most significant thing I found, and to me it was an amazing discovery was that every part of the Reserve I saw appeared to have been cleared by fire within the last few centuries. The mineral soil under the humus, wherever it was exposed about the roots of windfalls, was overlaid by a layer of charcoal and ashes. Continuous stretches of miles without a break were covered with a uniform growth of Douglas fir from two to five feet in diameter, entirely unscarred by fire. Among them numerous rotting stumps of much larger trees did bear the marks of burning."

In the wettest west-side valleys, fires burn through the forests every 500 to 600 years. In the drier east-side valleys, fires are slightly more common, occurring every few hundred years. Douglas fir, a species that germinates and grows well in open sunlight, is highly dependent upon fire for its success throughout the West. Most of the Olympic Park lowlands are western hemlock forests. If undisturbed, eventually most of the forest would be dominated by western hemlock. Such a change doesn't occur overnight, however, and long before all of the Olympic Peninsula becomes hemlock forest, disturbance typically opens up the forest stands, permitting Douglas fir to dominate.

In fact, the magnificent forests seen today are a direct result of past fires. Fire ring and charcoal studies have documented the occurrence of a number of large fires that have swept the Olympic Peninsula during the past thousand years. In 1308 massive fires burned through the Olympics and nearby Cascades. These blazes burned through approximately half of the forests on the Peninsula. Many of the fine old Douglas fir stands on the Peninsula date from this burn. Around 1550 blazes again swept through the Pacific Northwest. In some instances, the flames torched some of the forest that had regenerated after the previous blaze 250 years earlier. Finally, dry east winds propelled another series of large blazes through the Olympic forests around 1700. More than a million acres of forest along the eastern and northern slopes of the Olympics were affected by these fires. In between these great conflagrations, many smaller fires burned patches of forest scattered here and there about the Peninsula.

Although logging does open up the forest, favoring Douglas fir, as previously pointed out, there are substantial differences between a logged forest and a fire-disturbed forest. Fires create many snags, which are entirely lacking in logged-over forests.

Fires burn in a mosaic pattern, seldom burning an entire drainage from ridgetop to ridgetop. In particular, existing stands of old growth are the least likely to burn due to a variety of factors, including the higher moisture content of downed woody debris beneath them and the higher humidity in the shady multistand ancient forests. Thus the very trees most likely to be cut for timber on managed forests are the ones least likely to be killed by fire. This demonstrates yet another significant ecological difference between the unhealthy and ecologically bankrupt forests created by foresters and forestry compared to natural forest ecosystems.

Fires also kill some forest pathogens either directly or through smoke, thereby reducing mortality in the remaining trees. Fires release nutrients for future plant growth and enhance the occurrence of nitrogen-fixing bacteria, increasing the amount of nutrients in soils over non-burned areas. Some of these nutrients are also released in streams, and some aquatic biologists believe that the pulse of nutrients resulting from fires is critical to the maintenance of stream productivity, particularly in higher headwater regions.

Many forest species have adaptations that permit them to survive all but the most intense blazes. Douglas fir, for instance, has very thick, corky bark that protects and insulates the inner living layer of the tree. Self-pruning is another adaptation to fire. The loss of lower branches means fires can't jump easily into the canopy. Some plants like rhododendron sprout from suckers or roots after a blaze. And lodgepole pine cones often remain unopened unless heated by a fire. They then open, dropping seeds on the bare mineral soil that often results after a blaze.

Indeed, there is no such thing as a "destructive" fire within the context of a forest ecosystem. Even large, hot blazes occur occasionally under natural conditions and have their ecological role. Indeed, it can be said that almost no forest on the Olympic Peninsula is immune from blazes. Rather than viewing fires as destructive, within the context of western landscapes, fires are a natural and necessary ecological process. Fires are like a wolf that preys upon the trees. The giant forests of the Olympic

Peninsula have not only survived past fires, but thrive as a consequence of them. It is not fire that destroys forests, but the lack of fire. Indeed, if one allows a slight amount of anthropomorphism, it can be said that a forest ecosystem lives in mortal fear of fire suppression and timber harvest, rather than a fear of fires.

Major Plant Communities

Within the Olympic Mountains, there are four major plant communities: lowland temperate forests, midelevation forests, subalpine forests, and alpine plant communities. Further subdivisions might include subalpine meadows, coastal prairies, and riparian habitats.

Sitka Spruce–Western Hemlock Forests

The most spectacular of these communities, and the reason for the park in the first place, are the lowland temperate rain forests that are found along the coastal strip and along the major west-side valleys such as the Hoh, Queets, Bogachiel, and Quinault. The abundant rainfall is responsible for these luxuriant forests. The tall, straight bole of Sitka spruce (*Picea sitchensis*) is a major tree species here, mixed with western hemlock (*Tsuga heterophylla*). Western red cedar (*Thuja plicata*) and Douglas fir (*Pseudotsuga menziesii*) are also found here, primarily on the steeper slopes. Associated subdominants include the moss-festooned big-leaf maple, which tends to grow on shallow, stony soils such as the rocky areas where tributary streams cross the river valleys. Many epiphytes live on these maples and weigh about 6,000 pounds per acre, or more than four times the weight of leaves. Moreover, the trees send tiny root mats into the epiphytes to obtain extra moisture and nutrients.

The vine maple (*Acer circinatum*) has lovely, small, seven- to nine-lobed leaves and delicate branching. With its green bark and brilliant scarlet autumn leaves, it adds color to the understory vegetation. Shrubs common in this forest include salmonberry, with its lovely salmon pink blossoms; oval-leaf and red huckleberry; and trailing blackberry. Wood sorrel, sword fern, false lily of the valley, and other plants cover the forest floor.

Western Hemlock–Douglas Fir Forests

In drier northern and eastern valleys, Sitka spruce disappears. Western hemlock is still the climax species, but Douglas fir assumes a more prominent role in the forest makeup. From the Sol Duc Valley eastward, grand

The delicate, lacy branches of western red cedar and vine maple along the North Fork of the Skokomish River.

Moss-strewn big-leaf maple along the Dosewallips River. Big-leaf maple hosts a greater load of epiphytes, mosses, and ferns than any other species of tree.

fir (*Abies grandis*) becomes more abundant in the lowland forests, often growing in mixed stands with Douglas fir. The thin-barked grand fir is very susceptible to fire and seldom survives a large blaze.

Another species found in this mixed forest is western white pine (*Pinus monticola*), a five-needled pine that grows straight and tall. The beautifully tapered boles were once popular as masts for sailing ships. The western white pine has gray bark and narrow, six- to eight-inch-long cones. White pine has been dramatically reduced over much of its range by the introduced blister rust, a disease that kills mature trees.

Pacific madrone along Crescent Lake. Madrone is one of several California species that reaches its northern limits in the rain-shadow areas along the northern and northeastern fringes of the park.

Understory species in these valleys are predominantly salal, Oregon grape, and Pacific rhododendron, which cloaks the slopes with beautiful pink blossoms in spring.

A unique tree common along Hood Canal and the drier areas along the northern slopes of the Olympics is the Pacific madrone (*Arbutus menziesii*). At one time, Garry oak (*Quercus garryana*) and prairie grasslands were common in the rain-shadow area around Sequim. This habitat type is still common in the undeveloped portions of Oregon's Willamette Valley. Most of the oak savanna around Sequim was plowed and converted to agricultural fields. Today, these fields are falling prey to urban sprawl.

Riparian Forests

Red alder (*Alnus rubra*) is common along river gravel bars and other disturbed sites. It often invades after logging. It has gray bark that is often blotched with white lichen, giving it a mottled appearance. The leaves are elliptic, with blunt teeth along the margins. Red alder is short-lived, with a fifty-year-old tree considered quite ancient. These trees are important in forest succession because they host nitrogen-fixing bacteria, which add significant amounts of nitrogen to the soil.

Black cottonwood (*Populus trichocarpa*) is another common tree along rivers. Cottonwoods easily colonize gravel bars and can grow from even small pieces of branches.

Hiker among a red alder forest. The light gray–barked red alder dominates river terraces. The open parklike nature of the forest floor is maintained by winter browsing of Roosevelt elk.

Montane Forests

At around 1,000 feet elevation on western valleys, and slightly higher elsewhere, the dominant tree is Pacific silver fir *(Abies amabilis)*, also called lovely fir. Other trees often mixed with silver fir include western hemlock and Alaska cedar *(Chamaecyparis nootkatensis)*. At higher elevations, silver fir eventually gives way to mountain hemlock *(Tsuga mertensiana)* in the subalpine zone. On the northern and eastern slopes of the Olympics, silver fir disappears altogether or is confined to a narrow band where cool air drainage and shade favor it.

Also found in the silver fir forest are giant old Douglas firs, relics of past climatic conditions. A warming period combined with large fires allowed Douglas fir to move upslope into what is now the silver fir zone. Since then, the climate here has turned cooler and wetter, with more snow. The old Douglas firs persist, but they no longer reproduce in much of this zone.

Subalpine Forests

As elevation increases, the silver fir zone fades into the subalpine zone, which is well represented in the Olympic Mountains. As a region, it experiences the deepest snows, and most of the subalpine terrain in the Olympics was previously glaciated.

West of the Bailey Range, the most common subalpine species are the mountain hemlock and Alaska cedar, which grow between 3,000 and 5,000 feet elevation. Understory species include white rhododendron and oval-leaf huckleberry.

Mountain hemlock is a common timberline species from Yosemite National Park to Alaska, wherever snow depth exceeds ten feet. Alaska cedar, also known as yellow cedar, is a timberline species from northern California to Alaska. In the drier regions of the eastern Olympics, the mountain hemlock–Alaska cedar forest gives way to subalpine fir *(Abies lasiocarpa)*. These forests are found between 4,000 and 6,000 feet.

Unusual tree occurrences include Rocky Mountain juniper *(Juniperus scopulorum)*, an uncommon relict in the northeast part of the park. Whitebark pine *(Pinus albicaulis)*, a species that is more favored in the drier Rockies, grows only at timberline in the Upper Dungeness Valley. Aspen *(Populus tremuloides)* and Englemann spruce *(Picea engelmannii)* are both very rare species in the Olympics and are confined to the drier northeastern side of the park. Interestingly, a spruce located along Cameron Creek, at 179 feet tall and 7 feet in diameter, is the second-largest

Englemann spruce known, even though the tree's major range is in the Rockies, where there are millions of acres of Englemann spruce forest. Lodgepole pine *(Pinus contorta)* is found near Deer Park and at a few other sites. It grows in dense stands, often regenerating after fires. This two-needled pine has small, round cones that typically don't open unless subjected to the heat of a fire.

Subalpine Meadows

Subalpine meadows are common at or near timberline. Their occurrence is controlled by a number of factors. In many areas, cold air drainage prevents successful colonization by trees. In some places, snows are so deep

Lupine frames subalpine meadow in the Upper Royal Basin. Meadows often dominate basin floors where saturated soils and cold air drainage preclude the establishment of trees.

that only flowers can successfully complete their life cycle in the short summer season. Growing among these lush meadows are lupine (*Lupinus* spp.), Indian paintbrush (*Castilleja* spp.), glacier lily (*Erythronium grandiflorum*), avalanche lily (*Erythronium montanum*), red heather (*Phyllodoce empetriformis*), and numerous others.

Alpine Tundra

Alpine vegetation in the Olympics is restricted to a few locations. Steep slopes, abundant snow and glacial ice, and the generally low elevations of these mountains limit the amount of alpine tundra. The best examples of tundra are found in the northeast corner of the park on Elk Mountain, Observation Peak, and Blue Mountain. Conditions on these peaks may not be as extreme as alpine terrain in the Rockies or elsewhere, but they still present serious limitations on plant growth. Alpine plants usually grow in rock crevices or on south-facing, well-drained slopes where snow doesn't accumulate. By midsummer droughty conditions often prevail on these sites. Plants living here have several adaptations that permit them to thrive in this environment. They begin growth as soon as temperatures rise above freezing and the snow melts. Nearly all alpine plants grow low to the ground, thereby reducing their exposure to the nearly constant winds and allowing them to benefit from soil heating on sunny days. Because of the severe growing conditions, most alpine plants require several years to flower and produce viable seeds, and thus all Olympic alpine species are perennials. Most alpine plants are wind or insect pollinated. Flies and bumblebees are among the major insect pollinators here.

Olympic alpine zone plants include thread-leaf sandwort, small-flowered blue-eyed Mary, mountain lover, Olympic Mountain synthyris, Olympic rockmat, spotted saxifrage, tufted saxifrage, Piper's bellflower, mountain oxytropis, silky phacelia, and spreading phlox.

Species Accounts

Trees

SITKA SPRUCE
(Picea sitchensis)

Description. Light green needles stiff and sharp, up to an inch in length, projecting outward on all sides of the twig. If you grab the branch and it hurts, it's probably a spruce. Needles are four-sided and can be rolled in the fingers. Cones 2 to 3 inches long, with thin, papery, irregularly toothed scales. Scaly, purplish brown bark. Base of mature tree trunks often buttressed. Trunks very straight, with little taper, reaching nearly 300 feet in height and 10 feet or more in diameter, with a record tree 19 feet in diameter.
Distribution. Common along the coast and west-side valley bottoms, often mixed with western hemlock. Very common in Queets, Hoh, and Quinault Rain Forests.
Remarks. Sitka spruce is named after Sitka, Alaska, where the tree is extremely common. The species is the fourth tallest tree in the world and is common in the cool, wet coastal belt from northern California to Alaska's Kodiak Island. Selective browsing of its major competitor, western hemlock, is thought to help maintain Sitka spruce's dominance of rain-forest sites.

PACIFIC SILVER FIR
(Abies amabilis)

Description. Needles deep green on top with two white stripes beneath, up to 1¼ inches long, lying in horizontal flat plane, with smaller ½- to ¾-inch needles on top of the twig pointing upward and forward in a herringbone pattern. Cones barrel-shaped, 3 to 5 inches long and 1 to 2 inches wide. As with all firs, cones are borne pointing up from the tips of branches, rather than hanging down.

Pacific silver fir.

Cones are green until maturity, when they turn purplish brown. Cones disintegrate on the branches so are seldom found whole on the ground. The light gray bark is resin-blistered and is smooth on all but the largest trees. Tree has a tall, dense, conical shape.

Distribution. Typically found between 1,000 and 3,500 feet, where it is gradually replaced by mountain hemlock. Occasionally found below 1,000 feet in west-side valleys, particularly in the Bogachiel, where it seems to replace Sitka spruce on the valley floor. Distribution broadest on the west-side slopes, where it is the most common species of midelevation forests. Its distribution is narrower on the east side of the mountains, where it is typically confined to cool, moist stream bottoms. It is nearly absent from the rain-shadow northeastern portion of the park.

Remarks. *Amabilis* means lovely fir, and the species is one of the more graceful trees of the forest. A shade-tolerant species, it comes to dominate moist areas where fires are uncommon.

GRAND FIR
(Abies grandis)

Description. Needles are broad, ¾ to 2 inches, spreading in a flat plane from twig. Tips of needles often notched. Dark green above, with two distinct white stomatal stripes below. Cones are cylindrical, 2 to 4 inches, greenish, and borne erect on tips of branches. Bark is gray to light brown; smooth and resin-blistered when young but becomes more furrowed with age.

Distribution. Mixed with other conifers from lowlands to mid elevations; most common on the northern and eastern sides of the Olympics.

Remarks. Grand fir is often intermixed in Douglas fir forests, where it is more shade tolerant than Douglas fir but less resistant to drought.

Grand fir bough.

DOUGLAS FIR
(Pseudotsuga menziesii)

Description. Blunt, pointed needles ½ to 1½ inches, radiating around the twig. Light brown (green when immature) cones 2 to 4 inches with three-pronged "rat's tails" sticking out from under thin scales. Bark light gray and smooth in young trees, becoming corky, deeply furrowed, thick, and brown with age. Height nearly 300 feet, with diameters of 14 feet. Broad, rounded crown; long, branch-free lower trunks in mature trees.
Distribution. One of the most widely distributed trees in the Pacific Northwest; common throughout Olympic National Park at low to mid elevations.
Remarks. *Pseudotsuga* means "false hemlock"; however, this is not a hemlock, nor is it a fir. It is named for botanist David Douglas, who collected its seeds

Douglas fir, pictured here, is a sun-loving species that can't reproduce successfully under a dense forest canopy. Most of the ancient Douglas firs, like this one in the Quinault Rain Forest, were established after wildfire removed the forest canopy. Even in the west-side rain forests, large forest fires occur on an average of every 600 years.

while on a plant-collecting expedition to the Pacific Northwest in 1825. The common giant of the old-growth forest, Douglas fir can live over 1,000 years. Its thick bark makes it highly resistant to fire. Intolerant of deep shade, the seedlings often establish themselves on sites after fires. The origins of most giant Douglas fir stands can be traced back to a previous forest fire.

WESTERN HEMLOCK
(Tsuga heterophylla)

Description. Needles vary from ¼ to ¾ inch. Soft, light green with white stomatal stripes beneath. Needles spread in delicate, flat sprays. Cones oblong, ¾ to 1 inch, hanging from branch tips. Cones are purplish green when young, turning brown when mature. Gray bark, thick and furrowed in mature trees. Top leader of tree conspicuously drooped; lower branches bend gracefully downward. Height to 200 feet.
Distribution. Low-elevation forests, particularly on the western slopes of the Olympics.
Remarks. Highly shade tolerant. Most common understory species in mature forests, where it eventually replaces other species such as Douglas fir and Sitka spruce in climax forests. Browsed heavily by elk in winter.

MOUNTAIN HEMLOCK
(Tsuga mertensiana)

Description. Needles ½ to ¾ inch. Bluish green with white stomatal stripes on top and bottom. Needles radiate from all sides of the twig. Cones 1 to 2½ inches, usually larger than those of western hemlock. Cones borne on upper branch tips, often purplish in immature individuals, turning brown with age. Bark dark brown and furrowed. Mature crown rather broad, with drooping branches that sweep upward toward the tips. Height to 100 feet.
Distribution. Subalpine up to timberline throughout the park, though more common in the western and central portions of the Olympic Mountains.
Remarks. A timberline species from California's Sierra Nevada north to Alaska. It typically grows in wet, snowy environments. Its flexible branches can sustain heavy snow loads without breakage.

SUBALPINE FIR
(Abies lasiocarpa)

Description. Needles bluish green with one broad stomatal stripe above and two faint ones below. Needles usually curve upward. Cones are purplish and barrel shaped, 2 to 4 inches long. As with all firs, the cones stand upright on the tips of branches and disintegrate on the tree. Bark is resin-blistered and typically smooth except on the largest trees. Mature tree has a narrow, spire-shaped profile.

Distribution. Replaces mountain hemlock as the dominant subalpine species in the drier parts of the park, such as the northeast corner, and on drier, south-facing slopes in the central parts of the Olympics.

Remarks. The most common timberline species throughout the Cascades and the Rockies. At the extreme limits to growth, it will assume a stunted, dwarf, prostrate form known as krummholz. Moister summer conditions during the 1940s to 1980s permitted subalpine fir to invade meadows in the northeast part of the park. Can spread by layering, with ground-hugging branches putting down new roots. Branches and needles contain highly flammable resins. Even when green, it will burn as though soaked in gasoline, giving off a dense, black smoke. Because of its extreme flammability, the species persists only where fires are uncommon.

LODGEPOLE PINE
(Pinus contorta)

Description. Yellow-green needles in sets of twos 1 to 2½ inches in length. Egg-shaped cones up to 2 inches long will persist on trees for years, with even young trees bearing cones. Bark is thin and scaly, reddish brown to gray.

Distribution. Rather uncommon, but found on drier slopes at mid elevations to nearly timberline in the eastern parts of the park. A good place to see this tree is at Deer Park. Also scattered along the coast.

Remarks. Lodgepole pine is one of the most adaptable trees, growing in nutrient-deficient, boggy soils along the coast as well as dry, cold environments near timberline. There are two forms of lodgepole pine, both occurring in Olympic National Park. The coastal form, sometimes called shore pine, often assumes a shrubby, twisted stature. The straight-growing Rocky Mountain form, which occurs near timberline in the northeastern part of the park, gave rise to its common name, lodgepole, for its use by the Plains Indians for tepee lodge poles.

WESTERN RED CEDAR
(Thuja plicata)

Description. Scalelike needles in opposite pairs tightly pressed against the twigs. Has one pair of folded needles and second pair of nonfolded needles. Branches are flattened and appear limp, with an upward turn at the tips. Bark is light gray and can be ripped off in long, fibrous strips. Cones ½ inch in open clusters. Will reach heights of 200 feet with diameters of up to 20 feet.
Distribution. Moist soils. Common in west-slope low-elevation rain forest, but occurs on the eastern slopes of the Olympics as well.
Remarks. This rot-resistant tree was used by Native Americans for a variety of purposes. The wood is soft and easily worked, making it ideal for totem poles and canoes. The wood splits easily into flat sheets and was used for house construction. Early white settlers often made roofs of cedar shakes.

ALASKA YELLOW CEDAR
(Chamaecyparis nootkatensis)

Description. Scalelike, blue-green needles encase the twig, which is slightly wider than thick. Four rows of scalelike leaves, all having the same appearance. Needles prickly to touch. Flattened branches appear limp and seem to hang vertically. Berrylike, ½-inch cones ripen to brownish, mushroom-shaped scales. Bark grayish strips. Height up to 130 feet.
Distribution. Moist soils. Typically above 3,000 feet in avalanche chutes, rocky areas, and ridgelines in the subalpine zone up to timberline, sometimes even mixed among Pacific silver fir. More common in the western Olympics.
Remarks. A slow-growing, long-lived tree, with older individuals living more than 1,000 years.

Boles of Alaska yellow cedar.

WHITEBARK PINE
(Pinus albicaulis)

Description. Needles 1 to 3 inches long, occurring in groups of five. Egg-shaped cones are purple when immature, turning brownish when mature. Bark is thin, scaly, and grayish white. The trunk is typically multistemmed with a broad, airy crown.

Distribution. Rare in the Olympics; primarily found in the northeast corner of the park on dry, rocky areas near timberline. A good place to see this species is on rocky ridges of the Upper Dungeness drainage and Royal Basin.

Remarks. The seeds of whitebark pine are large and nutritious. Bears, squirrels, and birds such as the Clark's nutcracker collect and eat the seeds.

BIG-LEAF MAPLE
(Acer macrophyllum)

Description. Largest of all maples, reaching heights of 65 feet and diameters of 30 inches. Large, multistemmed, deciduous tree with opposite, five-lobed maple leaves. Leaves turn yellow in fall. Grayish brown bark often festooned with mosses, lichens, and ferns. Paired winged seeds called samaras.

Distribution. Found in lowland forests throughout the Olympics, particularly on old river terraces. A particularly well-developed stand is found in the Hall of Mosses on the Hoh River.

Remarks. Big-leaf maple carries a greater load of mosses, lichens, and other epiphytes than any other species. May develop roots in the soil and organic debris found on their moss-strewn branches, absorbing extra nutrients from the load of growing plant matter.

QUAKING ASPEN
(Populus tremuloides)

Description. Tree to 40 feet, with heart-shaped, point-tipped leaves, 1 to 2½ inches, on flattened leaf stems. Bark smooth, greenish white, becoming grayish and rough along the base of very old trees.
Distribution. Rare in the Olympics; occasionally found in the rain shadow of the northeast Olympics.
Remarks. Common in the Rockies and east of the Cascades, but unusual west of the Cascades. Flattened leaf stem causes leaves to vibrate in the slightest breeze, giving rise to the common name quaking aspen. Aspen are able to sprout from root suckers, and a single stand may consist of a clone of genetically identical individuals.

PACIFIC DOGWOOD
(Cornus nuttallii)

Description. Much-branched, smallish tree reaching 60 feet in height. Leaves opposite, oval, with pointed tips, with curving parallel views to the margin of the leaf. Deep green above, grayish green below. Turns red in autumn. Smooth, black-brown bark. Large, white flowers in spring.
Distribution. Common understory species in the drier east-side forests.
Remarks. Named for botanist Thomas Nuttall, who explored the Pacific Northwest in 1834.

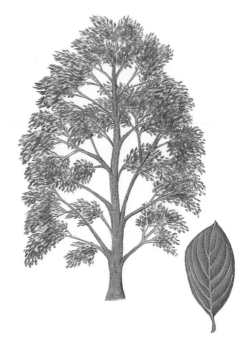

ROCKY MOUNTAIN JUNIPER
(Juniperus scopulorum)

Description. Smallish trees, up to 30 feet tall; rounded crown. Tiny, yellowish green leaves are scalelike, encasing the twig. Cones are bluish black and berrylike. Gray-brown, fibrous bark.

Distribution. Rare on the Olympic Peninsula; confined to the dry, rain-shadow side of the mountains. Can be seen in Upper Dungeness drainage.

Remarks. Common east of the Cascades, but occurs in only a limited number of places in the Puget Sound region.

PACIFIC MADRONE
(Arbutus menziesii)

Description. Appealing woodland tree. Older trees have rose-colored, peeling bark. Leaves are evergreen, leathery, shiny dark green above with whitish green below. In spring, the tree produces clusters of small, white, urn-shaped flowers, replaced by reddish orange fruits in the fall. Reaches heights of 90 feet.

Distribution. Low elevations on dry, rocky soils in the rain-shadow areas of the northern and eastern sides of the Olympic Peninsula. There are some beautiful stands of Pacific madrone along the shore of Crescent Lake.

Remarks. A California woodland species that reaches its northern limits in Puget Sound. Pacific madrone is a fire-adapted species, sprouting from the roots after a fire has killed the aboveground boles.

GARRY OAK
(Quercus garryana)

Description. Also called Oregon white oak. The only native oak in the region. A smallish, picturesque tree reaching diameters of 36 inches and heights of 80 feet. The alternate, 3- to 6-inch-long leaves have a typical oak-leaf shape with wavy margins. Dark green above and greenish yellow below. Acorns ¾ to 1½ inches long. Bark gray and furrowed.
Distribution. Reaches its northern limits in Puget Sound and Vancouver Island, British Columbia. Rare on Olympic Peninsula; confined to the low-elevation, rocky, dry areas and prairie grasslands in the rain shadow near Sequim.
Remarks. Indians once collected the acorns, soaked them to get rid of the tannin, and then ground them up into a flour used in baking.

BLACK COTTONWOOD
(Populus trichocarpa)

Description. The 3- to 6-inch-long alternate leaves are somewhat heart-shaped but more long than wide, with pointed tips. Dark green above and light gray beneath. Turns golden in autumn. Bark is grayish brown, becoming furrowed in older trees. Tall tree, with straight, limbless trunks that tower up to 150 feet, and V-shaped crown. In spring, new growth has a strong, perfumy fragrance.
Distribution. Streamsides and river bottoms at low to mid elevations.
Remarks. Seeds covered with white fluffy hair that looks like cotton. Fast growing; can reach heights of 100 feet in twenty years on a good site.

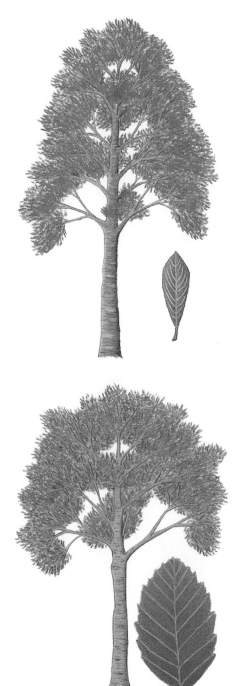

BITTER CHERRY
(Prunus emarginata)

Description. A smallish tree up to 80 feet, usually less. The alternate 1- to 3-inch-long leaves are oblong to oval, finely toothed, and rounded at the tip. The ½-inch flowers are white, with 20 to 30 yellow stamens in the center, and borne in loose clusters. Cherries are ½ inch and reddish. Bark reddish brown with horizontal rows of pores.
Distribution. Low elevations along streams or in recently logged areas.
Remarks. Cherries are so sour they are inedible. Birds, however, love the fruit.

RED ALDER
(Alnus rubra)

Description. A fast-growing tree that may reach heights of 100 feet. Looks something like the white-barked paper birch of the north woods. Leaves are opposite, oval, coarsely toothed, and 3 to 4 inches. Male and female catkins or flowers appear on the same tree. Female catkins are conelike, small, and brown. Bark is smooth and often covered with light-colored lichens.
Distribution. Gravel bars and river terraces. Forms open, airy glades.
Remarks. Often invades recently logged land and other disturbed sites. Roots host bacteria that convert atmospheric nitrogen into a form available to other plants and are critical to soil development.

Red alder along the East Fork of the Quinault River. Red alder is a pioneering species that colonizes gravel bars and other disturbed sites, such as clear-cuts. The tree enriches soils by taking atmospheric nitrogen and chemically changing it so it is usable by other plants.

Shrubs to Small Trees

DOUGLAS MAPLE
(Acer glabrum douglasii)

Description. Small tree or shrub, sometimes reaching 35 feet in height. Leaves opposite, toothed, three- to five-lobed maplelike leaves. Red-orange in fall. Winged seeds, seldom over 1 inch. Bark light gray.

Distribution. Dry ridges to well-drained seep sites. Usually drier, sunnier sites than vine maple.

Remarks. Related to Rocky Mountain maple, a favorite food of elk, deer, and other species. Named for botanist David Douglas.

VINE MAPLE
(Acer circinatum)

Description. Green, multistemmed shrub or small tree up to 20 feet tall. Leaves opposite, seven- to nine-lobed, and toothed; turn red to yellow in autumn. Winged fruit forms straight line rather than V-shaped like those of Douglas maple.
Distribution. The most ubiquitous understory species.
Remarks. A favorite food of elk and deer.

Vine maple.

SITKA ALDER
(Alnus sinuata)

Description. Shrub to small tree up to 20 feet tall. Leaves 1 to 4 inches, oval with pointed tips. Margins double-toothed. Male and female catkins appear on the same shrub. Female catkins ½ inch long, oblong, and conelike. Bark grayish.
Distribution. Common on avalanche chutes and along mountain streams. Found in basins up to subalpine zone.
Remarks. Named for Sitka, Alaska, where it is abundant. Like red alder, Sitka alder has root bacteria able to fix atmospheric nitrogen, making it available for other plant growth.

COMMON CHOKECHERRY
(Prunus virginiana)

Description. Small tree to 20 feet, but typically less. The 2- to 4-inch-long leaves are oval with fine-toothed margin. White flowers are ⅜ inch and borne in long racemes or clusters. The black fruit is edible.
Distribution. Common in disturbed sites and sunny forest openings.
Remarks. Fruit makes excellent jellies and syrup.

WESTERN SERVICEBERRY
(Amelanchier alnifolia)

Description. Shrub to small tree up to 15 feet. Smooth, gray bark. Alternate, round-oval leaves with teeth on the upper half. Flowers white. Fruit dull red, turning purple-black; looks something like a blueberry.
Distribution. Forest edges, rocky talus slopes, and other openings.
Remarks. Fruit is edible, if not tasty. Wildlife loves this plant. The berries are relished by black bears and birds; elk and deer browse the branches in winter.

KINNIKINNICK
(Arctostaphylos uva-ursi)

Description. Forms ground-hugging, trailing mats of leathery, evergreen, dark green, oval leaves. Bark reddish brown. Flowers urn shaped with pinkish cast and hang down from branches, often several to a cluster. Bright, hard, red berries.
Distribution. Well-drained, often rocky, dry sites at all elevations.
Remarks. Native Americans used to smoke the leaves.

OREGON GRAPE
(Berberis nervosa)

Description. Not a grape at all. Erect, hollylike evergreen leaves, each of which consists of nine to twenty leaflets. Flowers yellow. Clustered blue fruit.
Distribution. Dry to moist forests at low-mid elevations. Strongly associated with Douglas fir forests.
Remarks. The Indians used the bark and stems to make a yellow dye.

RED OSIER DOGWOOD
(Cornus stolonifera)

Description. Spreading shrub with multiple beautiful, smooth, wine-red stems. Leaves are opposite, with five to seven veins that converge toward the pointed leaf tip. The small, white flowers form dense, flat-topped terminal clusters. Terminal cluster of white, berrylike fruits.
Distribution. Moist soils along forest edge from low to mid elevations.
Remarks. Elk and deer browse heavily upon the stems in winter. Widely planted as an ornamental shrub.

Salal.

SALAL
(Gaultheria shallon)

Description. Erect shrub with alternate, sharply toothed, leathery, evergreen leaves. Often forms thickets. White-pink, urn-shaped flowers on terminal branches. Dark purple fruits. Often forms thickets.

Distribution. One of the most common understory species in drier coniferous forests on the eastern side of the Olympics; also found along the coast.

Remarks. One of the most important fruits for Native Americans of the region. The berries were eaten raw or dried into cakes.

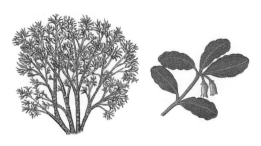

FOOL'S HUCKLEBERRY
(*Menziesia ferruginea*)

Description. Also known as false azalea, this spreading shrub has alternate, oblong, light green, deciduous leaves that are clustered along branches and have wavy margins. When crushed, has an aromatic smell. Pinkish yellow, urn-shaped flowers in drooping terminal clusters. Fruit an oval dry capsule.
Distribution. From low to high elevations in shady to semiopen coniferous forests.
Remarks. Leaves turn bright orange in autumn. Called fool's huckleberry because flower resembles that of huckleberry, but the fruit is an inedible dry capsule.

INDIAN PLUM
(*Oemleria cerasiformis*)

Description. Shrub to small tree. Alternate, pale green, lance-shaped leaves that are not toothed. Flowers white with greenish tinge, in an elongated bell shape. Fruit ripens to bluish black; resembles small plum.
Distribution. Open woods and streambanks at low elevations.
Remarks. One of the earliest shrubs to flower in the spring, often blooming by mid-February.

DEVIL'S CLUB
(Oplopanax horridus)

Description. Erect, thick, untapering stem armed with numerous spines. Large, maple-shaped leaves also have spines on the undersides. Whitish green flowers in a compact terminal cluster. Clusters of bright red berries.

Distribution. Moist woods along streams and seepage areas, as well as avalanche chutes.

Remarks. The aptly named devil's club often forms dense thickets that are difficult to move through. The spines contain a mild toxin and can cause swelling.

Devil's club frames Bogachiel Falls.

NINEBARK
(Physocarpus opulifolius)

Description. Erect to spreading with angled branches that have brown shredding bark on mature stems. Leaves have three to five lobes and are shiny green above, lighter below. Small, white flowers in terminal clusters.
Distribution. Streamside thickets and edge of moist woods.
Remarks. Was called ninebark because there appeared to be nine layers to the shredding bark.

WHITE RHODODENDRON
(Rhododendron albiflorum)

Description. Erect shrub up to 8 feet tall. Young twigs covered with coarse, reddish hairs. Leaves alternate in clusters on branch. Upper surface of the yellowish green leaves has rusty hairs. Large, showy, creamy white flowers grow in clusters of two to four. Fruit a dry capsule.
Distribution. Mostly found in subalpine meadows along the edge of tree clumps and on well-drained sites.
Remarks. The terminal cluster of leaves looks something like fool's huckleberry.

PACIFIC RHODODENDRON
(Rhododendron macrophyllum)

Description. Erect to spreading shrub, up to 20 feet tall. Leathery, evergreen, thick, oblong leaves. Showy pink to rose, bell-shaped flowers grow in terminal clusters.
Distribution. Common in dry coniferous forests on eastern side of Olympics.
Remarks. Sprouts after fires. Beautiful floral displays in late spring.

Rhododendron in bloom along the Dosewallips River. Although rhododendrons are usually associated with wet climates, on the very wet Olympic Peninsula, rhododendrons are found on the drier, eastern side of the mountains.

NOOTKA ROSE
(*Rosa nutkana*)

Description. Spindly shrub to 10 feet tall. Two large prickles at the base of each leaf, but seldom any other spines on plant. Compound leaves with odd numbers of toothed leaflets. Large, solitary, pink flowers typically borne at branch tips. Fruit reddish, round, berrylike rose hips.
Distribution. Open habitat along meadows, streamsides, and clearings.
Remarks. Rose hips are high in vitamin C and were often consumed by Native Americans.

WESTERN THIMBLEBERRY
(Rubus parviflorus)

Description. Erect, dense thickets. Looks something like devil's club but without spines. Large, deciduous, maple-shaped leaves with four to seven lobes. Large, white flowers with yellow centers. Domed, raspberrylike, bright red berries.
Distribution. Open sites in avalanche chutes, roadsides, edges of trails at low to mid elevations.
Remarks. Berries are sweet and edible.

SALMONBERRY
(Rubus spectabilis)

Description. Erect shrub, often forming dense thickets. Leaves dark green and sharply toothed, typically lobed into three leaflets. Large, red flowers. Raspberrylike yellow or reddish fruit. Scattered prickles here and there on brown stems.
Distribution. Moist to wet places along streams, avalanche chutes, and roadsides.
Remarks. Forms extensive clones. Berries are edible; taste varies among clones.

Salmonberry blossom.

RED ELDERBERRY
(Sambucus racemosa)

Description. Shrub to small tree up to 18 feet. Soft, pithy twigs. Leaves opposite and divided in large, lance-shaped, sharply toothed leaflets. White flowers in terminal clusters. Fruits bright red, berrylike drupes.
Distribution. Streambanks and other moist areas in low to mid elevations.
Remarks. Bears love the berries, and tasty jelly can be made from them.

SITKA MOUNTAIN ASH
(Sorbus sitchensis)

Description. Small, erect tree with several stems. Leaves are alternate, divided into seven to eleven leaflets, with toothed margins and rounded tips. White flowers in round-topped terminal clusters. Bright orange-red berries in terminal clusters.
Distribution. Openings such as the edge of parklands at mid to high elevations.
Remarks. The berries are a favorite with birds, particularly in the winter.

DOUGLAS' SPIREA
(Spiraea douglasii)

Description. A much-branched erect shrub, often forming dense thickets. Alternate, oblong to oval leaves, toothed above the middle, dark green above and grayish and woolly below. Tiny, deep rose to pink blooms in compact terminal clusters.
Distribution. Damp meadows, lakeshores, and streamsides from low to mid elevations.
Remarks. Named for early Pacific Northwest botanist David Douglas, for whom the Douglas fir is also named. Shrub is often planted as an ornamental.

DWARF HUCKLEBERRY
(Vaccinium cespitosum)

Description. Low, spreading mat or small shrub. Alternate, bright green leaves oblong to lance-shaped with toothed margin and pronounced veins beneath. Whitish pink, narrow, urn-shaped flowers. Blue fruit.
Distribution. Subalpine wet meadows.
Remarks. Edible fruit.

BLUE-LEAF HUCKLEBERRY
(Vaccinium deliciosum)

Description. Similar to dwarf huckleberry, but with whitish bloom on undersides of nearly round leaves.
Distribution. Subalpine meadows.
Remarks. Considered the best-tasting huckleberry. In autumn, provides much of the russet red color in subalpine meadows.

OVAL-LEAF HUCKLEBERRY
(Vaccinium ovalifolium)

Description. Erect, spreading shrub. Young twigs reddish to yellowish, turning gray on older branches. Leaves oval, green above and pale beneath. Pinkish, urn-shaped flowers appear before the leaves. Large, blue-black fruit.
Distribution. Mid elevations to subalpine forest openings.
Remarks. Fruit is edible and usually occurs earlier than the other huckleberries.

EVERGREEN HUCKLEBERRY
(*Vaccinium ovatum*)

Description. Erect shrub to 12 feet.
Young stems sometimes hairy. Alternate,
evergreen, and leathery leaves dark green
above and lighter below, with sharply
toothed margins. Pink, bell-shaped
flowers. Deep purplish black fruit.
Distribution. Typically found in openings
close to tidewater.
Remarks. Remain on shrub late into fall.
Taste improves after first frosts.

RED HUCKLEBERRY
(*Vaccinium parvifolium*)

Description. Erect shrub to 12 feet, with
very strongly angled, bright green
branches. Alternate, oval leaves not
toothed. Yellowish green or pinkish bell-
or urn-shaped flowers. Bright red, round
berries.
Distribution. Associated with decaying
wood, growing on stumps of fallen logs.
Often grows under forest canopy.
Remarks. Fruit is edible but sparse.

Red huckleberry.

Ferns

MAIDENHAIR FERN
(Adiantum pedatum)

Description. Forms delicate, palmately branched, fan-shaped clumps. Leaves have dark brown to black stems. Oblong leaflets.
Distribution. Shady, moist sites on cliffs; spray zone around waterfalls; and seeps.
Remarks. Often forms dense colonies.

LADY FERN
(Athyrium filix-femina)

Description. Fronds clustered, up to 6 feet long, and spreading. Lance-shaped leaves narrow toward both ends. Twice or thrice compound leaves.
Distribution. Moist forests and streambanks.
Remarks. Native Americans used the leaves to cover food.

DEER FERN
(Blechnum spicant)

Description. Evergreen, tufted fern that forms clumps. Looks something like a small sword fern, except the leaflets are attached to the leaf axis along their bases. Two kinds of fronds: sterile ones, which are clustered about the fertile centerpiece and frequently pressed to the ground, and spore-bearing leaves, which are taller and stand at the center of each clump.
Distribution. Moist forests and streambanks.
Remarks. An important winter food for deer and elk.

SPREADING WOOD FERN
(Dryopteris expansa)

Description. Fronds clustered and erect, to 3 feet tall. Fronds broadly triangular and thrice pinnate.
Distribution. Moist forests, scree slopes up to subalpine.
Remarks. Native Americans consumed this plant as a laxative.

OAK FERN
(Gymnocarpium dryopteris)

Description. Small, lime green, delicate-looking fern, seldom more than 18 inches tall. Triangular and thrice compound. Appears to have three similar leaves.
Distribution. Moist forest and rocky slopes.
Remarks. Can sometimes form a more or less continuous carpet on forest floor.

LICORICE FERN
(Polypodium glycorrhiza)

Description. Evergreen fern, often growing on trunks of deciduous trees, such as big-leaf maple. Once pinnate leaves with finely toothed margins.
Distribution. Commonly epiphytic, growing on trees.
Remarks. Named for its licorice-flavored rhizome.

SWORD FERN
(Polystichum munitum)

Description. Large, evergreen, erect leaves. Lance-shaped blade. Sharp-toothed with incurved spine tips.
Distribution. Moist forests to mid elevations.
Remarks. Often planted as ornamental.

Sword fern.

BRACKEN FERN
(Pteridium aquilinum)

Description. Fronds up to 6 feet tall. More or less triangular in shape, with twice to thrice compound leaves. Undersides fuzzy.

Distribution. Common on sunny sites and disturbed areas such as avalanche chutes.

Remarks. Can grow several inches a day. Often invades after fires.

THE COASTAL REALM

Reefs, cliffs, secluded beaches, sea stacks, and headlands all characterize the wild Olympic coast. The outer coast, as opposed to the protected tidal waters found in Hood Canal or the Strait of Juan de Fuca, is one of the park's most prized landscapes. At about sixty miles long, this is the largest undeveloped stretch of coastline along the Pacific seaboard between Canada and Mexico. Only at the villages of La Push and Kalaloch is there any significant development. This tiny parcel of Pacific Northwest coastline was barely spared from development. Among the many proposals to exploit the coast were plans for logging, offshore oil drilling, and construction of a coastal highway. Fortunately, thanks to the persistence and tireless energy of numerous individuals, this portion of the coast has been preserved in its natural state.

Efforts to protect the coast began with the creation of several national wildlife refuges in 1907. In 1938, Olympic National Park was created, and the coastal strip was part of the original park legislation. But persistent opposition from those who wanted to develop the coast was successful in getting the coastal strip removed from the legislation. In 1953, the coastal strip was finally added to the park, although that still didn't offer complete protection. The strip was very narrow and has been expanded; the off-shore lands became protected in 1986 and 1988. Lake Ozette and several other pieces of the coast were added to the park in 1977. In 1986, the boundaries were extended seaward to take in the tidal zone. Finally, in 1994, a national marine sanctuary was established to preclude offshore development.

The Olympic coast is one of the more productive parts of the entire U.S. Pacific coast. During the summer, the prevailing winds blow southwest along the shore. This effectively moves surface water offshore and

Backpacker on coastal strip. The Olympic coast is the longest stretch of undeveloped coast in the U.S. outside of Alaska. The coast was originally proposed for inclusion in the park when it was established in 1938, but opposition from development interests eventually led to its elimination from the park bill. The coastal strip was added to the park in 1953 by executive order of President Truman. Protection of the offshore tidal areas was provided in 1994 when the Olympic coast was declared a national marine sanctuary.

allows deeper, colder, nutrient-rich waters to upwell along the coast. This seasonal burst of nutrients results in a huge bloom of plankton, which in turn feeds other life from seabirds to whales.

Though the sea may be bountiful, life along the shore isn't necessarily easy. Animals and plants living along the seashore are exposed to twice-daily tides and shell-cracking waves. Winter storms pick up logs and other flotsam and hurl them with great force against the shoreline. Rocky cobble beaches, made up of small stones, are common in the protected coves between headlands on the outer coast and along the Strait of Juan de Fuca. Cobble beaches are important habitat for a variety of clams, the most common being the native littleneck and butter clams, as well as the introduced Japanese littleneck.

Zonation

A notable feature of the rocky shore is the obvious horizontal banding of different life forms.

Spray Zone

The highest zone is called the spray zone. Influenced by salt spray and moisture, but not directly covered by the tides, this is the harshest environment for life, and few species are adapted to living here. Resident here are black encrusting lichen, an algae, and the pale green sea hare. Terrestrial birds may also forage in this zone.

Upper Intertidal Zone

The upper intertidal zone is normally flooded during high tides. This is the home of acorn barnacles, mussels, and black turban snails. Hermit crabs and shore crabs scurry about. Here you find the foot-long rockweed, a multibranched brownish seaweed with little bladders, and a pale green, translucent sea lettuce.

The middle intertidal zone is covered most of the time. It is jammed with California mussels, blue mussels, gooseneck barnacles, limpets, snails, whelks, black chitons, and ochre sea stars in a variety of colors, ranging from purple to orange or brown. Mussels are bivalves like clams but cling to rocks, whereas clams burrow into cobble or sand. Barnacles resemble small tepees with pointed plates all coming together at the roof. Limpets look like flat, quarter-sized plates on rocks. Chitons look something like sow bugs and have eight plates running down their longish backs. Whelks resemble snails.

The most common mussel in this zone is the California mussel. These animals live for up to twenty years and are such a stable feature of the intertidal zone that barnacles sometimes grow on their shells. Their color varies somewhat but is generally blue, though some brown or black individuals may be found.

Feeding on the mussels are ochre sea stars, five-legged creatures that may be as much as a foot in diameter. The ochre sea star is a voracious predator of mussels. Just as wolves thin a deer or elk herd, sea stars help regulate the numbers and distribution of mussels. Sea stars avoid exposure to air and consequently feed largely on the lower edges of the mussel zone. When sea stars are removed, mussels colonize deeper waters.

Seaweeds are common here. Seaweeds are algae and lack roots, flowers, stems, and even leaves. Instead, they have blades that do the photosynthesizing and absorb nutrients directly from the water. Sea palms and bright green sea lettuce are two common seaweeds of this zone. Sea palms are droopy when out of water and resemble palms.

Lower Intertidal Zone

The lower intertidal zone is normally covered by water except during the lowest tides. It is home to hundreds of animals, including the green sea anemone, purple sea urchin, red sea urchin, orange sea cucumber, and the colorful opalescent nudibranch, with its blue stripes. Sea anemones, commonly observed in tidepools, look like pink and green flowers when opened in the water, spreading out their tentacles to capture prey. When the tide goes out, they close up again. Some species of anemones are known to live a thousand years.

Sea urchins are spiny, like giant pincushions. They are grazers, feeding upon kelp. Urchins are the preferred prey of sea otters. In areas where sea otters are present, they control urchin numbers, allowing kelp beds to flourish.

Split kelp and bull kelp are found growing here, held to the rocks by their holdfasts. Split kelp is recognized by its ribbonlike blades. The golden-brown bull kelp is found in slightly deeper water and grows to forty feet in length, forming dense "forests" that are home to many fish. The bulbous, ball-like end of the bull kelp acts like a float, keeping the fronds near the water's surface. Bull kelp is frequently washed up on shore. As large as it grows, it seems amazing that bull kelp is an annual, dying back each winter and regrowing the following summer.

Life in the Intertidal Zones

Animals and plants living in the intertidal zones must be able to cope with two worlds: a terrestrial world when the tide is out and a watery realm when the tide is in. They must be able to withstand extremes in temperature from freezing cold in winter to searing heat in summer. So why would species leave the relative comfort of the deeper ocean realm and move up into the tidal zone? The answer seems to be that most species are seeking to avoid natural enemies that live in the less stressful oceanic environment. But it's a no-win situation for many forms of life. Mussels, for example, may avoid predators such as sea stars by moving up into the

Ocean shore at low tide. The alternating exposure to air and then water creates a zone of extreme stress for most forms of life. As a consequence, only a few life forms are able to colonize this region.

upper tidal zone, but then they are exposed to desiccation and terrestrial predators from raccoons to oystercatchers.

The biological diversity of the tidal zone of the Northwest coast is remarkable and exceeds that of most eastern U.S. coastal areas. Several factors account for this diversity. First, the Pacific Ocean is older than the Atlantic Ocean by a hundred million years, which has allowed for more biological diversity to occur. Second, there is more rocky coastline here than on most of the eastern coast or even farther south on the Pacific coast. All other things being equal, rocky coasts support more life than sandy areas because they are more stable and have more nooks and crannies to harbor life. Finally, the annual variation in temperature here is far less extreme than at a similar latitude on the eastern seaboard, providing a more equable environment for life to prosper.

Several major adaptations are required for life along the ocean's margin. The first problem is desiccation. Most species living at the edge of the sea, such as mussels, limpets, barnacles, and snails, have hard shells. They can seal their shells and thus protect themselves against dehydration.

Many plants also have adapted to this life zone. Some seaweeds can tolerate drying out and assume normal photosynthesis upon rehydration. Others have a slimy mucus that reduces water loss.

Another requirement is the ability to hold on to the rock so that the continuous movement of water and waves doesn't knock them loose. Mussels produce a gluelike substance that firmly attaches them to the rocks. Barnacles cement themselves permanently to the rocks. Sea urchins have hydraulic feet that grip the rocks like a vise.

Most of the sedentary intertidal animals, such as barnacles, mussels, and tubeworms, are filter feeders that remove plankton and other organic matter from the water column. They rely upon the tide to bring them their food and remove waste materials. Others, such as snails, black chitons, and limpets, are grazers, scraping algae from the rocks.

Predators of these animals include sea stars, whelks, and crabs. The ochre sea star, a common predator of mussels along the coast, uses hydraulic suction cups on its legs to pry open mussel shells. Once there is even the slightest opening, the sea star turns its stomach inside out and pushes its mouth into the prey's shell. It then begins to digest the soft tissues inside. Digestion may take two or three days. Nucella whelks drill small holes into the shells of prey, then feed on the soft insides.

Defenses against predators range from the hard shells of mussels and oysters to the spines of sea urchins. Some animals use flight to avoid predators. Turban snails will "dash away" from sea stars, moving at the blazing speed (for a snail) of three inches a minute. Another defense is the ability to lose an arm or leg to a pursuing predator without harm. Most crabs, for instance, can lose an appendage and regrow one later.

Animals of Offshore Waters

Seabirds

Seabirds, such as the puffins, murres, and guillemots, all originally evolved from land species. They, like marine mammals, have made the transition back to the sea from land. Advantages of ocean living include abundant food (usually) and few predators. This stable environment has led to long lifespans and low reproductive rates. Unlike songbird species, which experience as much as a 70 percent adult mortality rate annually, some seabirds may lose as little as 20 percent of their adult population a year.

Despite the relative ease of finding food for adults, raising young presents difficulties. Finding suitable nesting habitat close to food sources is not always easy, and many seabirds must travel relatively long distances between foraging areas and nesting habitat. As a consequence, there is a premium placed upon experience and age.

Furthermore, because of the rigors of providing for young, the age of first breeding is delayed with many seabirds, which may not reproduce until three to seven years of age. Many seabirds also tend to produce fewer eggs and thus fewer chicks, investing more in each young than a typical songbird. Most seabirds are monogamous, mating with the same partner year after year.

Seabirds appear to be particularly vulnerable to changes in food resources as a consequence of El Niño events. During El Niño winters, warm waters flow farther north along the west coast. This reduces upwelling and the availability of prime foods, with often catastrophic results for seabirds. It may well be that these periodic, though short-term, climatic changes control seabird populations in much the same way that El Niño events control fire frequency in Pacific Northwest forests.

Seabirds display a number of adaptations to their oceanic world. Maintaining salt balance in the body is a problem for birds that live entirely on the ocean, and nearly all of them secrete excess salt through nasal glands. Most seabirds along the Pacific Northwest coast are diving birds that capture prey underwater. The ability to navigate in fluids compromises flight. Most seabirds, such as puffins, have plump, chunky bodies; short wings; and webbed feet with legs set far back on the body to allow for maximum propulsion underwater. Birds that soar, like gulls, tend to have large, broad wings. The ability to dive underwater requires some adaptations for oxygen storage. Seabirds not only have a larger blood volume for their body size than similar-size land birds but also can slow their heart rate during deep dives to conserve oxygen in the blood.

Nearly all seabirds—98 percent—have evolved into colonial nesters, compared with just 13 percent of all birds. Nesting habitat, typically on offshore rocky islets and sea stacks, is somewhat limited. As a consequence, these landscapes are partitioned among different breeding species, with some birds, like puffins, digging burrows in soft soil; others, like common murres, nesting on cliff faces; and still others, like some species of gulls, nesting aboveground on grassy slopes. Only one species, the marbled murrelet, nests in trees.

Seabird predation significantly influences prey populations. Some computer modeling done of the energy demands of common Oregon seabirds found that they may consume as much as 22 percent of the annual production of small fish found in near-shore waters.

Most seabird concentrations worldwide are found where upwelling of cold waters from near-shore depths creates an abundance of food. The Pacific Northwest coast is one such place. The rich waters of the Olympic coast, combined with the sheltered nesting habitat, make this one of the richest seabird sanctuaries on the entire Pacific coast, home to fourteen species of seabirds. The isolated 870 islands, sea stacks, and rocky isles off the coast provide 80 percent of Washington's seabird nesting habitat and are protected within the Washington Islands National Wildlife Refuge. Commonly sighted here are glaucous-winged gulls, pigeon guillemots, puffins, cormorants, murres, and auklets.

Probably the most abundant birds along the coast are gulls. A number of species migrate through the area, but only the western and glaucous-winged gulls breed on outer coastal islands. Western gulls reach their northern breeding limits on the Olympic coast; glaucous-winged gulls are more abundant throughout the Peninsula. Both gulls have red spotted bills. The western gulls have sooty gray-black backs and black tips on the wings; the glaucous-winged gulls have pale gray plumage, white heads, and no black tips on the wings.

Three species of cormorants—pelagic, Brandt's, and double-crested—live along the outer coast. Cormorants are diving birds with webbed feet that swim underwater to capture fish. All have long necks and serrated bills and are dark in color. These birds lack waterproof feathers and are often seen drying their outstretched wings. Brandt's cormorant is the least common of the three, reaching its northern limits along the Pacific Northwest coast. One way to distinguish this species from the other cormorants is the blue and yellow throat pouch during the breeding season. Brandt's nest only on Destruction Island. The three-foot-long double-crested cormorant, which has an orange throat patch, is a northern species that reaches its southern limits on the Olympic coast. The pelagic cormorant is the most common and, at two feet long, smallest of the three species. It has a red throat patch and face with conspicuous white patches on the flanks below the wings in breeding season.

Unlikely to be seen from shore is the storm petrel. These birds usually feed far offshore and come close to shore only to breed. Even when breeding, they are not easily observed, since they lay their eggs in underground burrows and leave those burrows only under cover of darkness. Two species are found along the coast: the black-bodied, white-rumped Leach's petrel and the grayish fork-tailed petrel. These small birds fly just above the surface of the ocean skimming fish and other food.

A more easily spotted seabird is the slender-billed, black and white common murre. These birds look something like a penguin in stance and shape. They are relatively abundant along the coast year-round. In nesting colonies, the murres stand packed like cordwood, protecting their pear-shaped eggs. Murres are diving birds that pursue fish to depths of up to 500 feet. Another common seabird along the outer coast is the rhinoceros auklet. This little bird grows small, feathered "horns" during the breeding season. It has a light tan breast and brown body. It has small wings that enable it to swim after fish underwater. These birds nest in underground burrows. Major nesting sites are Protection Island in Puget Sound near Sequim and Destruction Island off the coast.

The tufted puffin, another small seabird related to the auklet, is one of the best-loved coastal species, but unless you go in a boat offshore, you're not likely to see these seabirds. With their black bodies, white heads, large multicolored bills, and yellowish tufts curling back from the head,

Tufted puffin in winter plumage. About 20,000 puffins are known to nest along the Olympic coast in more than twenty nesting colonies.

they look like miniature clowns. When they fly, their short wings beat rapidly while their orange webbed feet dangle behind them. The puffin, like many other seabirds, actually uses its wings to swim underwater in pursuit of fish. Puffins nest in burrows dug into soft soils on offshore sea stacks and islands. About twenty-five nesting colonies are located along the coast. A relict population of puffins is also found on Protection Island by Sequim.

Next to gulls, perhaps the most common group of birds to be seen along is the coast is the shorebirds. Sandpipers and other "surf" birds can be difficult to distinguish from one another, but one unmistakable bird of this region is the black oystercatcher. With its long, red bill and loud call, the oystercatcher soon makes its presence known to anyone strolling along the rocky coast. The oystercatcher uses its stout bill to cut the muscles holding shellfish to the rocks, then it opens the shells and consumes the insides.

Two other birds common along rocky shores are the black turnstone and the surfbird. Neither breeds here, but both are common during spring and fall migrations. The turnstone has a black head, back, and sides with a white belly, wing bars, and rump. The bird gets its name for its habit

Black oystercatchers are relatively common along rocky coasts, where they pry open shellfish to consume the soft inner meat.

of turning stones while foraging for barnacles, sand fleas, small crabs, limpets, and other small prey. The chunky, robin-size, gray and white surf-bird has black and white wing markings and tail obvious in flight. Surf-birds also forage for small shellfish in the rocky tidal zone.

Pigeon guillemots are pigeon-size, black diving birds with red feet and conspicuous white wing bars. Guillemots feed on fish.

The marbled murrelet is a small, dumpy-looking bird with a short bill and tail. When it tries to get airborne, it tends to bounce across the water like a skipping stone before it launches into the air. When it dives, the bird flips forward, exposing its white tail rump. The marbled murrelet is one of the most unusual seabirds around: It nests in trees. Indeed, for a long time it was not known where these birds nested, until the early 1970s, when a logger discovered a marbled murrelet's nest after felling a huge, old tree. Since then, more nests have been located—all in old-growth forests. These small birds fly far inland to nest in big trees, and the cutting of old-growth forests has threatened their future.

Marine Mammals

One of the most memorable experiences of most visitors to the coastal strip is the sight of a breaching whale. About 65 million years ago, the ancestors of today's whales made the first journey from land back to sea. They were joined about the same time by the forebears of today's mana-tees and dugongs. Then some 30 million years ago, the eared seals (sea lions) and earless seals (harbor seals) both entered the watery realm. Finally, just 5 million years ago, the sea otter made the transition back to the ocean.

The closest relative of whales are ungulates—sheep, deer, and elk. Over time, major modification of the body for life in the sea came about, including the rotation of the nostrils to the top of the head, streamlined body for movement through water, and paddlelike front limbs for locomotion. Whales have differentiated into two major evolutionary branches—toothed whales like the orca or killer whale, which capture fish and other prey, and baleen whales like the California gray and the humpback, which filter krill, small fish, and crustaceans from the sea or ocean bottom.

Collectively, seals, sea lions, and walruses are known as pinnipeds. Pin-nipeds evolved from two separate land carnivores that entered the oceans about the same time some 30 million years ago. One, a doglike animal, entered the Pacific and evolved into fur seals, sea lions, and walruses, while a second otterlike species evolved in the Atlantic into today's true seals. True seals and walruses are now found in both the Atlantic and Pacific Oceans, having spread across the globe via the Arctic Ocean.

Among the evolutionary changes common to both major groups is a modification of teeth from those designed for shearing, grinding, and catching into a shape adapted to holding and catching. Most pinnipeds swallow their prey whole, hence there is no need for chewing. A second common feature of all pinnipeds is the evolution of limbs into flippers.

Despite these similarities, there are distinct differences between these groups. Sea lions and fur seals use their front limbs for swimming. Hind legs are primarily used for steering. As a result, sea lions and fur seals have a great deal of muscle in their broad chests and shoulders. True seals, however, use their hind limbs for locomotion. As a consequence, their muscles are concentrated in the back, making for a more streamlined looking animal. This difference in limb structure and use manifests itself in another way. Sea lions and fur seals can lift themselves off the ground and swing their hind limbs forward, thus "walking" on land to a limited degree. In contrast, the hind limbs of true seals cannot be rotated forward, and they move by sliding forward on their bellies.

The sea otter is the most recent addition to the marine mammals fauna of the Pacific Northwest, having evolved from a land mammal some 5 million years ago. Among its adaptations to life in the sea is the evolution of rounded teeth for crushing shellfish like crabs, sea urchins, and other prey. Its hind feet are broad paddles that are used for swimming. Finally, unlike other marine mammals that have large amounts of body fat to help conserve heat, the sea otter relies upon its dense, thick fur for insulation. But the fur isn't as efficient as fat, and sea otters burn a lot of calories maintaining their internal body temperature. Consequently, they must consume approximately 20 to 25 percent of their body weight each day to maintain their weight.

Though marine mammals have moved back into the sea, they still must breathe air to survive. They have evolved a number of adaptations that permit prolonged diving up to an hour in the case of some whales. The first is the ability to store oxygen in the blood and muscles. The ability to hold oxygen in the blood is enhanced by the greater blood volume per body weight than other animals. For instance, whales have two to three times the blood volume per unit body weight of humans.

Second, marine mammals can store carbon dioxide and lactic acid in the muscles to a much greater degree without suffering disabling effects compared to land animals.

Third, marine mammals are stingy in their use of oxygen and can restrict blood flow to the heart and brain during prolonged dives.

A return to the ocean presented another major obstacle to land mammals—heat loss. Water absorbs body heat twenty times faster than air. Maintaining internal body temperature was a major evolutionary problem that marine mammals had to overcome in order to colonize the sea. Most marine mammals have a much higher basic metabolism than land animals of a similar size and hence a greater need for food intake as well. Second, large body size is an advantage in cold waters, since the greater volume-to-surface ratio helps to conserve heat. This is one reason why some of the largest mammals on earth are whales. Third, insulation in the form of both fur and fat is well developed in all marine mammals. In animals like the fur seal or the sea otter, the dense, oily fur traps air and helps to insulate the animal. However, since pressure increases the deeper one dives, the insulating value of fur is limited. As a result, sea otters are relegated to shallow near-shore waters, in part due to their sole reliance upon fur for insulation. In species that dive to greater depths, like whales and sea lions, a layer of noncompressible blubber is the primary insulation.

To reduce heat loss further, most marine mammals have evolved side-by-side vessels and veins so that warm blood being carried to the flippers and other extremities is immediately adjacent to cold blood coming back from them. Thus the outgoing warm blood is cooled, while the incoming cold blood is warmed. This heat exchange ensures that little heat actually leaks to the environment through limbs.

Finally, some marine mammal species migrate between warmer and colder seas to maintain a more equable seasonal environment. This may be one reason why gray whales migrate between the rich feeding grounds in Alaska and birthing grounds in Baja.

Only four species are year-round residents of the Olympic coast: the harbor seal, sea otter, Dall's porpoise, and harbor porpoise. Seasonal residents include the California sea lion, Steller's sea lion, orca, California gray whale, and minke whale. Rare but occasionally observed off the coast are the northern fur seal and elephant seal.

The most abundant sea mammal occurring year-round along the Olympic coast is the harbor seal, with about 5,000 individuals. The large-eyed harbor seal is gray to brown with spots and no ears. These animals look something like a sad-faced dog and are frequently seen bobbing above the waves just beyond the surf line. They feed close to shore and are often observed by hikers along the beach. Seals must come to shore to give birth. The pups are born in May and June and nurse for up to six weeks.

Of all marine mammals, perhaps the most lovable is the sea otter. Sea otters were once abundant along the Pacific coast from California to Alaska, but their dense, beautiful fur made them the target of the fur trade, and they were extirpated from much of their natural range. The last Washington sea otter was killed in 1906. Fortunately, sea otters survived in Alaska, and some of these animals were transplanted to the Olympic coast in 1969 and 1970. Estimates in the mid-1990s placed sea otter numbers at between 350 and 400. Sea otters are often seen at Cape Johnson, Sand Point, Cape Alava, and Destruction Island. They are strongly associated with kelp beds, where they feed upon sea urchins, which like to graze on kelp.

Sea otters differ from river otters, which also forage along the coast. Sea otters float on their backs, but river otters never do. Sea otters are larger, up to 100 pounds and five feet long; river otters are usually less than 30 pounds and less than four feet in length.

Occasionally seen along the coast are northern fur seals. Fur seals breed in two locations. Most breeding occurs in Alaska's Pribilof Islands, but a smaller population occurs on San Miguel Island in California. Fur seals migrate along the Olympic coast and are most often seen near Cape Flattery and Cape Alava. Like the sea otter, fur seals were prized for their luxuriant pelts and were hunted nearly to extinction. They were protected in 1911, and their numbers grew to an all-time high in the 1950s. Since then, there has been a decline in fur seal numbers. These animals are still hunted on their breeding grounds, where they are clubbed to death for their furs by Alaskan natives. This, along with competition for favorite prey species from commercial fisheries, has led to a decline in their numbers.

Two sea lions are found along the Olympic coast: the dark brown California sea lion and the larger Steller's, or northern, sea lion. One of the easiest ways to distinguish between the two is that the California sea lion barks, whereas the Steller's is silent. Both can haul themselves out and amble about on land. Sea lions along the coast of Washington are all nonbreeding animals from breeding grounds farther south. As many as 6,000 sea lions pass along the coast during peak migrations. Northern breeding populations of Steller's sea lions in Alaska have dropped precipitously, to the point where they were recently listed as a threatened species. The drop is believed to have been caused by competition from commercial fisheries for bottom-feeding fish that are the main prey species of the Steller's sea lion.

The greatest marine mammal attraction along the Olympic coast is the annual gray whale migration, the longest migration known for any mammal. The peak southward migration occurs in December and early January; the return journey occurs in late February and March for males, with females and calves moving northward during April and May. The whales travel an average of 80 miles a day on the southward journey and a more leisurely 40 miles a day during the northward movement. Migrating females with calves migrate closest to shore and are seldom more than half a mile off the coast. There is a small but growing resident population of gray whales that now remains year-round in the Pacific Northwest.

The California gray whale was protected by the 1940s and is the only whale to have recovered from the overhunting that has driven some species to the brink of extinction. The whales feed in Alaskan waters in summer and spend the winter in the warm waters along the Mexican coast. Gray whales are baleen whales, obtaining food by filtering it through a strainer. The gray whales differ from other baleen whales, however, in that they feed primarily on bottom sediments rather than straining plankton from the water column. Because they are bottom feeders, they seldom stray far from shore and thus are more likely than other whales to be seen by hikers.

Fish

Olympic National Park hosts a wide variety of fish species. The following discussion will exclude saltwater species, although a number, principally salmon and trout, occur in both salt and fresh water.

The family Salmonidae, which comprises a large number of species, including trout, char, steelhead, and salmon, is native to the north temperate zone. Salmon are the most sought-after game fish in the region and are restricted to the rim of the North Pacific on the North American and Asiatic coasts, and to a far lesser extent on the European and North American coasts of the North Atlantic.

Pacific salmon belong to the genus *Oncorhynchus*, Greek for "hooked snout." There are five species: sockeye *(O. nerka)*, pink *(O. gorbuscha)*, chum *(O. keta)*, coho *(O. kisutch)*, and chinook *(O. tshawytscha)*. Based on DNA analysis, steelhead/rainbow trout and cutthroat trout have been reclassified as salmon and their genus name is now *Oncorhynchus*. Nevertheless, these fish will not be included in this general discussion.

Pacific salmon are known as anadromous, meaning that they breed and spend part of their life in fresh water, before traveling to the ocean to feed until they reach maturity and return to fresh water to spawn. The life histories of the five Pacific salmon species vary greatly. Pink salmon spend only two years at sea, whereas chinook salmon typically stay in the ocean for up to seven years. Sockeye salmon typically require a lake in the spawning system, where they spend a prolonged juvenile period. Some species, like pinks, go to the ocean almost upon hatching; others, like coho, spend a year or more in their natal streams before migrating to the sea.

Salmon are born in gravel beds in streams anywhere from a hundred yards to several thousand miles from the sea. (The chinook salmon migrate from the Bering Sea up the Yukon River all the way into the

Yukon Territory to spawn.) Laid in the fall, the eggs incubate for several months and then hatch into what are known as *alevins,* tiny, fragile, almost transparent fish with huge eyes and saclike appendages holding food. When the food is completely absorbed, the alevins emerge from the gravel as inch-long *fry.* In the river or a nearby lake, depending on the species, the fry feed and grow for periods ranging up to a year or more. Then, in the spring, during the season of annual flood, they head downstream to the sea. They are called *fingerlings* during this phase of their lives and are up to four inches long. They spend up to five years in the sea, growing rapidly in the productive ocean feeding grounds. These feeding grounds are spread out over the North Pacific, although exactly where remains a mystery. It is known, however, that fish often roam a great distance from their natal streams. A steelhead tagged in the Sea of Japan was caught just six months later in the Skagit River of northern Washington.

Spawning sockeye salmon. The Olympic Peninsula is home to five species of Pacific salmon (actually seven, since both rainbow and cutthroat trout are now considered salmon). Salmon play a critical role in the forest ecosystem. Not only are the fish fed upon by a wide variety of animals from black bears to winter wrens, but they provide nutrients to everything that sustains aquatic invertebrates and to the trees themselves.

In early summer of their maturing year, they begin to head back to their home streams, navigating by sense of smell.

All salmon stop feeding as they enter fresh water, living on stored body fat. They work their way upstream to their natal birth site to spawn. Using her tail, the female digs a nest, or redd, in loose gravel. Spawning salmon usually choose a riffle, where the fast-running water will provide an ample supply of oxygen for the eggs. A female salmon may release up to 15,000 eggs, which are then fertilized by the male. Most species of Pacific salmon die after spawning.

The timing of spawning varies considerably. Even within one river, there may be several different seasonal runs of the same species. For instance, there are several distinct runs of chinook salmon in the Hoh River: a spring run followed by a summer run, and yet another flush of fish in the fall, which goes into winter. Biologists believe these different runs are genetically distinctive and biologically important populations. Thus a spring run of fish could be threatened with extinction, while fall spawners of the same species may not be in trouble.

Salmon Ecology

Like so many things in nature, we used to view salmon as separate from other parts of the ecosystem, believing that though the loss of salmon runs may be a tragedy for anglers or commercial fishermen, they were of no greater consequence. Recent research, however, has demonstrated that salmon play a much more important and expanded role in the ecosystem, even helping to sustain the forest itself.

For example, numerous animal species, including the black bear, raccoon, mink, and river otter, seek out and consume salmon on the spawning streams. Other animals and birds feed on an occasional salmon, including skunks, coyotes, shrews, deer mice, squirrels, winter wrens, dippers, bald eagles, and crows.

Salmon eggs and bodies also contribute to the continued productivity of the salmon themselves. Many of the upper reaches of salmon spawning streams are nutrient-poor environments. The extra protein delivered to small tributary spawning areas by dead salmon and spawn enriches the entire aquatic ecosystem. The nutrients help create an abundance of aquatic invertebrates, leading in turn to greater growth of young salmon and other fish.

The nutrients in dead salmon are even taken up by the roots of trees bordering streams. In this way, the salmon are in effect feeding the forest. The forest in turn feeds the salmon stream with large woody debris in the form of logs, which provide important fish habitat as well as return stored nutrients to the aquatic ecosystem as the large logs slowly rot over the centuries.

Most wild salmon runs in the Pacific Northwest are depressed, or even in danger of extinction, from a variety of factors, including dams, dewatering of streams, loss of large woody debris and shade along streams as a result of logging, and sedimentation resulting from logging. For a long time, it was thought that greater hatchery production of salmon could mitigate for the loss of wild fish.

Recent research has shown, however, that each salmon run or stock is genetically unique. This singular genetic signature of each salmon stock is tied to its own home stream, affecting the timing of runs and the downstream migration of fingerlings, among other things. Replacement with hatchery fish "pollutes" the gene pool of the wild fish. Furthermore, the hatchery fish are simply not as strong as wild fish and are even more vulnerable to natural or man-made habitat changes. They also are more likely to contract diseases, which can spread through all fish populations—wild or domesticated. For all of the above reasons, biologists believe the only way to save salmon in the Pacific Northwest is to save the wild fish stocks and their habitat.

Species Accounts

The following descriptions cover the species most likely to be caught by anglers or seen in fresh water on the Olympic Peninsula. A few species are not discussed. These include the Olympic mud minnow, which is so rare it is endangered, and largemouth bass and perch, both introduced species found in a few lakes.

CHINOOK SALMON (KING)
(Oncorhynchus tshawytscha)

Description. Largest of the Pacific salmon, may reach 100 pounds or more. Unlike the other Pacific salmon, body shape does not change much during spawning. Black gums at base of teeth. Numerous black spots on a blue-green back; tannish sides turning to white on belly. Black spots cover upper and lower tail. Skin color turns from bright silver of the sea life to a dark brown, sometimes approaching black the more time spent in fresh water. Male and female are very similar, except for the male's larger size.

Distribution. Favors large rivers. Chinook may be seen in upriver migrations almost any month of the year but favor spring and fall. Major chinook streams include the Hoh, Queets, Quinault, Gray Wolf, and Soleduck.

Remarks. Mature chinook will spend three to seven years at sea. Most are four to five years old when they return to spawn and range in weight from 10 to 50 pounds. Chinook are not often easily seen on the spawning grounds, as they normally choose deeper spawning areas.

COHO SALMON (SILVER)
(Oncorhynchus kisutch)

Description. Male gets hooked jaw during spawning season. Black dots on upper part of back and upper half of tail only. Blue-green on back, shading to a white belly. At spawning time, the body becomes darker and the sides take on a reddish tinge. Gum area at base of teeth of lower jaw pale. Average 28 to 30 inches long, 6 to 10 pounds.

Distribution. Cohos usually spawn in coastal rivers, sloughs, and side channels, entering streams in November and December. Upper Soleduck River is a prime coho spawning stream.

Remarks. Cohos are sometimes known as blueback when caught before full maturity, and also as silvers. They are the most popular game fish of the salmon family and are one of the most valuable commercial species. Coho spend their first year in a river, making them more vulnerable than other salmon to habitat degradation. This is one reason they are endangered or threatened over much of their natural range south of Washington State. Typically return to spawn their third year.

SOCKEYE SALMON (RED)
(Oncorhynchus nerka)

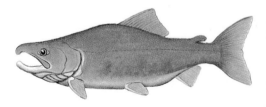

Description. Color in spawning males bright red with green head. Male develops a hooked jaw and pronounced humped back.

Distribution. Rarest of salmon on Peninsula. All sockeye spawn only in river systems with a major lake. Mature four-year-old sockeyes average 6 pounds, and older age groups reach 12 pounds. Large run in Quinault Lake, and another in Ozette Lake. Kokanee salmon are found in Crescent Lake.

Remarks. Juvenile sockeyes spend one to three years in a large lake before migrating to the sea. Completely landlocked sockeyes are known as kokanee.

CHUM SALMON (DOG)
(*Oncorhynchus keta*)

Description. Up to 38 inches long and 8 to 18 pounds. Strongly hooked jaw in spawning males. Breeding males are blackish above, reddish on sides, with vertical green bars. No black spots.
Distribution. Spawn in lower portions of Ozette, Quillayute, and Queets, as well as lower parts of some east-side streams. Not abundant.
Remarks. Chum salmon are called "dog salmon" in Alaska because they were commonly fed to sled dogs.

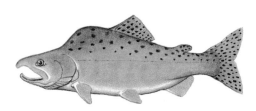

PINK SALMON (HUMPBACK)
(*Oncorhynchus gorbuscha*)

Description. Smallest of the Pacific salmon. Black oval spots on back and tail. Metallic blue back and silvery white belly. Mature spawning male develops a pronounced hump on back, hence the common name humpback or humpie, and takes on a gunbarrel gray color fading to yellowish white on the belly. Up to 30 inches long and 3 to 5 pounds.
Distribution. Pink salmon are scarce on the Olympic Peninsula, found primarily in northern-flowing streams and also in a few eastern-flowing streams like Dosewallips. Dungeness River has one of the best runs.
Remarks. Pink salmon live only two years. Most of their growth occurs in their second year at sea.

STEELHEAD OR RAINBOW TROUT
(Oncorhynchus mykiss)

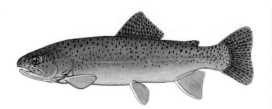

Description. Sea-run steelhead up to 45 inches long and 30 pounds; stream-dwelling rainbow trout much smaller. Usually bluish or greenish back, fading to silver-white on sides and belly. Distinctive red or pink lateral line down sides. Heavily spotted with black dots on back, sides, and tail.

Distribution. Nearly all Peninsula rivers host some runs of steelhead, including the Hoh, Bogachiel, Queets, Dungeness, Duckabush, Dosewallips, Skokomish, and others. Many runs are in steep decline from habitat destruction. A special subspecies of rainbow trout, the Beardslee trout, is found in Lake Crescent.

Remarks. Rainbow trout and steelhead are the same fish—one a sea-run version of the other. As a result of genetic analysis, the steelhead/rainbow was recently determined to be a salmon, not a trout. Unlike other salmon, steelheads do not die after spawning and can return to spawn two or three times. Steelheads have the most complicated life history of any of the salmons. Steelheads may spend anywhere from one to four years in fresh water and one to four (rarely a little more) years in salt water. These different combinations of freshwater and saltwater years create many possibilities for life cycles.

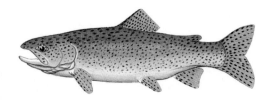

CUTTHROAT TROUT
(Oncorhynchus clarki)

Description. Bright red slash on either side of throat ("cut throat"); may be faint in fresh, sea-run fish. Dark greenish back, tannish sides, and white belly. Black spots cover tail, sides, and back. Although some subspecies can grow to 30 pounds or more, most usually not more than 1 to 4 pounds and 20 inches.

Distribution. Cutthroat trout live primarily in fresh water, including lakes, but some migrate to brackish ocean waters to live and feed.

Remarks. The species name *clarki* refers to William Clark, coleader of the Lewis and Clark Expedition, who was the first to describe the species to science.

DOLLY VARDEN TROUT
(Salvelinus malma)

Description. Green-blue back fading to reddish belly. Sea-run fish very silvery. Moderately long head, no wormlike markings on back, and pink or red spots on sides. Anal and pelvic fins have white edges.

Distribution. Coastal streams, with some stocks anadromous. Not common. Found in Quinault Lake and Lake Cushman.

Remarks. Genetic analysis has determined that Dolly Varden trout are a separate species from the inland populations now called bull trout. The bull trout is threatened with extinction across much of its natural range; the coastal Dolly Varden is only slightly better off.

EASTERN BROOK TROUT
(Salvelinus fontinalis)

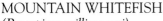

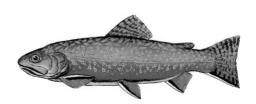

Description. Olive green back with wormlike markings. Red spots with blue halos on sides. Belly reddish, particularly in spawning fish. Maximum size is 14 pounds, but usually much smaller, less than a pound.
Distribution. Introduced fish, common in smaller creeks and some subalpine lakes.
Remarks. A fall spawner. Can be abundant in some lakes.

MOUNTAIN WHITEFISH
(Prosopium williamsoni)

Description. Troutlike body up to a foot, sometimes larger. Mouth small with no teeth. Long, pointed snout. Generally silver color with darker brownish back.
Distribution. Lakes and streams.
Remarks. Primarily a bottom feeder, eating aquatic insects.

TORRENT SCULPIN
(Cottus rhotheus)

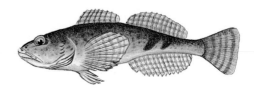

Description. Head and mouth large. Two small holes or pores on tip of chin, with prickles on head, sides, and back. Brownish back, with black speckling, to mottled silvery sides. Up to 6 inches but usually half that size.
Distribution. Swift water of large rivers.
Remarks. Usually found among rocks.

PYGMY WHITEFISH
(Prosopium coulteri)

Description. Slender, troutlike body. Usually under 6 inches in length. Mouth small with no teeth. Snout blunt but rounded. Pale tan above and silvery below.
Distribution. Rare. Lakes and streams.
Remarks. Eats aquatic insects and crustaceans.

PACIFIC LAMPREY
(Lampetra tridentatus)

Description. Eel-like. Adults 12 to 25 inches. No true jaws. Mouth like a sucking disk. Seven gill openings on the side of body behind head. Dark brown to bluish black color.
Distribution. Coastal streams from southern California to Alaska, including the Olympic Peninsula.
Remarks. The adults of this species feed on the blood and tissues of other fish, attaching themselves to the body of victims and sucking internal fluids from their prey. Many victims apparently survive these attacks. Like salmon, Pacific lampreys ascend freshwater streams and rivers to spawn and die after spawning.

RIVER LAMPREY
(Lampetra richardsoni)

Description. Eel-like. Adult body up to 6 inches. No true jaws. Circular sucking disk for mouth in adults. Seven gill openings on side of body behind head. Dark brown to black on top, fading to light gray on belly.
Distribution. Coastal streams from California to Alaska, including Olympic Peninsula.
Remarks. Unlike Pacific lamprey, the river lamprey does not feed upon other fish. In the adult stage, it does not feed at all, living only long enough to spawn.

LONGFIN SMELT
(Spirinchus thaleichthys)

Description. Slender silvery fish with short head. Upper jaw reaches below eye. Total length 6 inches.
Distribution. Anadromous; enters fresh water to spawn. Found from San Francisco to Alaska, including rivers on Olympic Peninsula.
Remarks. Spawns in fall between October and December.

REDSIDE SHINER
(Richardsonius balteatus)

Description. Compressed but deep body. Small mouth. Large eye. Silvery with dark green to blackish back. Black stripe bordered by lighter stripe on either side. Tinge of red behind gills. Up to 7 inches, but most smaller.
Distribution. Sluggish coastal streams and lakes with abundant vegetation from British Columbia to Oregon.
Remarks. Often schools.

NORTHERN SQUAWFISH
(Ptychocheilus oregonensis)

Description. Long head, narrow body, small eye. Up to 12 inches, although record fish up to 29 pounds have been taken. Back dark, fading to yellowish on sides.
Distribution. Prefers quiet water, typically lakes.
Remarks. Young feed on insects, but adults are fish eaters. Occasionally caught by anglers.

PEARMOUTH CHUB
(Mylocheilus caurinus)

Description. Long, narrow body with small barbel around mouth. Deeply forked tail with two lateral black stripes (one less prominent) along each side. Dark bronze back and yellowish white sides and belly. Length up to 14 inches, but most half that size.
Distribution. Lakes and slow, deep channels of rivers.
Remarks. Often the most numerous fish found in weedy zones of lakes.

PRICKLY SCULPIN
(Cottus asper)

Description. Total length up to 12 inches, but usually half that. Single pore under chin. Large spine. Prickling varies but can cover entire body. Olive-brown tinged with yellow. Black markings on sides. Spawning males almost black.
Distribution. Coastal streams. Can live in brackish waters.
Remarks. Species name *asper* refers to the rough prickles that cover the body. Feeds on plankton and aquatic insects. One of the chief foods of mergansers.

THREESPINE STICKLEBACK
(Gasterosteus aculeatus)

Description. Usually not more than 3 inches long. Head short. Large eye. Three erect dorsal spines—first two long, and third shorter.
Distribution. Found in both fresh and salt water from Baja to Alaska. Primarily brackish water on Olympic Peninsula.
Remarks. During spawning, male constructs nest made from twigs and other plant debris, held together by a mucilaginous secretion from male. Several females will contribute eggs to the nest.

LARGESCALE SUCKER
(Catostomus macrocheilus)

Description. Teardrop shape, with rounded head and thick body. Length to 24 inches. Lips thick and mouth located ventrally. Back and sides dark olive, fading to white or yellowish on belly.
Distribution. Occurs in lakes and streams from Oregon to British Columbia.
Remarks. Suckers are most likely to be seen during spawning season. Fish spawn in the spring at outlet streams or occasionally along lake margins.

REPTILES AND
AMPHIBIANS

Because of its overall cool temperatures, the Pacific Northwest is not a particularly good place for reptiles and amphibians. Temperature is particularly limiting for reptiles; they prefer warm, dry, arid environments and thus are not well represented here. Amphibians, which require moist conditions, fare slightly better, and all of the four endemic amphibians and reptiles found in the region are, not surprisingly, salamanders. Salamanders are also the most abundant species.

Species Accounts

Amphibians

The name amphibian comes from the Greek *amphi,* meaning double, referring to the two phases of its life cycle. Most amphibians are born in water bodies. The young have gills in the larva or tadpole stage. Eventually, most amphibians change into an adult form that can survive on land to some degree. Nevertheless, because their skins lack an adequate barrier against water loss, amphibians survive only in moist microenvironments. They are strongly associated with humid woodlands, seeps, and wetlands. Amphibians have thin skins that feel moist to the touch, whereas reptiles have scales and dry skin.

There are two major divisions within the amphibians: frogs and toads; and salamanders. Toads differ from frogs by being largely terrestrial as adults. Salamanders are tailed amphibians, but frogs and toads lack true tails. The former have fully developed fore and hind limbs during the larval stage, whereas frogs and toads have four limbs only after they mature into adults. Salamander larvae have teeth and are carnivorous, but frog tadpoles are herbivorous. Frogs and toads have eardrums; salamanders do not.

Because of its mild, wet climate, the Olympics support a large amphibian population. Fourteen species of salamanders and frogs, including two endemic species—Cope's giant salamander and Olympic torrent—are found here. Up to 250 amphibians per acre have been reported for some parts of the Olympic Peninsula, making them one of the major predators on invertebrates, insects, and other small prey. Their role in ecosystem dynamics is only now beginning to be appreciated, yet there has been a sharp decline in numbers. No one knows exactly why, although a variety of factors may be responsible. One may be the use of chemicals that break down the ozone layer, which has led to increased levels of ultraviolet radiation. Amphibian eggs may be more vulnerable to ultraviolet radiation than those of other animals. Habitat destruction in the form of logging and grazing has certainly had its impact, degrading waterways and wetlands on which some species are dependent. Even the introduction of trout and other fish to formerly fishless water bodies may be hurting amphibian populations. Trout and some other fish species prey upon both tadpoles and adult frogs. In California's Sierra Nevada, there has been a tremendous decline in frogs in lakes where trout have been introduced.

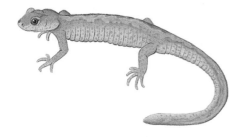

LONG-TOED SALAMANDER
(Ambystoma macrodactylum)

Description. Named for the very long fourth toe on its hind foot. Prominent grooves and ridges along sides. Smooth black or brown skin with greenish or yellow strip extending along head, back, and tail. White speckling on sides.
Distribution. One of the most widely distributed salamanders, living in a wide variety of habitats from lowland forest to the subalpine.
Remarks. Elsewhere, introduced fish, which consume the larvae, have decimated populations of this salamander.

ROUGH-SKINNED NEWT
(Taricha granulosa)

Description. Dark brown back and orange-yellow belly. Dry, glandular skin. Up to 7.5 inches total length including tail. In winter, males undergo change, with skin becoming smooth and moist. Tail becomes flattened.
Distribution. These are among the most widely distributed newts in the West. They are associated with wet forests, particularly riparian habitat. They tend to be found in hilly or mountainous country, from sea level up to subalpine. They are found in lakes, streams, or wandering around in forest duff.
Remarks. The skin of this newt contains a potent toxin, and thus it has few predators. There is enough poison in one newt to kill 25,000 mice. If disturbed, the newt reacts by curling up its back to display its orange belly, which is a warning about its toxicity. It is slow moving and more frequently seen in daylight.

NORTHWEST SALAMANDER
(Ambystoma gracile)

Description. Adult: rich brown color dorsally, with light gray belly. Lighter colored glandular areas behind eyes and along back and tail. Moist, smooth skin. Prominent grooves along sides. Total length including tail up to 9.5 inches.
Distribution. Low-elevation rivers and ponds.
Remarks. Seldom seen, as it spends most of its time in underground burrows. In dry summer months, seeks shelter in rotten logs, caves, and other moist areas. Potent poison from skin glands discourages predators.

OLYMPIC SALAMANDER
(Rhyacotriton olympicus)

Description. Small; total length of 4 inches. Huge, bulging eyes. Various colors, but most are plain brown dorsally and have yellowish bellies with a few black spots.
Distribution. Small, cold mountain streams, seeps, splash zone by waterfalls. Avoid fast water.
Remarks. This salamander secretes a mildly poisonous substance from its tail, which may discourage predators. Dependent upon cold water and has disappeared from many areas outside the park as a consequence of logging-induced water temperature changes.

WESTERN RED-BACKED SALAMANDER
(Plethodon vehiculum)

Description. Slender salamander about 4.5 inches long including tail, with an even-edged dorsal stripe running from tip of tail to head. Sides are gray or black, belly is gray with white speckling. Some coastal individuals are nearly all black; up to 10 percent of the western Olympic population are melanistic (have an increased amount of black pigmentation).
Distribution. This salamander is the most widespread in the Pacific Northwest and is strongly associated with coniferous forests. It does not tolerate cold, hence is seldom found in areas where snow is common. Tends to be found near rocks, talus slopes, beneath large logs.
Remarks. Eats primarily mites, spiders, and other invertebrates.

COPE'S GIANT SALAMANDER
(Dicamptodon copei)

Description. Large salamander with brown marbling on tan background. Similar to Pacific giant salamander but smaller, with shorter limbs and smaller head.
Distribution. Very rare; only three adult specimens ever described anywhere. Found on margins of ponds and streams in coniferous forest.
Remarks. Only discovered in 1970; largely confined to the Olympic Peninsula and coastal Washington. Can become sexually mature in a subadult form and seldom metamorphoses into an adult.

VAN DYKE'S SALAMANDER
(Plethodon vandykei)

Description. This small salamander averages about 4 inches total length including tail. It has fourteen costal grooves (grooves and ridges on its sides). Toes are slightly webbed. The color is variable, even within the same population. It can be yellowish or reddish, or have dark sides with white speckling and a light stripe down the back. The yellow phase is most common in the Olympics.
Distribution. This salamander is only found in three regions of Washington, including the Olympic Mountains. Though a woodland species and able to live far from water if in a moist environment, it is often found around seeps, waterfalls, and streams.
Remarks. Van Dyke's salamander is considered to be the most aquatic of woodland salamanders, nevertheless, lays its eggs on land. Larvae stage completed in egg, and young are born as miniature adults. Relatively rare in Olympics.

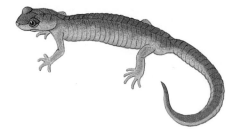

OREGON ENSATINA
(Ensatina eschscholtzii oregonensis)

Description. Stout-bodied with twelve costal grooves. Tail has a distinct constriction at base. No dorsal stripe. Reddish, orangish, brown, or tan overall.
Distribution. Commonly found under woody debris and logs. Prefers drier habitat and avoids wet places.
Remarks. When attacked, will wave its tail back and forth. Tail can break off and continue to wiggle, often distracting predator while ensatina makes its escape. The animal will grow a new tail.

WESTERN TOAD
(Bufo boreas)

Description. Large animal with horizontal eye pupils and dry, warty skin. Conspicuous oval parotid glands, enlarged areas at the back of the head where poison is excreted. Color ranges from reddish to greenish, but there is nearly always a white stripe down the back. Underside pale with dark blotches.
Distribution. Common by lakes and ponds but will travel through dry forest.
Remarks. Normally nocturnal, so seldom seen. Moves by crawling and climbing rather than jumping. If attacked, will secrete a poison. Western Washington populations have experienced significant declines.

TAILED FROG
(Ascaphus truei)

Description. Small, 2-inch frog. Grayish green, reddish brown, or brown, with yellow and gray mottling. Males have a prominent cloacal "tail." Eye has vertical pupil. Tympanum (eardrum) is absent.
Distribution. Near cold, rocky streams. Not found by ponds or lakes.
Remarks. Seldom seen; nocturnal. Hides under rocks in daytime and comes out to hunt under cover of darkness. Has hardened toes to assist in crawling along rocky streams. The lack of an external ear is an adaptation to its typically noisy environment along rushing mountain streams, where hearing acuity is relatively unimportant. This frog has suffered as a result of sedimentation from logging.

PACIFIC TREE FROG
(Pseudacris regilla)

Description. Less than 2 inches. Brown, green, pale gray, or reddish. Conspicuous dark mask from nose to shoulders. Often a Y-shaped pattern between eyes on top of head. Long, slender legs. Toes have round pads. (No other frog has toe pads.)
Distribution. The most common frog in Pacific Northwest. Found in a variety of habitats, from urban yards to deep forests. Often far from water.
Remarks. Males produce one prolonged note, particularly after rain, giving rise to common name "chorus frog."

RED-LEGGED FROG
(Rana aurora)

Description. Up to 4 inches. Reddish brown or brown in color, with small black markings and spots on back and sides. Irregular black bands across legs. Usually has dark mask on head. Ventral side of legs red, sometimes extending up into belly and sides. Creamy white throat.
Distribution. Woodlands adjacent to streams.
Remarks. It takes three to four years for frogs to reach sexual maturity.

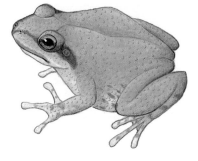

CASCADES FROG
(Rana cascadae)

Description. Total length up to 3 inches. Olive green, brown, or tan. Covered with black spots. Dark mask from eye to shoulder, with a lighter stripe along jaw from nose to shoulder. Ventral side of legs yellowish to gold.

Distribution. Associated with small pools and marshy areas adjacent to streams in subalpine terrain. Seldom found below 2,000 feet.

Remarks. Around the turn of the century, four specimens of this frog were collected near sea level on the Olympic Peninsula, a habitat where it is not found today.

BULLFROG
(Rana catesbeiana)

Description. Large frog up to 8 inches. Green or olive green, with black or dark blotches. A fold of skin extends from eye to shoulder. Belly is cream colored with dark marbling. Loud bass call.

Distribution. Highly aquatic; seldom far from water. Found at lower elevations around the Olympic Peninsula.

Remarks. An introduced exotic native to the Midwest. A voracious predator, eating almost everything from ducks to other frogs. The bullfrog may be responsible for the decline in spotted frogs in western Washington and Oregon, as well as declines in western pond turtles.

Reptiles

Turtles, lizards, and snakes are all reptiles. All have adaptations for life on land, although some species, such as the western pond turtle and the garter snake, may be strongly associated with water. All reptiles have scales and young that are born either alive or in eggs. In either case, they don't require a water environment to reproduce as do amphibians.

Lizards and snakes differ from one another in several ways. Most lizards have limbs with sharp claws, but snakes are limbless. Lizards have external ear openings and eyelids that can blink; snakes do not.

WESTERN FENCE LIZARD
(Sceloporus occidentalis)

Description. Up to 6.5 inches total length including tail. Brown, gray, or black. Lighter individuals have parallel triangular blotches on back. Blue throat patch and blue patches on each side of abdomen. Dorsal scales are pointed and keeled.
Distribution. Avoids humid forests. Found only along the eastern side of Olympic Peninsula, along Hood Canal.
Remarks. Common in logged areas, where it uses stumps and logs as perches.

NORTHERN ALLIGATOR LIZARD
(Elgaria coerulea)

Description. A stout lizard up to 10 inches total length. Dark brown or greenish brown. Longitudinal fold on each side of body. Square dorsal scales separated from a similar shaped scale by a mid-body line of small scales. Eyes brown.
Distribution. Moist forests, forest openings, and clearings. Most common along eastern side of Olympics, along Hood Canal and Strait of Juan de Fuca near Sequim.
Remarks. Bears a litter of fully formed lizards.

RUBBER BOA
(Charina bottae)

Description. Usually less than 24 inches. Rubbery look and feel to skin. Vestiges of hind limbs called anal spurs. Back is a uniform color of dark or light brown. Short, blunt tail that looks similar to the wedge-shaped head.
Distribution. Usually found near water, under logs, in rock crevices, and under leaf litter.
Remarks. Can climb and swim well. Usually nocturnal. Crushes its prey.

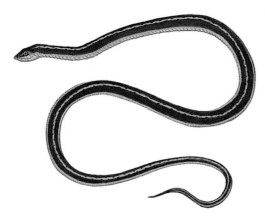

COMMON GARTER SNAKE
(Thamnophis sirtalis)

Description. May reach 52 inches in length. There is great color variation among garter snakes. In Olympic Peninsula, most common variety has black dorsal color with black head and yellow-green vertebral stripe. Belly is light green or blue near the head, darkening to black near the tail.
Distribution. Sea level to 6,000 feet. Wide variety of habitats, but usually associated with water, ponds, sloughs, and streams.
Remarks. If captured, garter snakes will release feces, urine, and musk to discourage predator.

WESTERN GARTER SNAKE
(Thamnophis elegans)

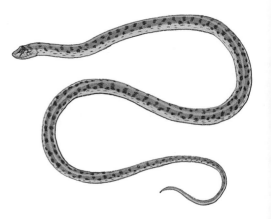

Description. Up to 40 inches in length. Light gray to light brown dorsally, with dull yellow vertebral and lateral stripes. Belly light gray.

Distribution. Usually near water. Common near human habitation.

Remarks. One of the most aquatic of the garter snakes. Also has the most varied diet of any snake, including leeches, snails, slugs, mice, voles, frogs, salamanders, and even small birds.

NORTHWESTERN GARTER SNAKE
(Thamnophis ordinoides)

Description. Small, usually less than 2 feet in length. Greatest color variation of any snake in Pacific Northwest, even among litter mates. Dorsal background color black, brown, gray, or olive. Vertebral stripe red, yellow, turquoise, white, or orange. Lateral stripes white or yellow. Relatively small head helps distinguish it from other garter snakes.

Distribution. Strongly associated with coastal fog belt. Primarily terrestrial and found among thickets, meadows, and forest clearings.

Remarks. Will forage in rain, seeking slugs, earthworms, frogs, salamanders, and snails.

BIRDS

Birds evolved from reptiles and still possess a few reptilian features, such as scaly feet. Birds are covered with feathers, which are modified scales. Feathers not only enable flight but also provide excellent insulation, an adaptation necessary for survival as a small-bodied, warm-blooded animal.

Several other features also enable flight. Most birds have a honeycombed bone structure, which creates structural strength but not much weight. They have no teeth, which would add weight, but have lightweight bills designed for specific foods: hooked bills in predators; stout, heavy bills for crushing seeds in seedeaters; stout, pointed bills for drilling wood in woodpeckers; and long, thin bills in birds that probe sand or mudflats.

Because of the great caloric demands of flying and the energy cost of maintaining their internal body temperature, most birds eat foods of a high calorie-to-weight value, including insects, seeds, nuts, and flesh. There are relatively few herbivores among bird species; most of these are larger ones, such as geese.

All birds are hatched from eggs and are given varying degrees of attention by the parents. Some species are precocial, able to run or swim almost immediately upon hatching. This includes some ducks, shorebirds, and chickenlike birds such as grouse. Most, however are altricial, requiring a degree of parental care. Baby birds remain in the nest for days or weeks until they are fledged (have the feathers necessary for flying).

Most birds have variation in plumage that changes with the season, sex, or state of development of the bird. For example, the male mallard duck possesses a green head, whereas the female is typically a mottled brown color. And some gulls have juvenile plumage that changes at different ages.

Flight provides birds with incredible mobility. More than any other animal group, birds are able to travel long distances relatively efficiently.

Migration is one way birds cope with seasonal food shortages, inclement weather, and competition with other birds, and there are few year-round residents in northern zones. Many of the birds in Olympic National Park are seasonal residents, breeding here in the summer but wintering elsewhere. Others breed farther north and are seen here only during spring or fall migrations.

Species Accounts

More than two hundred species of birds are known to reside in or migrate through the park. This is considerably fewer species than in some other, more southerly parks, which may host as many as four hundred or more species. There are several factors that account for this difference. First, as one goes northward, the number of species of most animal groups declines due to increasing cold and the seasonal nature of food resources. And Olympic National Park has less diversity of habitat than some of the southern parks, which means fewer niches available for different bird species.

Nevertheless, Olympic's mountains, forests, and waters are home to some species you are unlikely to see in as great an abundance in other parts of the country, such as bald eagles, tufted puffins, harlequin ducks, and a number of other species. Because of the relatively benign climate found on the Peninsula, quite a number of species are year-round residents, although some make migrations for the winter from higher to lower elevations or from inland locations to the coast. The following list does not include all the birds known to occur in the park but features the species most likely to be seen plus a few species that are rare but are of interest for other reasons, such as the marbled murrelet. The species descriptions are sketchy and may not be suitable for keying out each bird to the species level. For positive identification, consult a good birding guide.

Cormorants

Cormorants are large, dark, long-necked diving birds that feed on fish. They are usually associated with the ocean, although there are some inland freshwater populations in other parts of the West. They nest in colonies, typically on offshore sea stacks and rocky islets, although in some places, double-crested cormorants have taken to nesting in trees. There are three species of cormorants found within Olympic National Park: Brandt's, pelagic, and double-crested.

DOUBLE-CRESTED CORMORANT
(*Phalacrocorax auritus*)

Description. Up to 3 feet long, with long, snakelike neck. Adults generally black but with an orange-yellow throat patch.

Distribution. Found along rocky shorelines, particularly the outer coast.

Remarks. Year-round, breeding resident. The double-crested cormorant has less waterproofing of its feathers than other waterbirds and often assumes a spread-wing posture to dry the outer surface of its wings. The reduced water repellency of its feathers facilitates underwater pursuit of prey.

Herons and Bitterns

Birds in this group are generally waders that feed on fish. They tend to have long, daggerlike bills, slender necks, and longish legs.

AMERICAN BITTERN
(*Botaurus lentiginosus*)

Description. Body up to 32 inches. Black mark on side of neck. Stocky, brown body with tan belly and breast. Bill yellow, throat white. Dark outer wings obvious in flight.

Distribution. Associated with marshes and reedy shallows.

Remarks. Year-round, breeding resident. When alarmed, holds a stiff pose with bill pointing up, which tends to camouflage it among the reeds.

GREAT BLUE HERON
(Ardea herodias)

Description. Large, gray-blue bird up to
4½ feet tall, with long dark legs. Black
stripe extends back from eye.
Distribution. Shallow water such as
marshes and streams.
Remarks. Common year-round, breeding
resident. Flies with slow, steady wingbeats
with neck drawn in close to body. Stands
motionless when fishing and suddenly
spears prey such as fish and frogs.

Geese and Ducks

Geese and ducks are associated with water and typically have webbed feet. Geese
have blunt, triangular bills. Sexes are alike. Ducks are divided into subgroups
including dabblers, or puddle ducks, and divers. Dabblers, such as mallards, are
generally able to spring directly from the water into the air and can readily walk
on land. Diving ducks have the legs set farther back on the body, which aids in
underwater pursuit of prey but makes it more difficult to walk on land. When
taking flight, divers typically patter along the water's surface before becoming
airborne. More than a dozen duck and goose species have been reported for
Olympic National Park, but most are migrants.

CANADA GOOSE
(Branta canadensis)

Description. Large, gray bird up to 40
inches long with black head, neck, and
tail and white underparts.
Distribution. Found primarily on freshwater ponds, lakes, and marshes but also
on quiet bays.
Remarks. A few individuals are year-
round residents, but most seen during
spring and fall migration. Breeds in park.
Flies in V formation with loud honks.
Primarily an herbivore, feeding upon
grass and grains.

MALLARD
(Anas platyrhynchos)

Description. Medium size, 20 to 26 inches. Males grayish with a chestnut chest and glossy green head. Female brown. Both have purple wing bars with white edges, orange feet, and yellow bill.
Distribution. Widely distributed on freshwater ponds and marshes.
Remarks. Year-round, breeding resident. One of the most common ducks seen.

BLUE-WINGED TEAL
(Anas discors)

Description. Small duck, 14 to 16 inches. Fast flying. Males have white patch on rear of flank and white crescent by eye. Females brown. Both have distinctive pale blue patches on forewing.
Distribution. Freshwater ponds and marshes—rarely saltwater.
Remarks. Most abundant during migration, although a few individuals remain in the area and breed in the park. A common duck in the prairie pothole region but uncommon on West Coast.

HARLEQUIN DUCK
(Histrionicus histrionicus)

Description. Smallish duck, up to 16 inches. Short bill. Male blue-gray with colorful plumage. White patch in front of eye and other white bars and patches on head and neck. Female brownish with three round white spots on each side of head. Rapid flight.

Distribution. Nests on fast-moving streams and winters on coast.

Remarks. Year-round, breeding resident. Harlequin duck numbers are holding steady on the Olympic Peninsula but declining elsewhere across their range. Highest nesting population in park is found along Elwha River, but the ducks are also numerous on the upper Hoh, Queets, and other rivers. Less than 1,500 ducks are thought to reside in the entire state of Washington. They are being considered for listing as an endangered species.

COMMON MERGANSER
(Mergus merganser)

Description. Medium duck up to 27 inches. Male has greenish head, white body, and black back. When in flight, looks predominantly white. Female has crested rufous head, gray body, white throat and wing patch. Both have red serrated bill and red feet.

Distribution. Common on rivers, particularly larger west-side streams like the Hoh and Queets. Occasionally seen on lakes, rarely on saltwater except in winter.

Remarks. Year-round resident. Breeds in park. A fish-eating duck that captures prey by diving.

Hawks, Eagles, Ospreys, and Falcons

These are all birds of prey, capturing food with sharp bills and talons. Most have exceptional eyesight.

OSPREY
(Pandion haliaetus)

Description. Up to 2 feet long with 6-foot wingspreads. White crown, throat, and underparts and mostly white head. Black eye patch and black "wrist" on underwing. Long, narrow wings, held bent when flying. Only hawklike bird that regularly dives into water. Call is a series of sharp shrieks.
Distribution. Associated with larger rivers, lakes, and bays. Nests in tops of broken tree snags near water.
Remarks. Common summer breeder. The osprey captures fish by diving into the water. Often hovers before diving.

NORTHERN HARRIER
(Circus cyaneus)

Description. Medium hawk, 18 to 21 inches. Wingspread to 4 feet. Long, slim wings and long tail. White rump. Males gray above, females brown. Wings angled upward in flight.
Distribution. Open fields, marshes. Have been seen in the subalpine and alpine zones.
Remarks. Some are year-round residents, but most are seen during spring and fall migrations. Breeds in the region. Flies low, swooping over fields and open landscapes hunting for mice and other prey.

SHARP-SHINNED HAWK
(Accipiter striatus)

Description. Smallish hawk, up to 14 inches. Short, rounded wings and long tail that is squarish at corners but roundish when flared in flight. Bluish gray back with brown-barred breast.
Distribution. Coniferous forests.
Remarks. Most common during migrations, but some year-round, breeding residents. Preys on smaller birds, capturing them in flight.

COOPER'S HAWK
(Accipiter cooperii)

Description. Similar to sharp-shinned hawk but larger. Wingspread up to 3 feet, size to 20 inches long. Short, rounded wings and long, rounded tail. Grayish back with brown-streaked breast.
Distribution. Woodlands and streamside riparian forests.
Remarks. Most abundant during migration, but some year-round, breeding residents. Preys primarily on songbirds. Soars more than sharp-shinned hawk.

NORTHERN GOSHAWK
(Accipiter gentilis)

Description. Large, grayish hawk with a 4-foot wingspread. White line over eye, dark cap, and gray-barred breast.
Distribution. Coniferous forests and subalpine areas.
Remarks. Relatively common year-round, breeding resident. Very aggressive around nest; will attack hikers and others intruding upon territory.

RED-TAILED HAWK
(Buteo jamaicensis)

Description. Large hawk, up to 2 feet in length with a 4-foot wingspread. Broad wings, short tail. Often has black "wrist" marks on underwings. Top of tail reddish.
Distribution. Open country and open woodlands.
Remarks. Year-round, breeding resident. Preys primarily on rodents. Soars.

GOLDEN EAGLE
(Aquila chrysaetos)

Description. Large, brown bird, up to 40 inches with a 7- to 8-foot wingspread. Slight lightening at the base of tail (white in immature birds).
Distribution. Open alpine terrain, primarily in the northeastern part of the Olympic Mountains.
Remarks. Not common in park. Breeds here. Soars along ridge lines looking for marmots and other rodents.

BALD EAGLE
(Haliaeetus leucocephalus)

Description. Large, dark bird with prominent white head and tail in adults. Immature birds lack white head and have white on undertail and underwings. Wingspread up to 8 feet.
Distribution. Water bodies such as rivers, ponds, and coastal areas.
Remarks. Common year-round, breeding resident. Soars on horizontal wings. Feeds primarily on fish, birds, and carrion.

AMERICAN KESTREL
(*Falco sparverius*)

Description. Size 10 to 12 inches. Rufous back and sides, black and white markings on head. Male has gray wings.
Distribution. Open landscapes up to timberline.
Remarks. Uncommon year-round resident. Breeds in region. Hunts rodents, grasshoppers, and other small prey. Often seen hovering.

Grouse and Quail

Grouse and quail are chickenlike birds with precocial young able to run within minutes of being born. Often seen on the ground.

BLUE GROUSE
(*Dendragapus obscurus*)

Description. Chickenlike, up to 20 inches. Gray to blackish. Black tail with light band at top. Male has yellow-orange comb above eye.
Distribution. Coniferous forest, particularly near timberline in winter.
Remarks. Common year-round, breeding resident. Breeding males produce loud, low *hoo, hoo hoo* vocalizations.

RUFFED GROUSE
(*Bonasa umbellus*)

Description. Chickenlike, up to 19 inches. Red-brown; reddish tail with black band near tip.
Distribution. Coniferous forest, bushy woodlands, riparian areas.
Remarks. Year-round breeding resident. Breeding male drums wings on hollow logs, producing loud noise like a lawn mower starting up.

Shorebirds

Shorebirds, as their name implies, are common along water. Most are chunky and active birds.

KILLDEER
(Charadrius vociferus)

Description. Robin-size bird, with two black bands on breast. Brown back with white forehead, throat, and collar. Orangish rump.
Distribution. Mudflats, fields, beaches, near water.
Remarks. Common year-round breeding resident. Call a loud *kill-dee, kill-dee*.

BLACK OYSTERCATCHER
(Haematopus bachmani)

Description. Crow-size black bird with long, red beak.
Distribution. Coastal rocky shorelines.
Remarks. Year-round breeding resident. Uses its stout bill to pry loose mussels and other shellfish, which it then eats. Has sharp, loud cry.

SPOTTED SANDPIPER
(Actitis macularia)

Description. Small, 7 to 8 inches. Olive-brown above, white breast with black spots during breeding season, white line over eye, white wing stripe and tip of tail.
Distribution. Sandy and cobble beaches along lakes and streams, and ocean in winter.
Remarks. Uncommon year-round resident; greater numbers are seen during spring migration. Flies with stiff, rapid wingbeats.

Gulls and Terns

Gulls are fairly large, long-winged birds usually found near oceans. They soar well. Terns are smaller and more delicate. They often hover, and fly with a somewhat erratic motion. Twenty-three species have been reported for the Olympic Peninsula, but many are only infrequently seen during migration or tend to be winter residents. Only two gulls are common.

WESTERN GULL
(*Larus occidentalis*)

Description. Dark back with snowy white underparts. Legs pinkish. Black primary feathers.
Distribution. Coastlines.
Remarks. Year-round breeding resident. Tends to be found on outer coastline.

GLAUCOUS-WINGED GULL
(*Larus glaucescens*)

Description. Large, up to 27 inches. Pink legs. Gray mantle with white underparts.
Distribution. Coastal areas.
Remarks. Year-round breeding resident. Most common gull on the Olympic Peninsula.

CASPIAN TERN
(*Sterna caspia*)

Description. Large tern, up to 22 inches. White underparts, pale gray back. Thick red bill, black cap, forked tail.
Distribution. Coastal areas.
Remarks. Common summer breeder. Distinguished from other terns by its large size.

Alcids—Auks, Murres, Puffins

These small birds have short necks, short wings, short tails, and webbed feet. They are generally unable to walk on land and usually spend a lot of time at sea. There are eleven species of alcids reported for the Olympic Peninsula, but most are not likely to be seen, since they forage offshore.

COMMON MURRE
(Uria aalge)

Description. Duck-size black and white bird with long, thin bill. Head, throat, and upper part of body black, underparts white.
Distribution. Outer coast.
Remarks. Common year-round breeding resident. Nests on rocky islets and cliffs.

PIGEON GUILLEMOT
(Cepphus columba)

Description. Foot-long, black bird with red feet and white wing patch crossed by black bar.
Distribution. Ocean and rocky shores of outer coast.
Remarks. Common year-round breeding resident. Dives to bottom for food.

MARBLED MURRELET
(Brachyramphus marmoratus)

Description. Small, 9- to 10-inch brown bird with barred underparts during summer. More white on rump and flanks in winter.
Distribution. Coastal areas, but nests inland.
Remarks. Common year-round breeding resident. Often skips on the surface of water to get airborne. Tips forward when diving. Nests in old-growth forests. Becoming rare due to heavy timber cutting of old growth.

RHINOCEROS AUKLET
(Cerorhinca monocerata)

Description. Big head with heavy bill
and short neck. Brownish above, pale
gray-brown below. During breeding
season, has distinctive white plumes on
head and yellowish "horns" that grow
from bill, giving rise to its common name.
Distribution. Coastal seabird with largest
nesting colonies on Protection Island by
Sequim and Destruction Island off the
coast.
Remarks. Year-round resident, but most
abundant during the breeding season.
Nests in underground burrows.

TUFTED PUFFIN
(Fratercula cirrhata)

Description. Stocky body about 15 inches
long, nearly all black. White face, ivory-
colored ear tufts, large, orange-red bill.
Distribution. Rocky coastal areas.
Remarks. Year-round resident, but most
common in summer. Breeds offshore.
"Flies" underwater in pursuit of fish.

Pigeons and Doves

These are small-headed, plump, fast-flying birds that bob as they walk on the ground. There are three species of doves and pigeons resident year-round on the Olympic Peninsula, but only two are likely to be seen in the park.

BAND-TAILED PIGEON
(Columba fasciata)

Description. Resembles typical city pigeon, with broad, pale band across end of fanlike tail. Male is brown with pink-purple underparts and almost white abdomen.
Distribution. Forests, particularly those with some openings such as logged areas.
Remarks. Relatively uncommon year-round breeding resident. Higher numbers in summer. Strong, fast flier, often in flocks.

MOURNING DOVE
(Zenaida macroura)

Description. Buffy-gray body with brown head, long, white-edged tail, and long, pointed wings.
Distribution. Open woodlands, farmlands, and fields.
Remarks. Uncommon year-round residents. Musical *coo, coo, coo.*

Owls

Owls are nocturnal birds of prey that hunt primarily by sound. They have short necks and large, forward-facing eyes. Twelve species have been reported for the Olympic Peninsula, although only three—screech owl, pygmy owl, and saw-whet owl—are common.

WESTERN SCREECH OWL
(Otus kennicotti)

Description. Small, 7- to 10-inch reddish brown owl with ear tufts and yellow eyes.
Distribution. Coniferous forest.
Remarks. Common year-round breeding resident. Hunts in open areas but never far from trees.

GREAT HORNED OWL
(Bubo virginianus)

Description. Large owl, up to 2 feet, with ear tufts. Dark brown, heavily barred below, white throat, yellow eyes.
Distribution. Coniferous forest.
Remarks. Uncommon year-round, breeding resident. Voice a deep *hoo, hoo-oo, hoo.* Sometimes seen in daylight. Glides, but seldom soars.

NORTHERN PYGMY OWL
(Glaucidium gnoma)

Description. Very small, brown owl, lacking ear tufts. Neck has black eye patch on either side of head. Black streaks on whitish belly. Small, white dots around head and face. Tail long and barred.
Distribution. Coniferous forest.
Remarks. Common year-round, breeding resident. Very tame, easily approached. Often looks back with curious perky glance.

NORTHERN SPOTTED OWL
(Strix occidentalis)

Description. Medium size, up to 20 inches. Dark brown body with heavy white barring. Dark eyes.
Distribution. Old-growth forest.
Remarks. Year-round, breeding resident. The spotted owl is heading toward extinction due to the loss of old-growth forest habitat. The less than 100 spotted owl pairs left residing on the Olympic Peninsula may not be sufficient for a minimum viable population. Olympic spotted owls are now so isolated from other populations that local extinction is likely even if these owls persist elsewhere.

NORTHERN SAW-WHET OWL
(Aegolius acadicus)

Description. Small, 8-inch owl, reddish brown with brown and white streaks below. Whitish between the eyes and over nose. No ear tufts.
Distribution. Coniferous forest.
Remarks. Abundant year-round breeding resident. Very tame. In taking off, drops slightly.

COMMON BARN OWL
(Tyto alba)

Description. Heart-shaped, monkeylike face. Very long legs extending beyond the tail in flight. Size 14 to 20 inches. Pale overall, with a light brown back and white chest and belly.
Distribution. The edges of woodlands, common near barns and other buildings. A year-round resident of the Olympic Peninsula.
Remarks. The call is a discordant scream rather than the familiar *whoo, whoo, whoo* normally associated with owls.

Hummingbirds

These tiny birds with needlelike bills hover at flowers to sip nectar. There are just two species recorded for Olympic.

ANNA'S HUMMINGBIRD
(Calypte anna)

Description. Four-inch body. Green back with grayish underparts. Male has deep rose head and throat, female only hints of red.
Distribution. Shrubs and open landscapes.
Remarks. Uncommon year-round, breeding resident. Prefers nectar, a high-energy food necessary to maintain body temperature. Goes into torpor during colder weather.

RUFOUS HUMMINGBIRD
(Selasphorus rufus)

Description. Body 3½ inches long. Males has reddish brown body with white across chest, green crown, and iridescent orange-red throat. Female has green back, dull rufous on sides and base of tail; lacks the red throat.
Distribution. Forest and subalpine meadows and basins.
Remarks. Common summer breeder and migrant. Many migrating hummingbirds coming south from Alaska and elsewhere farther north concentrate on foraging for nectar among flowered subalpine basins.

Kingfisher

This short-legged, chunky bird with a crest and a large, stout bill is found near ponds and streams. Only one species of kingfisher is found in most of the United States.

BELTED KINGFISHER
(Ceryle alcyon)

Description. About a foot long. Slate blue with ragged crest on large head. White neck ring, chest, and belly with broad gray breast bands. Female also has rusty breast band.
Distribution. Near streams, ponds, and lakes.
Remarks. Common, year-round breeding resident. Hovers or rests in branch over stream or lake, then dives headfirst into water to capture fish.

Woodpeckers

Woodpeckers use their stout bills to chisel wood. They have stiff tail feathers, short legs, and strong claws. Nine woodpeckers are reported for the Olympic Peninsula, but only three are common.

RED-BREASTED SAPSUCKER
(Sphyrapicus ruber)

Description. Red head, breast, and neck. White wing patch, white rump with black back.
Distribution. Moist coniferous forests.
Remarks. Year-round, breeding resident. Feeds on ants attracted to sap from holes drilled in trees.

DOWNY WOODPECKER
(Picoides pubescens)

Description. Body 6 to 7 inches. Black body, white back, red on back of head. Two white patches on each side of head, one just behind eye. White outer tail feathers with a few black bars. Has smaller bill than hairy woodpecker.
Distribution. Riparian forests, mixed conifer forests.
Remarks. Common year-round, breeding resident.

HAIRY WOODPECKER
(Picoides villosus)

Description. Body 8 to 10 inches. Same coloration as downy woodpecker. Difficult to distinguish from downy other than larger size and longer, stouter bill.
Distribution. Coniferous forest.
Remarks. Common year-round, breeding resident. Diet 75 to 95 percent insects.

NORTHERN FLICKER
(Colaptes auratus)

Description. Up to a foot long. Brown-and-black barred back and wings, lighter belly with black spots, black throat patch, gray head with red mustache.
Distribution. Subalpine and lowland coniferous forests.
Remarks. Common year-round, breeding resident. Feeds primarily on ants. Often forages on ground.

PILEATED WOODPECKER
(Dryocopus pileatus)

Description. Crow-size black bird with pointed red crown, white stripes on face and down shoulder, white underwings visible in flight.
Distribution. Typically associated with old-growth coniferous forests.
Remarks. Uncommon year-round, breeding resident. Drills characteristic rectangular 2- to 4-inch holes in trees in pursuit of ants, its primary food source.

Flycatchers

Flycatchers have bristles around the base of the bill. Many of the species are difficult to distinguish from one another. Flycatchers sit on branches and swoop down to capture flying insects. Since they are dependent upon flying insects, not surprisingly, none of the nine species reported for the Olympic Peninsula are year-round residents.

WESTERN WOOD-PEWEE
(Contopus sordidulus)

Description. Body 6 inches, gray-brown above with olive-gray flanks and breast. Two narrow white wing bars.
Distribution. Low-elevation coniferous forest to subalpine forests.
Remarks. Common summer breeding resident.

HAMMOND'S FLYCATCHER
(*Empidonax hammondii*)

Description. Body 5 to 6 inches. Shorter tail than other flycatchers. Gray head and grayish olive sides, white eye ring, grayish white throat.
Distribution. Lowland coniferous and mixed deciduous-coniferous forests.
Remarks. Common summer resident. Nests in conifer forests.

Larks

Larks have musical voices and are generally a dull brown color with no differences between the sexes.

HORNED LARK
(*Eremophila alpestris*)

Description. Body size 7 to 8 inches. Overall brown color, but with black horns on head, black "whiskers" on face, and black breast spots, pale yellow flanks, and pale belly.
Distribution. Open fields, particularly in the subalpine and alpine terrain.
Remarks. A common breeding summer resident of the higher elevations. A few horned larks remain year-round on the Peninsula. Walks or runs instead of hopping on ground.

Swallows

Swallows are sparrow-size, streamlined birds with wide mouths and long, pointed wings. They spend most of their time in flight capturing insects on the wing. There are seven species of swallows, counting the purple martin, reported for the Olympic Peninsula. Four species are common. Due to their predominantly insect diet, none are year-round residents.

VIOLET-GREEN SWALLOW
(*Tachycineta thalassina*)

Description. Body 5 to 6 inches. Violet-green above, with clear white below extending up over eyes. White patches on rump.
Distribution. Usually near water, associated with fields and subalpine openings.
Remarks. Common summer breeding resident.

TREE SWALLOW
(*Iridoprocne bicolor*)

Description. Body size 5 to 6 inches. Green-blue above with white below.
Distribution. Near water, in open areas and fields, and around deciduous forests.
Remarks. Common summer breeding resident. A cavity nester, does well where there is an abundance of snags.

CLIFF SWALLOW
(*Petrochelidon pyrrhonota*)

Description. Upper parts blue except for white forehead, rusty throat, and rusty or buffy rump. Underparts white. Square tail.
Distribution. Near water by deciduous forest and farmlands. Nests on bridges and cliffs.
Remarks. Common summer breeding resident. Colonial nester building round, gourd-shaped nests.

BARN SWALLOW
(Hirundo rustica)

Description. Blue-black above, buffy underneath with rusty-red chin and throat. Deeply forked tail.
Distribution. Near water with open landscapes like farmland and fields.
Remarks. Common summer breeding resident. Often associated with houses, bridges, and other structures where it constructs mud nests under eaves.

Swifts

Swifts are fast-flying, insect-feeding birds with long, pointed wings bent close to the body. Two species are found in the park: the uncommon black swift and the more abundant Vaux's swift.

VAUX'S SWIFT
(Chaetura vauxi)

Description. Small, 4½-inch, grayish brown bird with pale white throat. Short, stubby tail, long, pointed wings.
Distribution. Coniferous forest up to timberline.
Remarks. Common summer breeder. Old-growth-dependent species. Nests in tree cavities. Cruises the treetops devouring insects.

Jays, Crows, and Ravens

These are medium to large, intelligent birds with pointed bills, rounded wings, and generally loud calls. Seven species have been reported for the Olympic Peninsula, but only four are common.

GRAY JAY
(Perisoreus canadensis)

Description. Body about a foot long. Gray overall, but darker on back. Dark cap. Throat, forehead, and collar white. Pale underparts.
Distribution. Low-elevation coniferous to subalpine forests.
Remarks. Common year-round, breeding resident. Very tame. Also called "camp robber" for its habit of invading picnic areas and campsites to pick up scraps.

STELLER'S JAY
(Cyanocitta stelleri)

Description. Body about a foot long. Dark blue color, almost bluish black on head. Crest on head.
Distribution. Coniferous forests.
Remarks. Common year-round, breeding resident. Has loud, shrieking call. Aggressive and will invade campgrounds for food scraps.

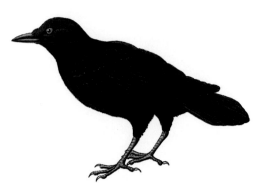

AMERICAN CROW
(Corvus brachyrhynchos)

Description. Body up to 18 inches. Entirely black. Stout black beak. Smaller bill than raven.
Distribution. Near the coast and water.
Remarks. Common year-round, breeding resident. Has familiar *caw, caw* vocalization.

RAVEN
(*Corvus corax*)

Description. Body 2 feet long. All-black bird with stout beak. Fan-shaped tail in flight distinguishes it from crow, which has square tail.
Distribution. Coastal and subalpine areas.
Remarks. Common year-round, breeding resident. Loud croak and other calls. Among the most intelligent of birds, has individualized calls for "friends."

Chickadees and Nuthatches

These are small, active birds with short bills. Seven species have been reported for the Peninsula, but only three are common.

CHESTNUT-BACKED CHICKADEE
(*Parus rufescens*)

Description. Body to 5 inches. Blackish brown cap and bib, rusty back and flanks, and white facial patch.
Distribution. Coniferous forest.
Remarks. Common year-round, breeding resident. Although the better-known black-capped chickadee is also found on the Peninsula, the chestnut-backed is by far the more common.

BLACK-CAPPED CHICKADEE
(*Parus atricapillus*)

Description. Solid black cap, white cheeks, black bib, gray back, and white below with pale tan wash on sides. Size 5 to 6 inches.
Distribution. Mixed forests and the edge of woodlands.
Remarks. Active little bird, flitting from shrub to shrub. Call is a cheerful *chickadee, dee, dee*.

RED-BREASTED NUTHATCH
(Sitta canadensis)

Description. Body less than 5 inches. Small, needlelike bill. Gray-blue back, rusty breast and flanks, black crown, black stripe through eye and white stripe just above it, white cheeks.
Distribution. Coniferous forest up to subalpine.
Remarks. Common year-round, breeding resident. Voice sounds like a tiny tin horn. Cavity nester.

BROWN CREEPER
(Certhia americana)

Description. Body up to 5 inches. Brown back with small white streaks, white underparts, white stripe just above eye. Stiff tail, braced when climbing.
Distribution. Coniferous and mixed forests.
Remarks. Common year-round, breeding resident. Spirals upward from base to top of tree, feeding on insects in bark.

Wrens

Wrens are small, chunky birds with slender bills. Their tails are often tipped at a jaunty angle. Five species are reported for the Olympic Peninsula, but only one is common.

WINTER WREN
(Troglodytes troglodytes)

Description. Body almost 5 inches. Stubby tail, brown body with barring on belly.
Distribution. Dense forests, among downfall, and dense riparian vegetation.
Remarks. Common year-round, breeding resident. Active little bird that aggressively defends territory. Song is melodious trill.

Dippers

These stocky birds are common along mountain streams. There is only one species in North America.

AMERICAN DIPPER
(*Cinclus mexicanus*)

Description. Body up to 8 inches. Gray-blue body with short tail and wings.
Distribution. Along fast mountain streams.
Remarks. Common year-round, breeding resident. Has musical, wrenlike trill. Walks underwater feeding on aquatic insects.

Kinglets

Kinglets are tiny, active birds with small, slender bills and short tails.

GOLDEN-CROWNED KINGLET
(*Regulus satrapa*)

Description. Body 4 inches. Plump little bird with grayish olive upper body and white underparts, two white wing bars, and white eye stripe. Male has orange-yellow crown patch and female has yellow.
Distribution. Coniferous forest.
Remarks. Common year-round, breeding resident.

RUBY-CROWNED KINGLET
(*Regulus calendula*)

Description. Body to 5 inches. Plump grayish olive bird with two white wing bars and white eye rings. Male has red crown patch, but it is seldom visible unless the bird is excited.
Distribution. Coniferous forest.
Remarks. Resident throughout the year. Breeds locally, but most common during fall, winter, and spring months when migrants gather.

Thrushes

Thrushes are familiar melodious songbirds generally of woodlands.

SWAINSON'S THRUSH
(*Catharus ustulatus*)

Description. Body to 7 inches. Gray-brown above with streaked buff cheeks and upper breast, white underparts, buffy eye ring.
Distribution. Moist woodlands and riparian vegetation.
Remarks. Common during the breeding season.

HERMIT THRUSH
(*Catharus guttatus*)

Description. Body to 7 inches. Brown above, brown-streaked breast, white belly, reddish tail, white eye ring.
Distribution. Moist riparian habitat, up to subalpine forests.
Remarks. Year-round resident, but greatest numbers during breeding season. Clear flutelike song.

AMERICAN ROBIN
(Turdus migratorius)

Description. Body to 10 inches. Gray-brown back, reddish belly, white near legs.
Distribution. Mixed woodlands.
Remarks. Common year-round, breeding resident. Lovely spring song.

VARIED THRUSH
(Ixoreus naevius)

Description. Body to 10 inches. Male back grayish blue, female brown. Underparts brown-orange with black band across breast in male, gray band in female. Both have orange eyebrows and wing bars.
Distribution. Old-growth coniferous forest up to subalpine.
Remarks. Common year-round, breeding resident. The haunting song of the varied thrush is a distinctive springtime feature of West Coast forests.

Pipits

Pipits are sparrow-size birds of open terrain.

AMERICAN PIPIT
(Anthus spinoletta)

Description. Body to 7 inches. Brown-gray back with faint streaking on breast. White outer feathers on tail. Pumps tail when walking.
Distribution. Strongly associated with the subalpine-alpine terrain in summer. Winters on coastal beaches.
Remarks. Resident throughout the year, but most common in summer.

Waxwings

All waxwings have yellow-tipped tails and plumed crests.

CEDAR WAXWING
(Bombycilla cedrorum)

Description. Body to 7 inches. Brownish crested head and upper back fading to gray with black margins on wings. Gray, yellow-tipped tail. Black eye stripe. The similar Bohemian waxwing seldom occurs in the Olympics.
Distribution. Riparian and shrubby habitat.
Remarks. Year-round resident, but more common during breeding season. Often seen in foraging flocks in the fall and winter.

Vireos and Warblers

These small songbirds forage among vegetation for insects. Vireos are generally a bit plumper than warblers. Four vireos have been reported for the Olympics, but only two are common. Thirteen warblers have been seen, with eight commonly observed.

HUTTON'S VIREO
(Vireo huttoni)

Description. Body 5 inches. Grayish brown back, pale gray underparts, two white wing bars, and a white eye ring that is broken above eye.
Distribution. Moist woodlands, coniferous and mixed hardwood-conifer forests.
Remarks. Year-round, breeding resident.

WARBLING VIREO
(Vireo gilvus)

Description. Body 5 to 6 inches. Grayish olive back, brownish wings and tail, pale yellow flanks, and whitish belly. Lacks wing bars. White eye stripe above eye and black line behind eye.
Distribution. Shrubs, deciduous woodlands, and riparian vegetation.
Remarks. Common summer resident and local breeder. Voice is melodious warbling song.

RED-EYED VIREO
(Vireo olivaceus)

Description. Black and white stripe over eye. Generally olive green overall with white underparts. No wing bars. Red eye is visible if close.
Distribution. Lowland mixed-conifer forests.
Remarks. A summer resident. Sings all day long and very late into summer.

ORANGE-CROWNED WARBLER
(Vermivora celata)

Description. Olive back and yellowish green underparts with pale rust-colored breast streaks. Lacks wing bars. Male has a faint orange crown.
Distribution. Shrubs, thickets, riparian areas.
Remarks. Year-round resident, but most common during the breeding season. Nests on the ground. Generally feeds low in branches.

YELLOW WARBLER
(Dendroica petechia)

Description. Body 5 inches. Yellow bird with olive back, wings, and tail. Rusty streaks on breast of male.
Distribution. Common in shrubby riparian-alder vegetation.
Remarks. Common nesting species in summer. Frequently flicks tail.

YELLOW-RUMPED WARBLER
(Dendroica coronata)

Description. Gray-black back and sides, white underparts, yellow throat, yellow patches on crown, sides, and rump.
Distribution. Coniferous forest up to subalpine.
Remarks. Year-round resident, but more common during the breeding season. The similar myrtle warbler now considered to be the same species.

BLACK-THROATED GRAY WARBLER
(Dendroica nigrescens)

Description. Gray-black back and wings, white underbelly, black head with two white stripes.
Distribution. Shrubs, riparian vegetation, woodlands.
Remarks. Common breeder in summer.

TOWNSEND'S WARBLER
(Dendroica townsendi)

Description. Dark crown, dark ear patch around eye, black throat, pale belly, yellowish breast with black streaks.
Distribution. Coniferous forests.
Remarks. Year-round, breeding resident. Tends to feed in tops of trees.

MACGILLIVRAY'S WARBLER
(Oporornis tolmiei)

Description. Grayish olive back, wings, and tail. Male has bluish gray head and bib with black on lower part of throat and upper breast. Belly yellow. Female head is lighter gray with no black on breast or throat.
Distribution. Dense shrubs and thickets.
Remarks. Common summer breeder. Nests on ground.

COMMON YELLOWTHROAT
(Geothlypis trichas)

Description. Body up to 6 inches. Olive-brown crown, back, wings, and tail, yellow throat and flank, white belly. Male has black mask on face.
Distribution. Streamside thickets.
Remarks. Common summer breeding resident. Voice distinctive *witch-ity, witch-ity.*

WILSON'S WARBLER
(Wilsonia pusilla)

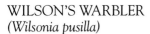

Description. Body 5 inches. Bright yellow underparts, olive-brown back. Male has black cap.
Distribution. Woodland thickets along streams.
Remarks. Common summer breeding resident. Nests on the ground amid brush.

Tanagers

Tanagers are thick-billed birds that feed on insects and berries. Males are often brightly colored.

WESTERN TANAGER
(*Piranga ludoviciana*)

Description. Body 6 to 7 inches. Male is yellow with red head and black back, wings, and tail. White wing bars and yellow shoulder bars. Female yellowish below, olive above; lacks red head.
Distribution. Coniferous forests.
Remarks. Common summer breeding species. Tame around people.

Towhees

Towhees are thick-billed birds that scratch the ground in search of food.

RUFOUS-SIDED TOWHEE
(*Pipilo erythrophthalmus*)

Description. Head and back black in male, brown in female. Both have rufous flanks, white belly, and white-tipped outer tail feathers.
Distribution. Streamside thickets, open woodlands.
Remarks. Common year-round, breeding resident. Often scratches the ground with both feet, looking for grubs and other insects.

Sparrows and Juncos

This is a large group of small to medium-size birds with conical bills. Most species are difficult to distinguish by casual observation. There are fourteen sparrow and junco species listed for the Olympic Peninsula, but only five are common.

SAVANNAH SPARROW
(Passerculus sandwichensis)

Description. Olive-brown back streaked with black, black-spotted chest, white underparts, pink legs and feet.
Distribution. Open country such as marsh, field, beach.
Remarks. Year-round, breeding resident, but more common in summer. Hops, rarely walks.

FOX SPARROW
(Passerella iliaca)

Description. Dark brown back, head, wings, and tail. Whitish underparts with black dots, large central breast spot.
Distribution. Dense undergrowth in coniferous forests.
Remarks. Common year-round, breeding resident. Highly variable, with many subspecies. The Pacific Northwest form is the darkest of all.

SONG SPARROW
(Melospiza melodia)

Description. Reddish brown back, wings, and tail. Streaked whitish breast with prominent black spot, long, rounded tail. White throat with broad dark stripes, grayish eyebrow.
Distribution. Streamside thickets.
Remarks. Common year-round, breeding resident. Pumps tail up and down when flying.

WHITE-CROWNED SPARROW
(*Zonotrichia leucophrys*)

Description. Body to 7 inches. White crown bordered by black stripe, then white stripe, and black again. Brown back, wings, and tail, pale underparts, whitish throat.
Distribution. Open woodlands, tundra.
Remarks. Year-round, breeding resident. Most common in summer.

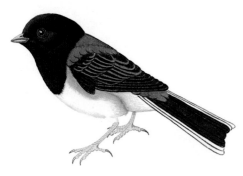

DARK-EYED JUNCO
(*Junco hyemalis*)

Description. Brown back, gray rump, rusty brown sides, white belly. Male has black head, female dark brown. White outer tail feathers visible in flight.
Distribution. Coniferous forest to subalpine.
Remarks. Common year-round, breeding resident. Often sings in winter.

Blackbirds

Blackbirds are medium-size birds with sharp-pointed, conical bills.

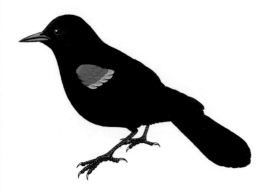

RED-WINGED BLACKBIRD
(*Agelaius phoeniceus*)

Description. Male has jet black body, red shoulder bordered by yellow. Female is dark brown with heavily streaked breast.
Distribution. Near water, particularly with cattails and reeds.
Remarks. Common year-round, breeding resident. Dominant males with better territories will often mate with two or three females.

BREWER'S BLACKBIRD
(Euphagus cyanocephalus)

Description. Body about 9 inches. Male has black body with purplish gloss, whitish yellow eyes. Female dark brownish gray with dark eyes.
Distribution. Open habitat, particularly near fields.
Remarks. Common year-round, breeding resident. Often forms huge flocks.

Finches

Finches are seedeaters with an undulating flight.

PINE SISKIN
(Carduelis pinus)

Description. Body to 5 inches. Brown-streaked body with yellow wing marks visible in flight. Yellow at base of tail.
Distribution. Coniferous forest.
Remarks. Common year-round, breeding resident. Often forms large flocks in winter.

PURPLE FINCH
(Carpodacus purpureus)

Description. Body is not purple, despite name. Rose red over most of male body, back streaked with brown, pale white belly, wings brownish. Female heavily streaked brown bird with pale, streaked underparts. Notched tail. Stout bill.
Distribution. Coniferous forest, open woodlands.
Remarks. Common year-round, breeding resident.

HOUSE FINCH
(Carpodacus mexicanus)

Description. Male has brownish back and cap with reddish forehead and bright red breast. Streaking on pale flanks and belly. Female is brown and streaked over back and breast. Tail only slightly notched; squarer than that of purple finch.
Distribution. Open habitat and shrubs.
Remarks. Common year-round, breeding resident.

RED CROSSBILL
(Loxia curvirostra)

Description. Male dull red with brown wings. Female yellow-brown. Distinctive feature is crossed bill. Notched short tail.
Distribution. Coniferous forests.
Remarks. Uncommon, but year-round, breeding resident. Uses its crossed bill to extract pine seeds from cones.

AMERICAN GOLDFINCH
(Carduelis tristis)

Description. Breeding male is bright yellow with black cap, wings, and tail and white rump. Female duller with light greenish brown above and pale underparts.
Distribution. Weedy fields, roadsides.
Remarks. Year-round resident, but most common during summer breeding season and afterward when foraging flocks are formed.

MAMMALS

Mammals are warm-blooded animals that bear young alive (with the exception of the duck-billed platypus) and have fur that provides insulation. Warm-bloodedness was a major evolutionary step forward, since it permitted activity during cooler weather, allowing the exploitation of habitats not available to cold-blooded animals, such as the Arctic and higher mountains, as well as year-round activity in colder climates.

Because mammals are warm-blooded and able to tolerate cooler temperatures, many species are more active at night. This is one reason why the mammals of Olympic National Park, though abundant, are seldom seen by visitors.

Since Olympic National Park has both a mountain and a forest component, plus a marine environment, the diversity of mammal life within the park is much greater than in most other parks.

Species Accounts

The following species are known to occur in Olympic National Park or adjacent lands. Included are brief descriptions of each species, giving key identification marks; notes on their general distribution in the park; and remarks about their behavior or status, or otherwise interesting information. Marine mammals are discussed in the chapter on the coastal realm.

Shrews

Shrews are small, mouselike animals, typically with very pointed snouts and small eyes and ears. They can also be distinguished from mice by the canine nature of their upper incisor teeth. They are largely insectivores, feeding on insects and other invertebrates. They are, however, fierce predators and will take larger animals like salamanders or earthworms. In many species, the life of adults is very short—most species live no more than a year and a half. After breeding and the young are weaned, most of the adults die, and almost the entire population consists of juveniles. They live hidden beneath the forest litter, spending most of their life searching for food. Shrews have a very high metabolic rate and must eat every two to three hours to maintain their body temperature. As a consequence, they must consume their own weight in prey every day or they will starve.

MASKED SHREW
(Sorex cinereus)

Description. Pointed snout. Fur velvety with light tan belly and sides, gray to brown back, and bicolor tail. Total length 5 inches with tail.
Distribution. Humid forested habitat from coast to mountains.
Remarks. One of the smallest of shrews. Eats insects, snails, earthworms, and other invertebrates.

WANDERING SHREW
(Sorex vagrans)

Description. Small size, 4.5 inches total, with tail about 1.5 inches long. Strikingly different summer and winter fur color. Summer is gray-brown with pale grayish wash to undersides. Winter sooty, almost black.
Distribution. Widely distributed, under logs and in dense vegetation in forested habitats, as well as in wet prairies and meadows from sea level to the subalpine.
Remarks. Species name vagrans refers to wandering habit. Eats earthworms, insects, and other invertebrates.

TROWBRIDGE'S SHREW
(Sorex trowbridgii)

Description. Overall length 5 inches or so, half of which is tail. Pointed snout. Sooty gray color, only slightly lighter on the belly. Distinctive white-tan feet. Sharply bicolored tail brown above, white below.
Distribution. Forest dweller. Found in a wide variety of habitats, generally at lower elevations, although found into the subalpine zone. Forest floor litter, under logs, and other cover, often far from water. More common than other shrews in drier forests, particularly Douglas fir–rhododendron areas.
Remarks. Eats insects and other invertebrates but also consumes conifer seeds. It was named for W. P. Trowbridge, who collected the first specimen near Astoria, Oregon, in 1855.

NORTHERN WATER SHREW
(Sorex palustris)

Description. A large black or dark brown shrew often with paler undersides. Tail bicolored, dark above, light below. Feet whitish, conspicuously fringed with stiff hairs.
Distribution. Seldom found more than 3 feet from water. Generally along streams, lakes, wetlands at higher elevations.
Remarks. The water shrew has a silver-colored bubble of air it traps in its fur to provide buoyancy while swimming. It uses its sense of feel and large whiskers to find prey.

DUSKY SHREW
(Sorex monticolus)

Description. Difficult to distinguish from other shrews. Dull brown above, underparts pale whitish. Tail slightly bicolored.
Distribution. Primarily associated with streams and wet meadows in forested zones at higher elevations.
Remarks. Sometimes called montane shrew because of its preference for higher-elevation habitat.

PACIFIC WATER SHREW
(Sorex bendirii)

Description. Dark brown or black above, with only slightly lighter belly and sides. Tail unicolored. Largest of the shrews, often more than 6 inches in length.
Distribution. Near streams, in swamps, marshes, wet areas at lower elevations, and along the coast.
Remarks. Stiff hairs on hind feet used for swimming distinguish this shrew from all others except northern water shrew. Water shrews dive into streams to hunt for aquatic insects such as dragonfly nymphs, mayflies, and stoneflies.

Moles

Moles are small, compact burrowing animals with outwardly turned feet that act as scoops for digging. (This feature is less pronounced in the shrew mole.) Since they spend all their time underground, their eyes and ears have become almost nonfunctional. All moles have pointed snouts and essentially no neck. Their fur is very soft, and they can move forward and backward with equal ease—a real advantage in the underground world they inhabit. One sign of mole presence is the snaking piles of dirt lying on the surface of the ground when the snow melts. Moles eat earthworms, insects, and some roots.

TOWNSEND'S MOLE
(*Scapanus townsendii*)

Description. Compact body, 6 to 7 inches long. Short, rounded tail 1 to 2 inches long. Flat, broad, pale front feet. Minute eyes and long, tapering naked pink snout. Metallic luster to velvety smooth, dark brown-black fur.
Distribution. Damp, easily worked soils in fields, meadows, coastal prairie, and, to a lesser extent, forest environments.
Remarks. There is a variety of Townsend's mole found only on the Olympic Peninsula: *Scapanus townsendii olympicus*.

SHREW MOLE
(*Neurotrichus gibbsii*)

Description. Smallest mole in North America. Total length about 5 inches, including a 1.5-inch tail. Often mistaken for a shrew. Unlike other moles, feet longer than broad. Fur iridescent gray to black. Tail scaly with bristlelike hairs.
Distribution. Lower-elevation humid forests in coastal areas.
Remarks. Unlike other moles, the shrew mole does not create a burrow system but makes shallow, loose tunnels under logs and near the surface of loose soil thatched with decaying vegetation. Unlike other moles, may forage above ground in daylight. Able to swim well.

COAST MOLE
(*Scapanus orarius*)

Description. Smaller than Townsend's mole, less than 5.5 inches. Fur brownish black. Tail and snout nearly naked. Front paw as broad as that of Townsend's mole, but claws more slender.
Distribution. Primarily a forest dweller but reported in a wide array of habitats, from meadow to forest.
Remarks. Owls are among the coast mole's biggest predators, even though they almost never leave their subterranean burrows.

Bats

Bats are small animals that resemble mice with wings. They are the only mammal that can truly fly (other animals, such as flying squirrels, glide). Bats are nocturnal and evolved to take advantage of a vacant niche, the air space occupied by birds in the daytime. Most bats in North America are insectivores, but in other parts of the world, they also eat fruit, nectar, and even fish. Like birds, bats have wings. Bats' wings are thin membranes of skin stretched between four greatly elongated "fingers" on each arm and the hind legs. The sternum is keeled like those of birds to accommodate the large flight muscles.

Although bats have good eyesight—the old cliché "blind as a bat" is inaccurate—they do rely upon an extraordinary sense of hearing and echolocation (locating invisible objects by means of reflected sound waves) to catch prey and avoid obstacles in the dark. So acute is their echolocation ability that in laboratory studies, bats have demonstrated an ability to distinguish between real and fake insects. Depending on hunting styles and prey, bats differ in ear size and the kinds of sonar signals emitted. Fast-flying bats, such as hoary bats, emit loud, high frequencies and have small ears. The western big-eared bat, which locates nonmoving insects on leaves, has very large ears and emits a faint, soft signal.

Although most people associate bats with caves, many species crawl under the rough bark found on large trees or roost inside hollow snags. Old-growth forests are important not only for spotted owls, but also for bats.

LITTLE BROWN MYOTIS
(*Myotis lucifugus*)

Description. Smallish bat. Fur glossy, yellowish brown to dark brown on back, undersides paler. Ears moderate size; when laid forward, almost touch nostrils.
Distribution. Forested habitat.
Remarks. One of the most common bats. Often roosts under tree bark and in snags.

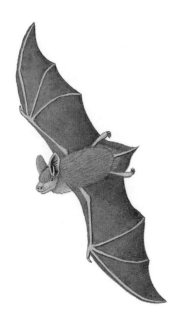

YUMA MYOTIS
(Myotis yumanensis)

Description. Fur dark brown to brown on back, fading to pale tan on belly. When laid forward, ears reach nostrils. It is difficult to distinguish Yuma bats from little brown bats in the field.
Distribution. Open areas, particularly around streams, lakes, and other water bodies, from sea level to subalpine.
Remarks. The Yuma bat was named for the capture site of the first specimen, at old Fort Yuma along the Colorado River by Yuma, Arizona.

KEEN MYOTIS
(Myotis keenii)

Description. Small. Ears long; when laid forward, extend beyond end of nose. Fur long and silky, dark brown.
Distribution. Prefers humid forests.
Remarks. Usually flies late at night.

LONG-EARED MYOTIS
(Myotis evotis)

Description. Ears blackish and large. When laid forward, extend 0.2 inch beyond nose. Upper parts light brown to brown, ears conspicuously darker.
Distribution. Not common. Coniferous forests.
Remarks. Prefers to roost under slabs of bark on old trees.

CALIFORNIA MYOTIS
(Myotis californicus)

Description. Small bat in western Washington, with the smallest feet. Fur reddish brown, with bases of hairs much darker than the tips. Ears and wings dark brown.
Distribution. Found in a wide variety of habitats, from coast to subalpine.
Remarks. Flight is erratic, with abrupt changes in direction.

LONG-LEGGED MYOTIS
(Myotis volans)

Description. Largest of smaller bats. Dark brown fur. Only brown bat with belly hair extending onto wings. Ears shorter than those of other bats.
Distribution. Forested habitat.
Remarks. Forages early, well before dark.

WESTERN BIG-EARED BAT
(Plecotus townsendii)

Description. Enormous ears, more than 1 inch long. Medium-sized bat, 4 inches long. Dull, longish fur, brown to black on back, paler undersides. Two prominent lumps on either side of nose.
Distribution. Prefers drier habitat than other bats, and roosts in caves.
Remarks. A high-flying bat, seldom near ground when foraging.

Rabbits and Hares

Unlike young rabbits, which are naked at birth, baby hares are fully furred, with eyes open and the ability to run. Also, hares do not dig burrows like rabbits, but hide among vegetation. There is only one member of the rabbit and hare family in the Olympics—the snowshoe hare, which exhibits periodic population cycles of nine to ten years.

SNOWSHOE HARE
(Lepus americanus)

Description. A medium-size hare with short ears and huge feet. Over most of its range, snowshoe hares are brown in summer and white in winter, but those found along the coast of Washington remain brown year-round.

Distribution. Throughout the Olympic Peninsula, from coastal forest to subalpine.

Remarks. Has a variety of vocalizations and communications, including a chirp, a birdlike warble, and a distress cry, and will thump the ground with foot.

Mountain Beavers

The mountain beaver is not related to beavers at all. This compact, medium-size rodent is the sole survivor of a line of very primitive rodents.

MOUNTAIN BEAVER
(Aplodontia rufa)

Description. Rabbit-size rodent, about a foot long. Dark brown fur with white spot by each ear. Small eyes and ears. Almost no tail.

Distribution. Creekside thickets, dense forest.

Remarks. Burrowing rodents with extensive burrow system close to surface. Ferns are the most important food. Mountain beavers produce two kinds of fecal pellets. Soft pellets are reingested as soon as they are expelled. This secondary digestion allows for maximum nutrient intake.

Tree Squirrels

Tree squirrels are primarily arboreal but are also found on the ground. They do not hibernate. There are two species found in Olympic National Park.

DOUGLAS SQUIRREL
(*Tamiasciurus douglasii*)

Description. Head and body up to 7 inches, with 5-inch tail. Upper body grayish brown, usually with rusty brown sides. Black line along sides in summer. Bushy tail.
Distribution. Coniferous forests.
Remarks. Active in daytime. Only squirrel likely to be seen. Sometimes known as chickaree. Vociferous and noisy, especially over territorial disputes. Call is loud *chirrr*.

NORTHERN FLYING SQUIRREL
(*Glaucomys sabrinus*)

Description. Broad folds of skin between front and back legs form "wings." Grayish with brownish wash. Large, dark eyes. Broad, flat tail.
Distribution. Old-growth coniferous forests.
Remarks. Flying squirrels do not truly fly but glide. They climb to an elevated point, then jump, spreading their legs, which opens out the flaps of skin to create "wings." These squirrels nest in hollow snags. They are strictly nocturnal, thus are seldom seen, even where abundant. Fungi are an important summer and fall food. These squirrels are a primary prey of northern spotted owls.

Chipmunks

Chipmunks are small, active rodents with striped bodies. They have internal cheek pouches to carry food. Chipmunks spend most of their time on the ground but are good climbers. They live in underground burrows.

TOWNSEND'S CHIPMUNK
(Tamias townsendii)

Description. Size 5 to 6 inches. Can be distinguished by wide, longitudinal dark and light stripes on head and back, with brownish background. White patch of fur on back of each ear. Tail white edged.
Distribution. Forested areas, but particularly along streams.
Remarks. Shy and seldom seen. Birdlike call.

OLYMPIC CHIPMUNK
(Tamias amoenus caurinus)

Description. Inner white stripes more conspicuous than outer white stripe. Rusty-yellow sides. Tail buffy edged.
Distribution. Prefers drier forests on eastern side of Olympics.
Remarks. This is the Olympic version of the yellow pine chipmunk, a species common in ponderosa pine and other forests in the western United States.

Beavers

Beavers are among the largest rodents in North America, with a stocky dark body, broad tail, and webbed feet.

BEAVER
(Castor canadensis)

Description. Stocky body, dark, almost black-brown fur. Webbed feet and dorsally flattened tail.
Distribution. Along streams and rivers.
Remarks. Can remain submerged for up to fifteen minutes. Builds dams by cutting riparian trees such as alder to back up flowing water to create ponds for its stick-and-mud lodges, which have underwater entrances. Beavers along bigger rivers live in bank burrows. Beaver ponds eventually fill in and are responsible for the creation of wet meadows.

Muskrats

The muskrat is the largest member of the vole family and is at home in aquatic environments.

MUSKRAT
(Ondatra zibethica)

Description. Body 8 to 14 inches, tail 8 to 10 inches. Grayish to brownish, with silver underparts. Vertically flattened tail scaly, black, and naked.
Distribution. In slow-moving, reed-filled ponds or streams.
Remarks. Builds conical mound of mud and vegetation that looks something like a beaver lodge.

The Olympic marmot, one of six species found in North America, is endemic to the Olympic Mountains. Marmots are active only in the summer months, hibernating the remaining seven to eight months of the year, when deep snow covers the high country where they reside.

Marmots

Marmots are members of the groundhog family. They are burrowing animals found in the alpine and subalpine.

OLYMPIC MARMOT
(Marmota olympus)

Description. Head and body 18 to 21 inches. Furry tail. Brownish color. Brown feet.
Distribution. Restricted to subalpine meadows and rockslides of Olympic Mountains.
Remarks. The Olympic marmot is endemic to the Olympic Mountains and is the only marmot found there. Marmots live in colonies and give shrill alarm whistles when frightened.

Porcupines

Porcupines are dark-colored, slow-moving rodents covered with quills.

PORCUPINE
(Erethizon dorsatum)

Description. Head and body 18 to 22 inches. Tail 8 to 9 inches. Compact, stocky body with short legs. Light tan to dark brown. Covered with sharp quills, or spines.
Distribution. Forests. Relatively rare in the park.
Remarks. Porcupines are slow and seemingly dim-witted. They eat the bark off trees and climb readily.

Pocket Gophers

Pocket gophers are small animals with external cheek pouches that open on either side of the mouth. Large, yellowish incisors are always exposed at the front of the mouth. Front claws are large and curved for digging.

NORTHERN POCKET GOPHER
(Thomomys talpoides)

Description. Head and body 6.5 inches. Tail 1 to 3 inches. Gray-brown with black patches behind ears.
Distribution. Rare. Deep soils, usually in meadows, particularly near streams.
Remarks. Pocket gophers are active all winter under the snow. When the snow melts in summer, the dirt of their casings remains on the ground's surface.

Deer Mice

There are a number of deer mouse species in the Pacific Northwest, but only one on the Olympic Peninsula. Deer mice are easy to distinguish from other mice by their large ears and long tails.

DEER MOUSE
(Peromyscus maniculatus)

Description. Head and body 3 to 4 inches. Tail 2 to 5 inches. Gray-brown above, white below. White feet. Bicolored tail, usually less than 90 percent of head and body length.
Distribution. Forests, meadows, at all elevations.
Remarks. Deer mice are among the most abundant and widespread mice in North America, ranging from Alaska to Mexico.

Wood Rats

BUSHY TAILED WOOD RAT
(Neotoma cinerea)

Description. Looks like a giant mouse with a bushy, squirrel-like tail. Head and body 8 to 9.5 inches, tail 5 to 7.5 inches. Body gray to black above, white feet.
Distribution. Rocky outcrops, rockslides, in mountains.
Remarks. Also known as pack rat for habit of randomly collecting materials from surrounding area and storing them under rock ledges and in crevices. Wood rats may use the same caches for generations, and such collections have been used to determine past vegetation and climate.

Voles

Voles are little, mouselike creatures strongly associated with grass and meadows. Their runways are sometimes visible in grass. They have small, beadlike eyes.

RED-BACKED VOLE
(*Clethrionomys gapperi*)

Description. Head and body 3.5 to 4.5 inches. Tail 1.5 to 2 inches. Distinctive red back with gray sides.
Distribution. Cool, moist forests, common among decaying litter and under logs.
Remarks. Plays critical role in forest ecosystems by dispersing fungi spore in its feces.

HEATHER VOLE
(*Phenacomys intermedius*)

Description. Head and body 3.5 to 4.5 inches; tail 1 to 1.5 inches. Body grayish with a wash of brown, silvery underbelly. White feet. Short ears.
Distribution. Grassy-heather habitat in mountains, rocky slopes.
Remarks. This vole does not make its own runways, but uses runways made by other mice and voles.

TOWNSEND VOLE
(*Microtus townsendii*)

Description. Body and head 5 to 6.5 inches. Tail 2 to 3 inches. Large, dark brown vole with gray belly. Tail dark brown to black. Ears large enough to protrude over fur.
Distribution. Tidal flats, moist meadows from coast to alpine.
Remarks. Species named for J. K. Townsend, a naturalist at Fort Vancouver, Washington, who collected the first specimen in 1835. Good swimmers; will swim across small streams.

LONG-TAILED VOLE
(*Microtus longicaudus*)

Description. Head and body 4.5 to 5.5 inches. Tail 2 to 3.5 inches. Large vole with long, bicolor tail. Dark gray tinged with brown.
Distribution. Primarily streamsides and mountain meadows.
Remarks. Species name from the Latin *longus*, meaning "long," and *cauda*, "tail."

OREGON VOLE
(*Microtus oregoni*)

Description. Head and body 4 to 4.5 inches. Bicolored tail 1.5 inches. Ears almost hidden in fur. Brown back and silver belly.
Distribution. Meadows and forests, particularly low-elevation riparian areas.
Remarks. Prefers protective cover; seldom ventures into the open.

Jumping Mice

These are small to medium-size mice with large hind feet and long tails. They can leap up to 6 feet. They hibernate in winter.

PACIFIC JUMPING MOUSE
(*Zapus trinotatus*)

Description. Head and body to 4 inches. Tail up to 6 inches. Generally tannish on back and sides with white belly. Tail brown above and white beneath.
Distribution. Moist, grassy areas or riparian woodlands with ferns or grassy understory. Fairly well distributed at low elevations throughout park.
Remarks. Hind legs allow this mouse to leap up to 6 feet. Hibernates through the winter.

Dog Family

All members of the dog family are opportunistic hunters that travel widely, hoping to encounter prey. They capture prey by running it down, as opposed to stealth, as used by members of the cat family. In good habitat, both coyotes and wolves will assume a social structure and hunt in packs.

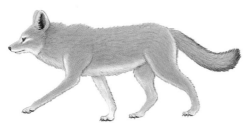

COYOTE
(Canis latrans)

Description. Doglike carnivore with bushy tail, sharp-pointed face, and sharp, prominent ears. Up to 52 inches long and 50 pounds, but most smaller. Fur generally grayish with pale underparts.
Distribution. All kinds of habitat, from alpine meadows to dense forest.
Remarks. Hunts mostly smaller rodents and birds, particularly voles. Is capable, however, of taking down a deer or even elk under some conditions, such as when prey is floundering in heavy snow.

WOLF
(Canis lupus)

Description. Large, doglike animal. Broader snout than coyote, shorter ears, shorter bushier tail. Long legs with broad paws. Black to gray to white.
Distribution. Extinct on Olympic Peninsula; last documented wolf killed in Elwha drainage in 1920.
Remarks. As early as 1935, biologist Olaus Murie was calling for the reintroduction of wolves on the Olympic Peninsula. A source for wolves exists on Vancouver Island, and there is increasing political discussion about reintroducing wolves into Olympic National Park. Reintroduction of wolves is important not only to reestablish a genetic line in the Pacific Northwest, but also because wolf predation exerts a major evolutionary force upon prey and consequently ecosystems.

RED FOX
(*Vulpes vulpes*)

Description. Slender, doglike animal up to 4 feet, including 18-inch tail. Sharp-pointed face and erect ears. Color is variable and not always red. Tail tipped in white.

Distribution. Edge and fringes of meadows and fields.

Remarks. Uncommon. Non-native to Olympic Peninsula. There is a native red fox found in the higher elevations of the Cascades, but all red foxes found at lower elevations, including those of the Olympic Peninsula, have been introduced from the East.

Bears

Bears have large, compact bodies, short tails, and powerful limbs. They have small eyes and round erect ears. Coat color varies from black to white. (A rare color morph on the British Columbia coast is nearly pure white.)

Bears are not true hibernators, since they do not reduce their body temperature significantly. Indeed, a hibernating bear can be rather easily awakened in its den.

There is only one species of bear on the Olympic Peninsula, the ubiquitous black bear. One of the oddities of the Olympic Peninsula is that grizzly bears never colonized the area.

BLACK BEAR
(*Ursus americanus*)

Description. Compact body, with short tail. Small, beady eyes, pointed snout, and erect ears. A big black bear can weigh more than 700 pounds, but most are considerably smaller, in the 200- to 300-pound range. Though most black bears are black, there are other color variations, including brown and reddish brown.

Distribution. Throughout the Olympic Mountains from lowlands to alpine.

Remarks. Black bears hibernate in hollow trees, old snags, and dens dug in the ground. The first big snowfall in autumn usually sends them into hibernation. But even those bears living on the mild coastal areas of the Olympic Peninsula enter a midwinter hibernation period of about three months.

Raccoons

Raccoons have plantigrade (flat) feet and ringed tails.

RACCOON
(*Procyon lotor*)

Description. Generally grayish brown, with black mask over eyes and complete black rings on a bushy tail. Weigh 10 to 15 pounds, sometimes up to 25 pounds.

Distribution. Along streams and waterways from sea level; Olympic coast to subalpine.

Remarks. Will den up in a hollow tree in colder weather, but does not hibernate. Omnivorous, eating everything from crabs and mussels along the shore to berries, insects, and bird eggs. Raccoons like to wash their food before eating.

Weasel Family

Weasel family members are slender carnivores, including minks, martens, fishers, weasels, skunks, and otters.

MARTEN
(Martes americana)

Description. Martens are 16 to 20 inches long, with an 8- to 9-inch round, bushy tail. Light to dark brown on top, with orangish throat patch. Prominent ears.
Distribution. Coniferous forests, particularly old-growth. Good tree climber.
Remarks. Feeds primarily on voles, squirrels, and other small mammals. Also consumes berries in season. Active all winter.

FISHER
(Martes pennanti)

Description. Cat-size animal that looks similar to marten but is larger, up to 36 inches, and has bushier tail. Dark chocolate brown to nearly black.
Distribution. Was found in mixed coniferous forests but is likely extinct in park.
Remarks. Thirty-seven fishers were trapped in the Queets Valley in 1920, and another twenty the following year in the Quinault Valley. One trapped in 1969 was the last documented occurrence of this animal in or near the park.

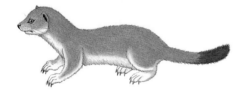

SHORT-TAILED WEASEL
(Mustela erminea)

Description. Thin, lithe 6- to 9-inch body with a 2- to 4-inch tail. Short legs. Blunt nose. Seasonal coat change from brown with white underparts in summer to white in winter. Black-tipped tail.
Distribution. Meadow borders, bushy riparian alder patches, and forests at all elevations.
Remarks. Also known as ermine. Weasels living at lower elevations remain brown year-round. Curious; will investigate people in its territory.

LONG-TAILED WEASEL
(Mustela frenata)

Description. Thin, lithe body up to 18 inches, including 5- to 6-inch tail. Summer pelage usually dark brown with yellow underparts. Turns white in winter at higher elevations. Black-tipped tail.
Distribution. Found in a wide variety of habitats, from sea level to mountaintops.
Remarks. Preys upon small rodents but will take prey up to rabbit size.

MINK
(Mustela vison)

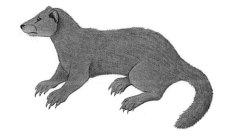

Description. Head and body up to 17 inches. Dark chocolate brown fur with white chin patch.
Distribution. Nearly always associated with rivers and streams.
Remarks. Preys on fish, frogs, and shellfish.

RIVER OTTER
(Lutra canadensis)

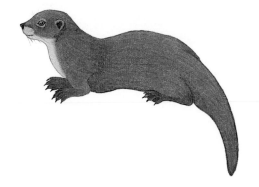

Description. Long, thin body about 4 feet, including thick, tapered 15- to 20-inch tail. Dark brown. Short legs with webbed feet. Head broad and rather flat, with very small ears and eyes.
Distribution. Rivers, lakes, and coastal estuaries.
Remarks. Otters living inland feed primarily on fish captured by pursuit. Those by the coast eat more crustaceans, such as crabs. Otters are at home in water but den on land. They will sometimes travel long distances from one water body to another and have been seen more than a mile from water.

SPOTTED SKUNK
(*Spilogale putorius*)

Description. Smallish body 15 to 16 inches long, with a bushy, 6-inch tail. Black with four white lines, a spot on head, and other irregular markings from head to tail.

Distribution. Thickets and heavy cover at lower elevations. Likes hollow logs, crevices, and abandoned buildings.

Remarks. The Olympic Peninsula represents the northwestern edge of this animal's range, which barely reaches into southwestern British Columbia. The spotted skunk can climb trees but prefers to forage on the ground. Feeds on bird eggs, earthworms, grubs, and anything else it can catch.

STRIPED SKUNK
(*Mephitis mephitis*)

Description. Cat-size, black-and-white animal 14 to 18 inches long, with a 7- to 10-inch tail. Two broad, white lines down back. Bushy tail. Well-developed scent glands.

Distribution. Brushy thickets and dense vegetation mixed with open areas like meadows and prairies, from coast to mountains. Dens in rocks and hollow logs.

Remarks. Along Puget Sound, the purple shore crab is one of the staples of the striped skunk's diet, but it will eat anything from insect grubs to bird eggs, wasps, and carrion.

Cat Family

The members of the cat family are among the most purely carnivorous animals in the West. They have specialized teeth designed for cutting and shearing meat. Members of the cat family hunt by stalking and pouncing. They seldom chase prey.

MOUNTAIN LION
(Felis concolor)

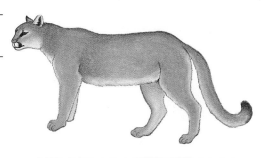

Description. Tawny, sand-colored cat up to 8 feet in length, including 30- to 35-inch black-tipped tail. Kittens spotted.
Distribution. Throughout the Peninsula, from coastal regions into subalpine.
Remarks. Preys mostly on deer and elk, but will take porcupines and other smaller prey on occasion. Also known as cougar or puma.

BOBCAT
(Lynx rufus)

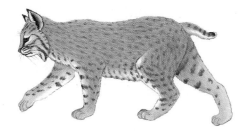

Description. Spotted cat with tufted ears and short, white-tipped tail. Weight 10 to 30 pounds.
Distribution. Found in all habitats, from coast to mountains.
Remarks. Preys on anything it can catch, from pocket gophers and mice to rabbits and birds. Has even been known to take down weakened deer.

Deer Family

There are two deer species on the Olympic Peninsula: the Roosevelt elk and black-tailed deer. In both species, only males have antlers. All deer are browsers and have no upper incisors. All have four-parted stomachs like a cow's and chew their cud. Both species are polygamous; dominant bull elk, in particular, form large harems in the autumn.

ROOSEVELT ELK
(Cervus elaphus roosevelti)

Description. Large, tawny-reddish animal weighing up to 800 pounds. Head and neck dark brown. Heart-shaped yellowish rump patch. Short mane on throat. Antlers on mature bulls are spreading and large, with numerous points, with 6 to 7 on one side being a large animal.
Distribution. Throughout the mountains, but more abundant in western valleys. Migrates from lowlands in winter areas to subalpine pastures in summer.
Remarks. Olympic National Park originally was set aside as a reserve to protect the relict populations of Roosevelt elk on the Peninsula.

BLACK-TAILED DEER
(Odocoileus hemionus columbianus)

Description. Males have branched antlers. Reddish in summer, grayish brown in winter. Black-tipped tail. Weight up to 250 pounds, but many, particularly females, quite a bit smaller.
Distribution. Throughout the park, from forests to meadows. Hurricane Ridge is usually a good place to see deer in summer.
Remarks. Good swimmers. Browse is main component of diet.

Named for president and conservationist Teddy Roosevelt, the Roosevelt elk is a coastal variety of the species that ranges from British Columbia to northern California. There are an estimated 5,000 to 6,000 elk ranging on the Olympic Peninsula.

Mountain Goats

Mountain goats are actually related to antelope. They live on steep slopes and are remarkably agile climbers. Their chief defense against predators is their ability to scale sheer cliffs. Both sexes have horns (as opposed to antlers, which are shed each year). Females with kids occupy the best habitat and staunchly defend it against all other goats, including males. Their sharp horns are lethal weapons, and female goats are able to discourage most other goats from advancing onto their territory. Avalanches and falling are two of the chief causes of mortality.

Mountain goats were never native to the Olympic Peninsula. Twelve mountain goats were introduced into the Olympic Mountains, beginning in 1924, and the population has grown to over 1,200. Native vegetation has suffered from this exotic herbivore population boom. The Park Service is currently attempting to remove goats from the park ecosystem.

MOUNTAIN GOAT
(Oreamnos americanus)

Description. Stocky, white animal with foot-long, pointed black horns in both sexes.

Distribution. Largely confined to high alpine areas in the east-central region of park.

Remarks. Mountain goats are not native to the Olympic Peninsula, but were introduced. They have done considerable damage to alpine flora. Attempts to remove them have been controversial, however.

THE FUTURE OF THE OLYMPICS

The Olympic Peninsula is a special place; there's no other place like it in the world. In general, it hasn't been treated well, particularly from an ecological perspective. There's no doubt that as a fiber farm it's exceptional, but as good as it is at growing trees for timber harvest, it is even better at growing salmon, spotted owls, Roosevelt elk, large trees, and old-growth forest ecosystems. There are many other, lesser-known ecosystem functions we are only beginning to appreciate. The future of the Olympic Peninsula lies in ecosystem restoration rather than continued resource extraction.

As I hope has been demonstrated by earlier chapters, logging has not been compatible with the protection of landscape values, nor has the dominance of the timber industry been good for the human communities of the Peninsula. Technology changes have led to declining employment in the wood-products industry. In addition, overharvest and export of raw logs overseas have led to a decline in jobs and jeopardize future employment. While timber jobs are in steep decline, employment based upon ecosystem restoration and human enterprises that are compatible with the nonconsumptive use of the landscape is on the rise. Not that an expanding human population both on the Peninsula and elsewhere doesn't pose some long-term problems for the landscape, but many of these issues are more easily addressed, and may have fewer long-term consequences, than the continued unraveling of the forest ecosystem.

As poorly as we have treated the Olympic Peninsula, partly through ignorance and partly through greed, the core of the Peninsula has been protected within Olympic National Park and represents a solid core zone that can aid the recovery of the rest of the landscape. A number of changes in land use and policy can effectively lead to a more complete Olympic landscape.

Fish Restoration

The first involves the restoration and recovery of native species. For instance, the deconstruction of dams on the Elwha River could lead to the restoration of one of the most important salmon streams on the entire Peninsula. Since most of the Elwha drainage lies within Olympic National Park and remains high-quality habitat, the Elwha could once again become a major salmon producer.

Lake Mills was created by construction of the Glines Dam on the Elwha River. The Elwha River is home to all five species of Pacific salmon, Dolly Varden trout, steelhead (a sea-run rainbow trout), and sea-run cutthroat trout. Glines Dam, along with the Elwha Dam a few miles downstream, effectively blocked access to spawning habitat for hundreds of thousands of salmon that once ran up the Elwha River and its major tributaries. Conservationists are calling for the removal of both the Grimes Canyon and Elwha Dams to permit restoration of salmon runs.

Other runs can also be nurtured back to life with programs designed to restore the forest habitat, which is so important to successful salmon and steelhead production. Greater reliance upon hatcheries is not the solution. Rather, long-term landscape restoration, including the production of large woody debris, reduction in sedimentation, and reduction in commercial fish harvest, is necessary to bring about the recovery of ailing fish stocks.

Not only could the restoration of salmon lead eventually to restored commercial fisheries and tremendous sport-fishing opportunities, but salmon have been shown to be critical to the life of the forest itself. Salmon are consumed by numerous species, from black bears to shrews. Nutrients from the dead fish enrich the aquatic ecosystem as well and are even taken up by the roots of trees. In a sense, the restoration of salmon is also about the restoration of the forest itself.

Wolf Restoration

Another species awaiting restoration is the gray wolf. These wolves were once native to the Peninsula, but the last ones were killed in the 1920s, in a federal government–sponsored nationwide wolf eradication program on behalf of the livestock industry, the same program responsible for the extirpation of wolves from Yellowstone and other national parks. At present there is much discussion about bringing wolves back to the Peninsula. If approved, wolf restoration could happen quickly. A likely source of wolves is Vancouver Island, where a subspecies of wolves similar to those that once resided on the Peninsula still roams. The Vancouver Island wolves prey upon the same species they would likely capture in Olympic National Park: Roosevelt elk and black-tailed deer.

Restoration of the wolf is as much about restoration of a major ecological process as it is about restoration of a species. The wolf is the consummate predator, and as such, it has shaped the evolution of many of the Peninsula's other wildlife, including both prey species like elk and other predators as well. It has been demonstrated elsewhere that the presence of wolves can reduce the number of medium-size predators, which feed on ground-nesting birds, duck eggs, and other smaller animals.

It would be incorrect to assume that wolves, if restored, would remain within the bounds of the park—nor should they. They are important to the ecological health of the entire landscape and will and should be permitted to roam throughout the Peninsula. Given the decline in rural

Wolves were extirpated from the Olympic Peninsula by 1920. Today there is a movement to restore the wolf to the Peninsula.

homesteads and livestock production on the Peninsula, there are potentially fewer conflicts with livestock producers than in the past. Though there's no doubt that wolves will at times reduce prey numbers, the greatest long-term threat to elk and deer is not predators, but the habitat loss represented by increased logging roads, loss of old-growth forests, and inappropriate rural development that may threaten wildlife migration corridors and habitat.

Fire-killed snags on Blue Mountain. Wildfire is a natural evolutionary force that greatly influences most western plant communities. Even in the wet Olympics, periodic fires occur.

Wildfire Restoration

Wildfire is a natural periodic disturbance of all forest ecosystems. Fire, along with windstorms, snowstorms, disease, insects, and other natural occurrences, is critical to the full functioning of native forests. On the wet western slope of the Olympics, fires burned across the landscape every 400 to 600 years. On the drier side of the mountains, they were more frequent, occurring every few hundred years.

The entire structure of the forest is dependent upon occasional disturbance from fire. The dead snags that result from a fire aren't a wasted resource. Snags are critical for many cavity-nesting birds, and ones that fall into a stream or lake provide long-term fishery habitat and nutrient cycling. Fires also cleanse forests of pathogens. Allowing fires to assume their natural ecological role will take some understanding, patience, and tolerance.

Restoring the Olympic Ecosystem

Environmentalists have had to expend a lot of energy just to hold on to the Olympic forests within the park and protect the coast from development. But now is the time to think about a proactive program to reclaim and restore the entire Olympic Peninsula. This would include buying up much of the private timberland and combining it with existing state lands on the western edge of the park to reconnect the coastal strip with the mountains. On the eastern side of the Peninsula, existing Forest Service land could be removed from timber production and the roads closed. A similar restoration program to bring wildlands down nearly to Hood Canal should also be explored. Forest restoration, along with the reintroduction of the wolf, elimination of dams on the Elwha River, and restoration of salmon runs, would gradually bring about the ecological restoration of the entire Olympic Peninsula.

The original plans for protecting the Olympic Peninsula called for the inclusion of the entire forested lowland, from the ocean to the highest peaks. These plans were never realized as timber corporations and their supporters in Congress worked to remove all the best timber-producing lands from park protection. Timber companies now control 915,000 acres on the Peninsula. The state of Washington owns another 364,700 acres, and the Forest Service lands amount to 632,324 acres. Taken together, these lands offer a tremendous opportunity for ecosystem recovery and completion.

It's not entirely clear whether the limited amount of old growth currently existing in Olympic National Park is sufficient to ensure the long-term viability of the remaining populations of many species now isolated in small, fragmented islands of old-growth habitat on the Peninsula. It is critical that the areas of old-growth habitat be enlarged and expanded. Only acquisition and protection of the lands and restoration of natural forest processes can ensure that this will occur.

The best places for private-land acquisition lie between the Queets and Bogachiel drainages. These lands form a critical link between the ocean and park border, and they are, biologically speaking, the best forest-growing sites. These lands will likely acquire old-growth characteristics in a few hundred years.

Most of the nonpublic lands are held by corporations, which makes acquisition of large parcels possible. These lands, along with the large state holdings in Washington's Clearwater State Forest, could easily be combined and added to Olympic National Park to recreate a sea-to-mountains park as originally envisioned by early preservationists.

Some timberland holders would likely be willing to sell their lands for an appropriate price, especially since many of them are heavily cut and not currently valuable for timber production. But even if they were not all willing sellers, there is no reason the federal government couldn't use eminent domain to acquire critical pieces. After all, we have no qualms about using eminent domain to obtain lands we deem necessary for highways, dams, and other public projects. Why shouldn't we use eminent domain on behalf of nature and the public good that an intact sea-to-mountains ecosystem would eventually provide?

The creation of Olympic National Park is only a halfway solution to the preservation of the Olympic Peninsula ecosystems. It was a good first step, but it doesn't go far enough to ensure the long-term preservation of ecosystem processes, native species, and even the elk herds and old-growth forests it was originally set aside to preserve. To ensure the long-term viability of the Peninsula's forests and all its inhabitants, including the human population on the Peninsula, restoration is necessary. The future is in our hands.

RECREATION

Hiking

Nearly 600 miles of trails traverse Olympic National Park, ranging from short, easy loops to long, difficult hikes along high passes or rugged ocean beaches.

Wilderness use permits are required for all overnight stays in the back-country. There is a fee for backpacking and overnight camping in Olympic National Park, and from Memorial Day weekend through Labor Day weekend, some areas require reservations. Reservations may be made up to thirty days in advance by calling the park's Wilderness Information Center at (360) 452–0300. At other times of the year and for areas that do not require reservations, wilderness use permits are available at all ranger stations and the WIC, which is located just behind the park's visitors center in Port Angeles.

Winter Hiking

There are many challenges to winter hiking, not the least of which is the generally terrible weather. Be prepared. Streams can swell to far beyond their normal size. Wet snow and cold rain can easily lead to hypothermia. Some trails in the park are usually snowfree, including the Skokomish River Trail, Elwha River Trail, Humes Ranch–Rica Loop, Sol Duc River Trail, Ozette Loop, Hoh River Trail, North Fork Quinault Trail, and Duckabush River Trail.

Backpacker on the Bogachiel River Trail.

Hikers on the High Divide Trail with Olympic National Park's highest peak, Mount Olympus, beyond.

COASTAL HIKES

Area	Trail Name	Length (in miles)	Trailhead Access	Features
Kalaloch			U.S. 101	short beach trails
Mora-LaPush	Third Beach Trail	1.4	LaPush Road, 12 miles west of U.S. 101	sandy beach 1.4 miles from trailhead
	Second Beach Trail	0.8	LaPush Road, 14 miles west of U.S. 101	sandy beach 0.8 mile from trailhead with tidepools and views of sea stacks
	Rialto Beach Trail	1.5	Mora–Rialto Beach, 14 miles west of U.S. 101	view of the beach, James Island, and Cake Rock
	Cape Alava–Sand Point Loop	9.3	Ozette Ranger Station, at the end of Hoko Road	most heavily used of all backcountry areas; primarily boardwalk
North Coast Hike	Rialto Beach to Sand Point	15.5	End of paved Rialto Beach Road, 13 miles from U.S. 101	difficult hiking; eagles, shorebirds, harbor seals, and sea otters often seen; gray whales sometimes observed in March, April, and October
South Coast Hike	Oil City to Third Beach Trailhead	15.0	Oil City Road; 15 miles south of Forks on U.S. 101	difficult hiking on both coastal route and overland trails

NORTHERN OLYMPICS

Area	Trail Name	Length (in miles)	Trailhead Access	Features
Lake Crescent	Moments in Time Nature Trail	0.5	trail located between Olympic Park Institute and Lake Crescent Lodge	views of lake; old-growth forest and former homestead sites
	Marymere Falls	1.0	Lake Crescent	90-foot waterfall; trail leads through old-growth forest
	Mount Storm King Trail	1.7	Marymere Falls Trail	steep climb to point on ridge; good views of Lake Crescent
	Pyramid Peak Trail	3.5	north shore of Lake Crescent	summit 2,600 feet; WWII aircraft spotter station; views of Lake Crescent and Strait of Juan de Fuca
	Spruce Railroad Trail	4.0	connects the North Shore and Lyre River Trailheads	flat; adjacent to WWI Spruce Railway bed; excellent Lake Crescent views
	Sol Duc Trail	6.8	end of Sol Duc River Road	Sol Duc Falls 0.8 mile through dense forest; Sol Duc Falls–Lover's Lane loop (6 miles of trail) is rough and rocky
	Mink Lake Trail	2.5	Sol Duc Resort	1,400-foot climb through dense forest to lake; trout fishing available
	Ancient Groves Nature Trail	0.5	off Sol Duc Road	loop through old-growth forest connecting two roadside turnouts
Seven Lakes Basin–High Divide	Seven Lakes Basin–High Divide Loop	18.2	end of paved Sol Duc Hot Springs Road, 14 miles from U.S. 101	subalpine meadows with views of interior mountain from High Divide; subalpine meadows and lakes in Seven Lakes Basin; old-growth forests below 3,500 feet

HURRICANE RIDGE–ELWHA REGION

Trail Name	Length (in miles)	Trailhead Access	Features
Heart of the Forest Trail	2.0	Loop E of Heart of the Hills campground	lowland forest with dense vegetation
Hurricane Hill Trail	1.5	end of Hurricane Ridge Road	at top of hill are mountain peak vistas, views of Port Angeles and Strait of Juan de Fuca; wildflowers are numerous in early summer
Meadow Loop Trails	varies	Hurricane Ridge Visitor Center	subalpine environment; trail continues to Klahhane Ridge
Elwha West Lake Mills Trail	2.0	Lake Mills boat launch parking area	follows river in forest
Griff Creek Trail	2.8	Elwha Ranger Station	sections of steep switchbacks; overlook at 1.8 miles
Krause Bottom Trail	2.0	end of Whiskey Bend Road, south of Elwha Ranger Station	traverses wooded ridge above the Elwha River, then drops to Riverside Bench
Madison Falls Trail	0.1	startds at Sweet's Cedarville Resort	meadow and forest grove, follows Madison Creek, falls cascade 100 feet down basalt cliffs
Lake Angeles Trail	6.5	Heart o' the Hills Trailhead is off Hurricane Ridge Road, 4.8 miles from Olympic Park Visitor Center and Wilderness Information Center	rocky climb beyond lakes—footing can be uncertain; Lake Angeles offers view of the Rocky Klahhane Ridge, interior Olympics; several species of endemic plants found on ridge
Appleton Pass Trail	10.2	5.3 miles beyond the Elwha Ranger Station	Olympic Hot Springs 0.1 mile from Boulder Creek campground; views of Mount Olympus, Sol Duc–High Divide area, Boulder Creek beyond Oyster Lake
Elwha River Trail	28.4	end of unpaved Whiskey Bend Road, 4 miles south of U.S. 101 on the Olympic Hot Springs Road, just south of the Elwha Ranger Station	trail grade overall is gradual; Douglas fir–western hemlock forest; last 2.6 miles ascend steadily to Low Divide in a subalpine setting; rustic cabins; subalpine flowers and views at Low Divide

HURRICANE RIDGE–ELWHA REGION (Continued)

Trail Name	Length (in miles)	Trailhead Access	Features
Long Ridge–Dodger Point Trails	16.7	trail leaves Elwha River Trail 2.4 miles from trailhead	steep, long, steady climb, challenging route finding; 360-degree views of interior Olympics at Dodger Point Lookout
Rica Canyon–Humes Ranch Trail	18.2	Sol Duc Trailhead	makes loop from Elwha trail down steep grade to Elwha River and back; Goblin's Gates funnel churning waters of Elwha River into Rica Canyon; homesteads, deer, elk, occasional bears

HIKING THE RAIN SHADOW

Trail Name	Length (in miles)	Trailhead Access	Features
Grand Valley Trail	7.8	end of Obstruction Point Road: 8 miles from Hurricane Ridge parking lot, which is 17 miles from Pioneer Memorial Museum	extended alpine views along entire route; marmots, wildflowers, brook trout in Grand and Moose Lakes; subalpine
Cameron Creek Trail	13.3	Deer Park or the Lower Gray Wolf Trail	gradual climb through mixed forest until subalpine zone just below Cameron Basin; ascends to Cameron Pass, the highest trail pass in the park
Royal Creek Trail	7.2	Dungeness Trailhead along USFS road #2860, one hour from Sequim	begins in dry, open forest, ascends to subalpine zone with beautiful meadows
Upper Gray Wolf River Trail	19.2	USFS Gray Wolf Trailhead, Slab Camp Trailhead, or Three Forks Trailhead	gradual climb through old-growth forests and forest-fire regrowth; Alaska cedar abundant

HOOD CANAL COUNTRY

Trail Name	Length (in miles)	Trailhead Access	Features
Staircase Shady Lane Nature Trail	3.0	across the bridge from the Staircase Ranger Station	low-elevation old-growth forest
Staircase Rapids Loop Trail	2.0	across the bridge from the Ranger Station	heavy virgin forest along Skokomish River, crosses Staircase Rapids; red cedar trees
Lake Constance Way Trail	2.0	go 14.3 miles on Dosewallips River Road to marked trailhead	extremely steep, rough scramble through rocks and forest
Skokomish River Trail	15.1	Lake Cushman Road leaves U.S. 101 at Hoodsport; 15 miles to park boundary, 1 mile to Staircase Ranger Station, campground, and trailhead	gradual ascent, passes through forest, along river, offers excellent views of peaks in southeast corner of Olympics, drops down to open meadows
Main Fork Dosewallips River Trail	15.4	Dosewallips River Road joins U.S. 101 at Brinnon; at 16 miles is NPS Dosewallips Ranger Station and trailhead	major access corridor to numerous other trails in the eastern Olympics
West Fork Dosewallips River Trail	10.0	Dosewallips River Road, at Ranger Station (see above)	provides access to spectacular high country
Duckabush River Trail	23.0	Duckabush River Road leaves U.S. 101 about 22 miles north of Hoodsport and continues 7 miles to Duckabush Trailhead	gradual then steeper grade; O'Neil Pass; Brothers Wilderness; alpine lakes
Lena Lake Trailhead to Upper Lena Lake	7.0	Hamma Hamma Road leaves U.S. 101 14 miles north of Hoodsport; at 8 miles is USFS Lena Creek Campground and Lena Lake Trailhead	steady ascent to wooded lower lake then ascending to subalpine upper lake; fishing

HOOD CANAL COUNTRY (Continued)

Trail Name	Length (in miles)	Trailhead Access	Features
Flapjack Lakes Trail	7.4	Skokomish River Trail	steady ascent; Flapjack Lakes lie in a cirque basin with a view of the Sawtooth Range above
LaCrosse Pass Trail	6.4	a section of the Ducka-bush River Trail	steep ascent; wildlife abundant in upper basins; gradual descent into Dosewallips
O'Neil Pass Trail	13.0	Start from Deer Park and come in via the Three Forks Trail	good views in upper section

WESTERN APPROACHES

Trail Name	Length (in miles)	Trailhead Access	Features
Hoh Rain Forest Hall of Mosses Trail	0.75	visitor center at the end of the Hoh Road	level walk through mossy big-leaf maple forest
Spruce Nature Trail	1.25	visitor center at the end of the Hoh Road	walk through old-growth forest
Sams River Loop Trail	3.0	Queets Ranger Station or the trailhead 1 mile east of station	passes Queets and Sams Rivers; former homestead meadows
Maple Glade Rain Forest Trail	0.5	across the bridge from the Quinault Ranger Station	about a 30-minute stroll
Graves Creek Nature Trail	1.0	Graves Creek Campground	loop trail through the temperate rain forest
Hoh River Trail	18.0	near the end of the 18.5-mile Hoh Road, near visitor center and ranger station	easy grade along river; ascent to Elk Lake, Glacier Meadows, and the moraine; major corridor leading up the Hoh River to the foot of Mount Olympus

WESTERN APPROACHES (Continued)

Trail Name	Length (in miles)	Trailhead Access	Features
Queets Trail	16.0	Take Queets Valley Road for about 14 miles east of U.S. 101	one of the least-traveled trails in the park; low-elevation rain forest; often wet and muddy
Bogachiel River Trail	23.2	Undie Road leaves U.S. 101 5.5 miles south of Forks; trailhead is 4.6 miles from U.S. 101	even grade along river with periodic short ascents; dense forest; elk; fishing
Skyline Trail	30	From Quinault North Shore Road (46 miles north of Hoquiam), 18.5 miles to North Fork Trailhead	difficult trail; outstanding views of remote peaks, lakes, meadows, and snowfields
East Fork Quinault River Trail	17.5	from Quinault South Shore Road (43 miles north of Hoquiam), 19.2 miles to trailhead	varied terrain; provides access to other trails in the headwaters of the Dosewallips and Duckabush drainages
North Fork Quinault River Trail	16.5	from Quinault North Shore Road (46 miles north of Hoquiam), 18.5 miles to North Fork Trailhead	gradual grade along river; ascends into subalpine zone; great views of surrounding high peaks at Low Divide
Graves Creek Trail	8.0	from Quinault South Shore Road (43 miles north of Hoquiam), 19.2 miles to trailhead	ascends from 650 to 4,000 feet; crossing of Success Creek can be difficult during heavy summer rain; lowland forest to alpine meadows

Fishing

Though it's not known for its fishing like Yellowstone National Park or Katmai National Park, Olympic National Park offers outstanding fishing opportunities. You don't even need a license to fish in the park. Bear in mind, however, that if you want to fish for salmon or steelhead, you'll need a Washington State punch card. Also, lakes shared by other jurisdictions, such as Cushman, Ozette, and Quinault, require state licenses.

Because Olympic National Park occupies the high middle ground of the Olympic Peninsula, as well as a long stretch of the wet western coast, most of the major rivers of the Olympic Peninsula have their headwaters in Olympic National Park, and a few, notably the Hoh and the Quillayute, meet the ocean at the park's coastal strip.

Salmon and steelhead fishing used to be the major attraction of the Peninsula. But habitat destruction, chiefly as a result of dams (some even in the park) and logging outside of the park, has significantly reduced the runs. Takes on anadromous, or ocean-running, salmon are very limited. One salmon species that remains abundant is the kokanee, a freshwater sockeye salmon that is caught in lakes.

Fishing for steelhead can be quite good in some of the rivers, and cutthroat and rainbow trout are abundant in nearly all major park waters. Though actually a char, and with a very limited take, the Dolly Varden can also be found in park waters.

Lakes

The following is a quick review of the major lakes.

Lake Crescent. At 5,000 acres, Lake Crescent is the largest water body in the park and the most famous. Not only is it exquisitely beautiful, it also has terrific fishing. Long isolated from other water bodies by an ancient landslide, Lake Crescent has developed its own resident varieties of trout: the Beardslee rainbow trout and Lake Crescent cutthroat trout. Lake Crescent also hosts populations of kokanee salmon.

Lake Mills. This lake was created by a dam on the Elwha River. The 451-acre reservoir has rainbow, brook, and cutthroat trout living in it.

Lake Cushman. This lovely lake, formerly a natural lake enlarged by a dam, is home to cutthroat, rainbow, Dolly Varden, and steelhead, along with several species of salmon.

Quinault Lake. Created by glacier scouring and a glacial moraine dam, beautiful Quinault Lake is home to cutthroat, Dolly Varden, and salmon, especially kokanee. Fishing is regulated by the Indians and requires a permit.

Ozette Lake. The third-largest natural lake in the state, Ozette Lake is home to steelhead, sockeye, salmon, and cutthroat trout. Fishing is reputed to be OK here, but not great.

Rivers

Hoh River. The mighty Hoh is the largest river on the Olympic Peninsula. Glacial fed, it runs clear only in the winter. Chinook salmon run April through November. Coho salmon start appearing in August, peaking in October. The river has both summer and winter runs of steelhead. March is the top steelhead month, but excellent catches are made from December through March. Chinooks are the star attraction at this river.

Soleduck River. One of the most accessible rivers, with U.S. 101 and a park road running parallel to this river. It is one of the few rivers on the Peninsula that has runs of all five major species of salmon, plus steelhead and sea-run cutthroats. It's the steelhead runs that make this river famous.

Bogachiel River. The Bogachiel has both summer and winter runs of steelhead, but winter is the big season. For those who want to try some wilderness-style fishing, there is good access to the stream in the park by way of the Bogachiel River Trail.

Queets River. The Queets has large runs of both summer and winter steelhead. It also is home to resident populations of Dolly Varden trout. One problem is that the river is seldom clear. It is a good boating river, particularly for drift boats. Most floaters start at a large gravel bar about a mile above the Salmon River and float down to the Clearwater Bridge Road. The biggest numbers of steelhead are caught in January and February, but fish can also be taken in March and April.

Quinault River. This river is mostly on reservation land, and the portions outside the park require a Native American guide. Good summer run of steelhead.

Salmon River. Only a small portion of this is in the park. Best known for sea-run cutthroat trout. Small river, but does have steelhead as well.

Duckabush River. Most of the Duckabush in the park is fishable, but the best steelhead fishing is outside the park. Inside, the emphasis is on rainbow trout in the smaller, headwater portion of the river.

Skokomish River. A rainbow trout stream, near the Staircase campground.

Dosewallips River. Good trout stream. A waterfall blocks the migration of steelhead.

Elwha River. Famous fly-fishing stream, especially for rainbows and Dolly Varden. Once a great salmon stream. If proposals to remove dams advance, salmon may again be the attraction here. A good trail follows the river into the park.

Gray Wolf River. Accessible only by trail, the Gray Wolf offers good trout fishing, but only some salmon.

Camping

Camping is prohibited outside authorized campgrounds within the park unless you are backpacking at least one-half mile into the backcountry. Wilderness use permits are required for all trail and beach camping, but not for automobile campgrounds. You can obtain a backcountry permit for a fee from all ranger stations, some trailheads, and the Wilderness Information Center. Camping at designated car campgrounds is limited to fourteen consecutive days.

The National Park Service operates sixteen campgrounds with a total of 910 sites. Camping fees vary depending on the services and amenities provided. Some remain open throughout the winter. RVs and trailers are not permitted at all campgrounds; check for the latest information.

Facilities

Most campgrounds provide water, toilets, and garbage containers. Individual campsites offer a picnic table and firepit or grill. No hook-ups, showers, or laundry facilities are available in park campgrounds. Some do have trailer dumping stations. Sites best accommodate trailers twenty-one feet or less. Major campgrounds have a few sites that will accommodate larger RVs. Laundry facilities are available in Port Angeles, Sequim, La Push, Forks, and some smaller towns along U.S. 101. Showers are available at Sequim Bay, Bogachiel, Dosewallips, and Lake Cushman State Parks. Contact local chambers of commerce for privately owned facilities.

Firewood

In campgrounds where wood is not available for sale by concession services, visitors may collect dead wood on the ground within one mile of campgrounds. Wood gathering is permitted along road corridors within

100 feet of the road. In the Deer Park area, firewood may be collected only in designated areas.

Pets

Pets are permitted on a leash (up to six feet in length) in park campgrounds and parking areas. Pets are prohibited in all park buildings, in the backcountry, and on most park trails.

Campgrounds

Deer Park (5,400 feet). This is a small campground with a limited number of sites. The views from Deer Park and nearby Blue Mountain are tremendous.

Dosewallips (540 feet). Good base while hiking trails on the eastern side of park from campground.

Elwha (390 feet). This campground lies just a few miles from Lake Mills along the Elwha River Valley.

Fairholm (580 feet). On Lake Crescent with a nice beach for swimming.

Graves Creek (540 feet). In the Quinault rain forest near trails for Enchanted Valley and Graves Creek.

Heart o' the Hills (1,807 feet). Major campground on the road to Hurricane Ridge.

Hoh (578 feet). Good site in Hoh rain forest. Access to Hoh River Trail and nature trails.

July Creek (200 feet). Walk-in campground on the shores of Lake Quinault.

Kalaloch (50 feet). Huge campground right on the ocean. More like a giant parking lot, but access to the beach is great.

Mora (50 feet). Pretty campground along Quillayute River within a few miles of the ocean.

North Fork (520 feet). Small campground among big trees.

Ozette (40 feet). Small campground on the shores of Ozette Lake near trails to the coast.

Queets (290 feet). Lovely campground on Queets River within beautiful rain forest. Off the beaten path.

Sol Duc (1,680 feet). Big campground along Sol Duc River near commercial Hot Springs.

Staircase (765 feet). Nice campground in big trees near Lake Cushman and trail up Skokomish River.

INDEX